D0208413

Culture and
Customs of
Ghana

Culture and Customs of Ghana

Steven J. Salm
and
Toyin Falola

Culture and Customs of Africa

GREENWOOD PRESS
Westport, Connecticut • London

Library of Congress Cataloging-in-Publication Data

Salm, Steven J., 1966–
    Culture and customs of Ghana / Steven J. Salm and Toyin Falola.
      p. cm.—(Culture and customs of Africa, ISSN 1530–8367)
    Includes bibliographical references (p.) and index.
    ISBN 0–313–32050–0 (alk. paper)
    1. Ghana—Social life and customs. 2. Ghana—Civilization. I. Falola, Toyin. II. Title.
    III. Series.
    DT510.4.S25   2002
    966.7—dc21   2001055614

British Library Cataloguing in Publication Data is available.

Library of Congress Catalog Card Number: 2001055614
ISBN: 0–313–32050–0
ISSN: 1530–8367

First published in 2002

Greenwood Press, 88 Post Road West, Westport, CT 06881
An imprint of Greenwood Publishing Group, Inc.
www.greenwood.com

Printed in the United States of America

The paper used in this book complies with the
Permanent Paper Standard issued by the National
Information Standards Organization (Z39.48–1984).

10 9 8 7 6 5 4 3 2 1

To our parents
and the wisdom of the generations that they represent

Contents

Series Foreword		ix
Preface		xi
Acknowledgments		xiii
Chronology		xv
1	Introduction	1
2	Religion and Worldview	33
3	Literature and Media	59
4	Art and Architecture/Housing	83
5	Cuisine and Traditional Dress	105
6	Gender Roles, Marriage, and Family	125
7	Social Customs and Lifestyle	147
8	Music and Dance	167
Glossary		193
Bibliographic Essay		199
Index		213

Series Foreword

AFRICA is a vast continent, the second largest, after Asia. It is four times the size of the United States, excluding Alaska. It is the cradle of human civilization. A diverse continent, Africa has more than fifty countries with a population of over 700 million people who speak over 1,000 languages. Ecological and cultural differences vary from one region to another. As an old continent, Africa is one of the richest in culture and customs, and its contributions to world civilization are impressive indeed.

Africans regard culture as essential to their lives and future development. Culture embodies their philosophy, worldview, behavior patterns, arts, and institutions. The books in this series intend to capture the comprehensiveness of African culture and customs, dwelling on such important aspects as religion, worldview, literature, media, art, housing, architecture, cuisine, traditional dress, gender, marriage, family, lifestyles, social customs, music, and dance.

The uses and definitions of "culture" vary, reflecting its prestigious association with civilization and social status, its restriction to attitude and behavior, its globalization, and the debates surrounding issues of tradition, modernity, and postmodernity. The participating authors have chosen a comprehensive meaning of culture while not ignoring the alternative uses of the term.

Each volume in the series focuses on a single country, and the format is uniform. The first chapter presents a historical overview, in addition to information on geography, economy, and politics. Each volume then proceeds to examine the various aspects of culture and customs. The series highlights the mechanisms for the transmission of tradition and culture across generations: the significance of orality, traditions, kinship rites, and family property distribution; the rise of print culture; and the impact of educational institutions. The series also explores the intersections between local, regional, national, and global bases for identity and social relations. While the volumes are organized nationally, they pay attention to ethnicity and language groups and the links between Africa and the wider world.

The books in the series capture the elements of continuity and change in culture and customs. Custom is not represented as static or as a museum artifact, but as a dynamic phenomenon. Furthermore, the authors recognize the current challenges to traditional wisdom, which include gender relations; the negotiation of local identities in relation to the state; the significance of struggles for power at national and local levels and their impact on cultural traditions and community-based forms of authority; and the tensions between agrarian and industrial/manufacturing/oil-based economic modes of production.

Africa is a continent of great changes, instigated mainly by Africans but also through influences from other continents. The rise of youth culture, the penetration of the global media, and the challenges to generational stability are some of the components of modern changes explored in the series. The ways in which traditional (non-Western and nonimitative) African cultural forms continue to survive and thrive, that is, how they have taken advantage of the market system to enhance their influence and reproduction also receive attention.

Through the books in this series, readers can see their own cultures in a different perspective, understand the habits of Africans, and educate themselves about the customs and cultures of other countries and people. The hope is that the readers will come to respect the cultures of others and see them not as inferior or superior to theirs, but merely as different. Africa has always been important to Europe and the United States, essentially as a source of labor, raw materials, and markets. Blacks are in Europe and the Americas as part of the African diaspora, a migration that took place primarily due to the slave trade. Recent African migrants increasingly swell their number and visibility. It is important to understand the history of the diaspora and the newer migrants, as well as the roots of the culture and customs of the places from where they come. It is equally important to understand others in order to be able to interact successfully in a world that keeps shrinking. The accessible nature of the books in this series will contribute to this understanding and enhance the quality of human interaction in a new millennium.

Toyin Falola
Frances Higginbothom Nalle Centennial Professor in History
The University of Texas at Austin

Preface

PEOPLE not closely associated with the continent of Africa often see it as a far-away place, as a land of many societies sharing a single "African" culture. Most of us have even heard the occasional slip of the tongue referring to the "country" of Africa. On a continent with many countries and almost one billion people, there are, of course, many variances that define the cultural landscape. One of these factors is the impact of historical migrations that brought people from one region to another, creating religious and cultural links between groups separated by great distances. The impact of colonialism, which drew borders based not on commonalities of people, but on arbitrary boundaries of European possessions, has also contributed to the diversity of culture within Africa as a whole, and within individual countries. Today, migration continues, both from rural to urban areas, from other countries into Ghana, and from Ghana to other countries, largely as a search for new employment and educational opportunities. The increasing mobility of people and ideas has hastened the rate of cultural change on the local and national levels by bringing world cultures into closer contact with one another.

This book elaborates on what not only makes the culture and customs of Ghana unique within the larger global cultural climate, but also identifies those characteristics that define the cultural values of the various ethnic and social groups within the West African country. The culture and customs of Ghana have adapted to their current shape over more than 1,000 years of settlement. The differences are complex, existing with multiple permutations in every corner of modern Ghana. Still, the decades of independence have strengthened the idea of a national Ghanaian culture that encompasses the shared similarities while leaving room for differences in social institutions, philosophies, attitudes, and ways of life.

The cultures and customs of Ghana today are a product of diversity in indigenous forms, influenced by a long history of Islamic and European contacts. The culture and customs are not static. They represent a dynamic process of adoption and adaptation, incorporating elements of outside cultures that are useful and discarding those that are not. The diversity of cultures in Ghana makes a discussion of every detail impossible. We will focus on salient cultural forms and customs, generally derived from Ghana's most prominent ethnic groups. This is not meant to slight any particular group, but only serves to make this book possible. We apologize in advance for any glaring omissions.

Acknowledgments

IN WRITING this book, we have benefited greatly from personal experiences as well as the insights, encouragement, and criticisms of many people. The most important of these experiences are the result of numerous interactions with many Ghanaians over the years. To the many people in Ghana who have granted us insights into their culture and customs we express our gratitude. For our most recent interactions, particular thanks go to Theodore Agyemang, Harold and Agnes Batsa, Jerry Pengwame, Jane Asante, Roger Allotey, John Collins, Frankie Laine, and Sandy Sackey for their wisdom, friendship, and support. Special thanks go to Francis Provencal, a friend and artist who represents everything that is fascinating and complex about Ghanaian culture. We can only hope that the reflections shared by them are conveyed effectively by us in the words and images of this book. The University of Ghana, Legon offered a venue to establish interpersonal relationships and access to invaluable documents. Steve received financial support to complete this project, in addition to collecting data for his Ph.D. thesis.

Many people have read and offered valuable comments on earlier drafts of this book. They played an important role in what you see before you now and to them we are indebted. Ann O'Hear, Edmund Abaka, Kwabena Akurang-Parry, Emmanuel Akyeampong, Rebecca Gámez, and Manuel Callahan took their valuable time to review and comment on the work. Sam Saverance assisted in map preparation, responding to our needs within a short time period. Scott Newton and Shelley Tanner helped with the cover photograph, while Akua Sagua-Boison generously gave her consent to appear on the cover. The remaining photographs belong to us.

For us, this book was a labor of love, but others suffered in the process of data gathering and writing. Writing a book is more trying for those with whom we share our daily routines. We were constantly reminded of the wise saying: "One who has not carried your burden knows not what it weighs." Steve would like to thank his family and friends, and most especially, Susan Ranheim, for allowing him the time to complete this project and for offering the necessary diversions. Susan's recent visit to Ghana, her excitement and inquisitiveness, offered yet another perspective on the many facets that comprise Ghanaian culture and customs. As always, Toyin thanks his large number of friends and family. The book marks the beginning of an intellectual journey for Ann Genova, Ann Cooper, and Kirsten Walles, and we wish them success. Hopefully, they will inherit the baton and pass it on to the next generation.

Chronology

10,000 B.C.	Earliest evidence of hunter-gatherer societies within modern Ghana found at site on the Oti River.
A.D. 1000	Guan begin migration southwards from modern Burkina Faso, along the Volta River, toward the Atlantic coast.
ca. 1298	First Akan kingdom of Bono founded.
1471	First Europeans arrive on the coast.
1482	Portuguese build Castle of St. George in Elmina.
1500–1807	Era of trans-Atlantic slave trade attracts more Europeans to the coast and produces a new economic order.
1697–1750	Rise and consolidation of Asante Empire under the leadership of Osei Tutu and Opoku Ware.
1822	The first newspaper, the *Royal Gold Coast Gazette and Commercial Intelligencer*, is established in Cape Coast.
1824	First confrontation between the Asante people and the British results in an Asante victory and the death of the British Governor.
1857	Charles Bannerman establishes the *Accra Herald*, the first African-owned newspaper in Ghana.
1873–74	Second major Anglo-Asante conflict results in British victory and capture of Kumase.

1874   Britain formally establishes Gold Coast Colony.
            First gold mines opened in Wassa and Asante.

1877   Capital of the Gold Coast colony moved from Cape Coast to
            Accra.

1878   Cocoa first introduced to Ghana from Fernando Po by Tetteh
            Quarshie.

1896   Last major Anglo-Asante conflict leads to British destruction
            of Kumase and exile of King Prempe to the Seychelles.
            British declare protectorate over Asante.

1897   Aborigines' Rights Protection Society established to protect
            the property rights of African elite from British intrusion.

1900   First Africans appointed to colony's Legislative Council.

1902   British proclaim protectorate over Northern Territories.

1911   The first West African novel, *Ethiopia Unbound*, by Ghanaian
            lawyer and journalist, J.E. Casely-Hayford, is published in
            London.

1915   *The Blinkards*, a play about Cape Coast society by Kobina
            Sekyi, is first performed. It is not published, however, until
            1974.

1919   German Togoland is mandated to the British by the League
            of Nations and ruled within the Gold Coast administration.

1920s   Highlife music begins to develop.

1920   The National Congress of British West Africa, a regional
            group calling for African-elected representation, is founded.

1925   The West African Students' Union founded in London.

1927   Achimota School opened near Accra.

1928   Completion of new harbor at Takoradi.

1931   J.B. Danquah establishes the *West African Times*.

1934–37   Nnamdi Azikwe, who later becomes the first president of Ni-
            geria, serves as editor of the *African Morning Post*.

1935   Ghana Broadcasting System begins airing news and music un-
            der the name Station ZOY.

1939	The British establish the Colonial Film Unit.
1946	The British introduce the *Burns Constitution* giving Ghanaians additional seats in the Legislative Council.
1947	United Gold Coast Convention (UGCC) founded in August.
1948	University College of the Gold Coast (now the University of Ghana) established.
1948	Riots at the Christiansborg crossroads on 28 February leave three dead, many injured, and scores detained.
1949	Kwame Nkrumah breaks from UGCC in June and forms the Convention People's Party (CPP).
1950	Nkrumah and CPP embark on "Positive Action" campaign. Nkrumah and other prominent CPP leaders detained and charged with sedition.
1951	New constitution leads to general elections in February. Nkrumah's CPP wins a two-thirds majority.
1952	Nkrumah is released from prison and becomes first Ghanaian prime minister.
	The Kumasi College of Technology (now the University of Science and Technology) established.
	The Boy Kumasenu, Ghana's first full-length feature film, is completed.
1954	New constitution expands assembly, grants broad powers to government over all internal affairs, and calls for national elections. CPP wins almost three-fourths majority.
	The National Liberation Movement (NLM), a largely Asante-based, political opposition group to the CPP, is founded.
1955	The NLM and other anti-CPP groups join to form the United Party (UP).
1956	A plebiscite favors the union of the former German Togoland with Independent Ghana.
	Another election is held and the CPP holds its strong majority. It is now faced, however, with a united opposition led by the UP.
1957	The Gold Coast becomes independent Ghana at midnight on 6 March and Nkrumah becomes its first prime minister.

Increasing fear of rebellion leads Nkrumah to pass the Deportation Act.

1958 Nkrumah and the CPP pass Preventive Detention Act, allowing the government to detain opponents without trial or appeal.

1960 Ghana becomes a republic and Nkrumah the first president in July.

1961 University of Cape Coast founded.
Ghana Broadcasting Corporation launches the External Service, popularly known as the "Voice of Ghana," to broadcast news and opinions throughout Africa.

1963 Organization of African Unity founded.

1964 Ghana declared a one-party state.
Construction of Akosombo Dam completed.

1965 Ghana Broadcasting Corporation introduces television service (GBC-TV).

1966 Armed forces stage coup on 4 February while Nkrumah is in Asia and establish the National Liberation Council.

1968 *The Beautyful Ones Are Not Yet Born*, a novel by Ayi Kwei Armah, is published.

1969 Kofi A. Busia and his Progress Party win National Assembly elections ushering in the era of the Second Republic.

1972 Lieutenant Colonel Ignatius Acheampong ousts the Busia government in January and establishes a second period of military rule under the National Redemption Council (NRC).

1975 The NRC is reorganized into the Supreme Military Council (SMC), reducing non-military participation in government even more.

1978 The leadership of the SMC replaces Acheampong with Lieutenant General Frederick W.K. Akuffo and schedules elections for July 1979.

1979 Junior officers, led by Flight Lieutenant Jerry John Rawlings, stage Ghana's first violent coup on 4 June and establish the Armed Forces Revolutionary Council (AFRC).

1979	The AFRC, after four months in power, holds elections resulting in victory for the People's National Party (PNP), led by Hilla Limann.
1981	The short-lived Third Republic is toppled on 31 December when Rawlings leads a second coup and establishes the Provisional National Defence Council (PNDC).
1981	Kwaw Ansah's *Love Brewed in an African Pot*, Ghana's best-known feature film, released.
1983	PNDC, under pressure from international funding agencies, introduces the Economic Recovery Program.
1985	Government enacts the Customary Marriage and Divorce (Registration) Law, which introduces a standard system of registration for customary law marriages.
1988–89	Elections held for new district assemblies.
1990	The Movement for Freedom and Justice is founded and calls for end to military rule.
1991	The PNDC agrees to create a Consultative Assembly to draw up a new constitution.
1992	An April national referendum approves a new democratic constitution and multiparty system. New political parties begin to register in May. The PNDC is transformed into the National Democratic Congress (NDC). Presidential election held in November results in victory for Rawlings. Major opposition parties boycott December parliamentary elections and the NDC coasts to a significant majority. The first Pan African Historical Theatre Festival is held in Cape Coast and Accra under the theme "The Re-Emergence of African Civilization."
1993	The Fourth Republic is inaugurated in January. Jerry Rawlings becomes president.
1995	The Frequency Registration and Control Board grants the first private FM license to a small college radio station, Radio Universe, at the University of Ghana.

1996   National elections return Rawlings and the NDC to power, but the opposition wins 65 seats in the 200-member parliament.

1997   Rawlings begins his second term as president.
            The first private TV Stations, TV 3 and Metro TV, begin to broadcast.

2000   John A. Kufuor and his New Patriotic Party (NPP) defeat Vice President John E. Atta-Mills and the NDC in December elections.

2001   Kufuor and the NPP take office, ending almost twenty years of PNDC/NDC government.

1

Introduction

GHANAIAN culture encompasses long-standing interactions between the past and the present, the traditional and the modern. It is a dynamic culture that reflects the "duality" inherent in the attempt to blend rich cultural institutions and customs with continuing adaptations to the political, economic, and social exigencies of the modern world.

Ghana holds a prominent place in African history and culture. The country was one of the first in sub-Saharan Africa to grant extended residence rights to European visitors in the fifteenth century. It was one of the first to be formally colonized in 1874, and it was the first sub-Saharan African country to earn its independence from European colonialism, in 1957. Prominent Pan-Africanists like George Padmore and W.E.B. Du Bois chose to reside in independent Ghana and their names remain well known on both sides of the Atlantic today. The independence years have brought both success and turmoil to Ghana. Kwame Nkrumah, the first prime minister and president, was ousted in a 1966 coup. The next fourteen years saw a continued deterioration of the economy and consequent political upheavals. Since 1981, however, the political scene has been stable. Economic progress and development have followed, but the economy continues to show signs of weakness and dependency. Falling prices of gold and cocoa, the two primary foreign exchange earners, and economic mismanagement continue to impede the growth of the country. Recent elections of a new president and parliament, however, bring new hope for Ghanaians at the beginning of a new millennium.

GEOGRAPHY

Ghana is situated along the coastline of the Gulf of Guinea. Burkina Faso is to the north of Ghana, Côte d'Ivoire is to the west, and Togo is to the east. The southern coast lies 465 miles north of the equator and the Greenwich Meridian passes through the port city of Tema, sixteen miles east of the national capital, Accra. The Republic of Ghana is home to 18.5 million people and its population continues to grow at the rate of 2.5 percent annually. It extends 420 miles northward from the ocean, spans 334 miles of coastline, and has a total area of 92,100 square miles, about the size of Oregon.

Geographically, Ghana consists of flat terrain and gently rolling hills, with more than half of the country less than 660 feet above sea level. The mountain range along the southeastern border with Togo contains the highest point in the country at 2,920 feet. The southern coastal region is generally drier, is relatively flat, and contains a number of salt water lagoons. Beautiful forested hills and plateaus rise in an escarpment at the edge of the Greater Accra Region and once served as a mosquito-free residence for colonial elites. The central areas are heavily forested, although the timber industry and cocoa farming have decimated much of the virgin rainforest that once covered a large area of the country. The northern third of the country is largely savanna and open woodland, but overgrazing by livestock and increased cultivation are gradually depleting the natural vegetation and the region is beginning to resemble the arid lands of the Sahel to the north.

Numerous rivers and streams crisscross the Ghanaian landscape. The Volta, the largest river, was dammed in the early 1960s as part of President Kwame Nkrumah's plan to build the Akosombo Dam, a mammoth hydro-electric project that would not only meet all of Ghana's electricity needs but allow for the export of some hydroelectric power to neighboring countries as well. What was once the main drainage basin for a large portion of the country became the largest man-made lake in the world, forced thousands of people to relocate, and consumed a significant portion of cultivable land. The lake begins forty miles from the estuary of the river and is navigable for almost 250 miles northward. Boats travel across it in every direction carrying goods and passengers daily. The dam was completed in 1964 and is still in operation today, although frequent droughts and deteriorating equipment limit its production capacity. Next to the Volta, the most important rivers are the Pra, the Tano, the Ankobra, the Birim, the Offin, and the Densu. Many smaller streams and rivers dry up or experience reduced flows during the dry season.

The only natural lake in Ghana is Lake Bosumtwi. Lying in a steep-sided caldera about twenty miles southeast of Kumase, the capital of the Ashanti Region, it reaches depths of almost 300 feet and is surrounded by crater walls standing more than 2,000 feet high. It is important to some local residents, who believe that their souls come here after death to say goodbye to their god.

Ghana has a tropical climate, with consistently high temperatures all year round. There are three distinct climate zones. The southern coastal belt is warm and humid, with temperatures normally in the mid to upper 80s F. The heat diminishes slightly in July and August, following the heavy rainy season. There are two rainy seasons in the southern and central areas. The first, from late April through June, is the heaviest. Lighter rains come in late

September, October, and November. The forested regions generally experience heavier rains and higher temperatures than the coastal areas, while the northern savanna area is hotter and drier, with daytime temperatures in the 90s for much of the year. In the northern savanna, there is only one rainy season, lasting from May to October, with the most rain falling in August and September, and one dry season. The period of the harmattan involves cold and dusty northeasterly winds that come down from the Sahara Desert, limiting visibility and decreasing the temperatures slightly, especially at night. The harmattan is most prevalent in the north between November and March, but reaches south to the coastal regions, usually for a few weeks to a month during December and January.

PEOPLES

Humans have occupied the area of what is now Ghana for at least 10,000 years, but little evidence remains of these early, hunter-gatherer societies. Between 5000 and 2000 B.C. inhabitants of what are today the Brong-Ahafo and Ashanti Regions began to settle in larger villages and employ agricultural techniques and animal domestication. By A.D. 1000, larger population centers, probably associated with the long-distance trading networks of the ancient empire of Ghana, developed in the northern and central areas. The northern trade routes, however, diminished in the fifteenth century with the demise of the Songhai Empire and the arrival of the Portuguese, diverting the economic focus to the coast.

Forty-five percent of Ghanaians are under the age of fifteen. About 70 percent of Ghanaians live in the southern and central areas of the country. The triangular-shaped region bounded by Accra and Tema to the east, Sekondi-Takoradi to the west, and Kumase to the north has the highest density, estimated at more than 200 persons per square mile. This area also contains the bulk of Ghana's mineral deposits, the main cocoa-producing regions, and all the major port facilities. The Northern, Upper West, and Upper East Regions, despite occupying more than 40 percent of the country's surface area, contain only about 25 percent of the population.

Variations in culture and economic development coincide with the population disparities. Groups in the southern and central areas have had a longer history of contact with Europeans. They are more likely to be Christian, to have had greater access to formal education, and to have a greater interest in Western goods. Islam, on the other hand, has a long history in the northern areas, and its influences there are more pervasive in everyday life. There are, of course, variances. Christian missionary groups continue to convert northerners, while branches of Islam, especially the Ahmadiyya movement, have established a presence in some of the southern regions. Indigenous religions prosper throughout Ghana, and often coexist with Christianity and Islam.

Ghana is a highly multicultural and multiethnic country. There are about one hundred ethnic divisions characterized by linguistic and cultural differences. The large majority of Ghana's population today, however, can be classified into five major groups: the Guan, the Mole-Dagbani (with the Gonja), the Akan, the Ewe, and the Ga-Adangbe. These groups migrated to the country over the last 1,000 years, most arriving from areas to the north, and a smaller number coming from the east.

The Guan

The Guan moved into modern Ghana along the Volta River and, apart from a few groups that followed the Volta gorge and moved westward to settle along the coast between Winneba and Cape Coast, they still live near what is now Lake Volta. The Guan began their migration from the Mossi region of modern Burkina Faso probably around A.D. 1000. Most scholars believe that they are the earliest of modern Ghana's ethnic groups to arrive. This notion is supported by Akan, Ga-Adangbe, and Ewe oral traditions, which suggest that the Guan were already present at the time of their migrations.

The Guan organized themselves into small independent states that extended over a wide area. As the Akan, Ewe, and Ga-Adangbe arrived over the next 300 years, they absorbed some of the Guan, while pushing others to settle in new areas. What were previously exclusively Guan areas became smaller Guan-speaking enclaves along the Volta, in Akuapem, and within the coastal plains. Many of the other early settler groups in Ghana were at least partly assimilated into the culture and social organization of the new migrant communities. The Larteh-Kyerepong of the Eastern Region, for example, although still a distinct group, speak a language that remains unique, but contains many words borrowed from Ga-Adangbe and Akuapem Twi. The social institutions, customs, and names used by the Larteh-Kyerepong also provide strong evidence of Akan influence, while certain Guan subgroups, such as the Anum-Boso, show a greater influence from Ewe language and culture.

The Mole-Dagbani and the Gonja

The two most populous groups in the northernmost states of Ghana are the Mole-Dagbani and the Gonja. Ghanaians often refer to the Northern, Upper East, and Upper West Regions as "the North," suggesting some degree of homogeneity of the geography and the people that differentiates them from the rest of the country. In contrast to the more forested and tropical south, the northern regions are situated in the hotter and drier Sahel, where vegetation is less dense. The peoples of these regions also rely on different food crops, such as yam and millet, and show a greater influence from Islam.

The Dagomba, the Nanumba, the Mossi, and the Mamprusi fall under the umbrella of the Mole-Dagbani group. Oral tradition describes how the Mamprusi and Dagomba peoples originated in Zamfara, a Hausa state in modern Nigeria. They moved from there to present-day Mali, and then to Gambaga in Ghana. Upon arriving in Ghana, some established the kingdom of Mamprusi, while others founded the Mossi and Dagomba states further to the north. The rulers of Dagomba and Mossi still regard Gambaga as their spiritual home. During the colonial era, more Hausa arrived to serve in the Hausa Constabulary Force, a force which later incorporated northern Ghanaians as well. The Hausa continue to migrate into Ghana, living in enclaves in many southern Ghanaian cities. Exhibiting traits that southern Ghanaians associate with Hausa society, many of them mistakenly refer to all northern Ghanaians as "Hausa."

Gonja tradition states that the ancestors of the present-day Gonja people originated in the area of the ancient Mali Empire and founded a kingdom in northern Ghana. Gonja culture supports this statement. The language contains several Mande words, the people continue to use Mande clan names, practice similar rules of succession and inheritance, and employ similar ethnic identification marks. They became part of the expanding Asante Empire in the eighteenth century and, after the British victory over Asante, were incorporated into the British protectorate of the Northern Territories in 1902.

The Akan

The Akan, the largest ethnic group in Ghana, compose about 48 percent of the population. They are made up of two main groups, the Fante and the Twi. The Fante came first, settling predominantly in the area around what is now Cape Coast, probably sometime in the thirteenth century. The Twi inhabited much of the central region, and the forest country to the south, between the Volta and Tano Rivers. Some Akan migrated east and created the Baule community in what is now Côte d'Ivoire. The first Akan kingdom, Bono, was established in the late thirteenth century, long before the Portuguese first arrived in 1471. Because of their position on the coast, the Fante were the first to form relationships with the Europeans and some, especially the Fante elite, adopted and adapted aspects of European culture. It is fairly common today, for example, to find prominent Fante families with European surnames.

From a number of small political groupings there arose several powerful states. The Akan states of Asante, Fante, Akwamu, Akyem, Akuapem, Wassa, and Denkyira emerged before the end of the seventeenth century by conquering and at least partially assimilating weaker groups. Asante, the most powerful of these states, continued to expand during the eighteenth and early nineteenth centuries. As Asante power began to wane, the British defeated them and established a protectorate over the region in 1896.

Although they spread over a large geographic area of Ghana, the various Akan subgroups share many cultural traits. Political alignments, however, have more often followed local interests. The development of the Asante Empire came largely at the expense of the independence of the surrounding Akan states, such as Denkyira and Akwamu. The British, seeking to limit the power of the Asante Empire, provided assistance to these groups, who quickly reasserted their autonomy after the Asante defeat.

The Ewe

The Ewe people came from northern Togo, though at an earlier time, they were probably a minority group within larger, more powerful kingdoms to the east such as those of the Fon and Yoruba. They initially settled around the mouth of the Volta. Subsequent groups followed the river and moved further upland. Today, they occupy much of southeastern Ghana and are separated from the Ga-Adangbe and Akan by the Volta. There are also many Ewe groups in the southern parts of neighboring Togo. During the early colonial era, the Ewe were included in German Togoland, but after Germany's defeat in the First World War, the territory was divided between France and Britain by the League of Nations. Voting in a 1956 plebiscite on whether to join with independent Ghana or remain with their brethren in French Togoland, the British-ruled Ewe voted for the former and their territory became the Volta Region.

The Ga-Adangbes

The Ga-Adangbes most likely traveled along the coast from Nigeria. Oral tradition tells a story of leaving Yorubaland because of political strife. Another line of thought, however, avows that they originally came from Egypt, where they left for similar reasons, and only later came into contact with the Yoruba. In any event, the Ga language shares some structural similarities with Yoruba, supporting those ties. Similarities in language, in circumcision rites, in the importance of priests in state affairs, and in child naming patterns suggest that the Ga and the Adangbe were originally one group.

Many historians believe that, after leaving the area of modern Nigeria, the Ada settled on the coast to the west of the Volta, while other Adangbe groups like the Krobo moved northward and settled in the Shai and Krobo hills. The Ga, on the other hand, settled on the Accra plains. The Ga inhabit the stretch of coast from Accra to Prampram, below the Akuapem escarpment, between the Laloi lagoon on the east and the Densu river on the west, in the Greater Accra Region. The Ga are a fishing and farming people organized into seven main towns: James Town, Ussher Town, Osu, La, Teshie, Nungua, and Tema. The oldest parts of Accra, James Town and Ussher Town, are largely Ga neighborhoods, and up to 75 percent of the Ga reside in coastal urban centers.

Like the Fante, the Ga had extensive contact with Europeans before the colonial era and entered into political alliances with them. The declaration of Accra as the colonial capital in 1877 further ensured that it became a center of learning and trade that attracted, and continues to attract, migrants not only from other Ghanaian towns but from all over West Africa. Returnees from the New World, mainly Brazil, also settled in the Ga urban complexes. Many of these migrants were absorbed into Ga society, but, because of its urban nature, the Ga language and culture also demonstrate a willingness to absorb external cultural traits.

LANGUAGES

Ghana is a highly multilingual country consisting of about sixty language groups. English is the official language, due to Ghana's colonial history. It is used in government, most large-scale business transactions, and the national media, but virtually everyone speaks other languages as well. The 1969 Constitution required that members of parliament speak, read, and understand English, but the 1992 constitutional debates did away with the requirement in order to increase the overall diversity of representation in government. In education, new guidelines enacted in the mid-1980s promote the use of local vernaculars at the primary levels, where learning one of nine Ghanaian languages is now mandatory. English, however, still remains the dominant language at more advanced levels.

Most Ghanaians are at least bilingual, and many others are able to speak three or more languages. It is not uncommon to hear a speaker, especially in the urban areas, use two or even three languages within a single conversation. The national radio and television media rely on English as their major language, but Akan, Dagbani, Ewe, Ga, and Hausa are also employed frequently, especially in advertisements, commentary, and public service announcements.

All the languages in Ghana belong to different branches of the Niger-Congo language family. In the north, languages belonging to the Gur branch of Niger-Congo predominate, and include three major subdivisions: Gurma, Grusi, and Mole-Dagbani. In the south, most languages, including Akan, Ga-Adangbe, and Ewe, belong to the Kwa branch. There are also a number of sub-divisions within these three. Akan includes Asante, Fante, Akuapem, Akyem, Akwamu, Ahanta, Bono, Nzema, Kwahu, and Safwi. Ga-Adangbe contains Ga, Adangbe, Ada, and Krobo. Even the language of the Ewe, who most closely resemble a single linguistic group, can be broken down into various subdivisions. The presence of Central Togo remnant groups, such as the Nkonya, Tafi, Logba, Sontrokofi, Lolobi, and Likpe, who live among the Ewe but speak a different language, further complicates linguistic categories. There is, in addition, some representation in Ghana of Mande languages more commonly found to the north and west in Côte d'Ivoire, Sierra Leone, Guinea, and Mali.

Twi, or Akan, is by far the most widely spoken African language in Ghana today. Almost 9 million people speak it as a first language and, because it has become the *lingua franca* and is used in many facets of life, many others have learned it on their own or in school. Pidgin, a language that incorporates aspects of English and local languages, is also quite popular, especially among younger and often more affluent urban residents. All the major languages of Ghana, however, are featured daily in radio and television shows.

EDUCATION

Informal education pervades many aspects of African life. Societal elders give moral and ethical instruction to children so that they can satisfy the needs of the community and understand its traditions. Informal education utilizes apprenticeship to teach professional skills such as blacksmithing, drumming, or medicine. Such education is still popular throughout Ghana, but formal, Western-style systems also have a long history.

Western-style education first arrived in Ghana with the coming of the missionaries. In the nineteenth century, many Presbyterian and Methodist schools were founded, though most were located in the southern areas of the country. By 1881, there were around 5,000 students attending more than 139 mission schools at the primary level. Secondary education was also introduced, with a number of private groups establishing schools before the end of the century. Under colonial administrations, especially that of Governor Guggisberg in the 1920s, new education policies emphasized improved

A young student beginning her school work.

teacher training, equal education for girls, and an increase in the provision of secondary school education. Achimota School, for example, one of the best secondary schools in Ghana today, opened its doors in 1927. Still, the colonial government could not satisfy the demand for education in the following decades and private groups and individuals established hundreds of additional schools.

After the victory of the Convention People's Party in the 1951 elections, the government introduced the Accelerated Development Plan for Education. Although it did not go into effect until 1961, the plan provided for free, compulsory education at the primary levels and intended to provide universal education to everyone. An education system that grew to be one of the best in Africa during the colonial era grew even stronger during the early years of independence.

Today, Ghana's public education system includes primary schools, junior secondary schools, senior secondary schools, polytechnic institutions, teacher training colleges, and universities. The system is based on that of the British, although there have been changes in recent years to improve the process and make education more accessible. Before the mid-1980s, a student graduating after six years of primary school, four years of middle school, and seven years of secondary education was often around twenty-five years of age. Most students, however, did not continue their education after middle school; less than 10 percent were able to advance to secondary or vocational schools. Educational reform sought to make education more useful by focusing on areas of study more relevant to the economic needs of the country. It also reduced the length of time spent at the middle and secondary levels. Junior secondary school replaced middle school and reduced the required time by one year. Senior secondary school now lasts for only three years before entrance to polytechnic institutions or universities. Gender and geographical disparities, however, remain today. At the primary level, the difference is slight, but the bias toward males increases at higher educational levels. In general, students in the southern regions of Ghana, with a longer history of Western education and easier access to schools, are more likely to attend formal schools at every level. Like the gender bias, this disparity grows as the level of education increases.

Reforms also aimed to improve postsecondary education to cater for the increased enrollment that would come from reforms at the lower levels. Before 1993, there were three institutions of higher education in Ghana: the University of Ghana, founded in 1948 as the University College of the Gold Coast; the University of Science and Technology, opened in 1952 as the Kumasi College of Technology; and the University of Cape Coast, founded in 1961. During the 1990s, the government also established the University of Development Studies at Tamale and upgraded the rating of the postsecondary teacher training college at Winneba, making it the University College of Education. There are also a number of specialized tertiary institutions in the country.

Within the last decade, fees have been reintroduced due to the desire to shift the financial burden away from government and to make up for deteriorating economic conditions. Throughout its short history, Ghana's national government has devoted a large percentage of its resources to education. Low wages, shrinking subsidies, and rising school fees have led to numerous strikes by faculty, staff, and university and polytechnic students during the 1990s. The government responded, in part, by instituting a student loan program to assist resident students to pay for their room and board at the universities. The protests have continued, but the proposed changes have been implemented. The universities are overcrowded today, with total attendance more than double the intended capacity. It is not uncommon to find up to five students living in a campus dormitory room intended to house only two. Senior secondary school graduates are often faced with the dilemma of waiting at least a year for entrance to the university and, even after embarking on their studies, they are faced with the prospect of spending an extra year or two making up for canceled semesters and missed time. Thus, those who have the means often choose to go abroad for university education.

Facilities, too, are suffering from lack of funding. New, affordable books are rare. Although most postsecondary institutions have at least a few computers with internet access, they are insufficient to meet the demands of even the intended student population. Ghanaian institutions are falling further and further behind the technological revolution. The country does not lack qualified intellectuals but, like so many other African scholars, the instability of the school calendar, deteriorating university infrastructure, and low wages have led many to seek employment overseas.

URBAN CENTERS

Thirty-three percent of Ghanaians live in urban areas today. Long-term and short-term migration continues to increase the size and diversity of urban populations, especially in the main urban centers. This diversity is augmented by significant numbers of people from outside Ghana as well. These include Nigerians, Lebanese, and Chinese who are mostly involved in retail trade and the service industry. It also encompasses numerous Europeans and Americans associated with business ventures, foreign diplomatic missions, and non-government organizations.

The British moved the capital of the Gold Coast colony from Cape Coast to Accra in 1877. Accra remains the economic, administrative, and judicial capital of the country, as well as the capital of the Greater Accra Region. Its population is estimated to be near 2 million, with a sizable number of residents living in the rapidly growing surrounding areas. The second largest city is the capital of the Ashanti Region, Kumase, with a population estimated at more than 1 million. Kumase was the capital of the former Asante Empire and remains the royal capital of Asante and home of the Asante king (the *asantehene*). Other urban areas of importance include Tamale, the capital of the Northern Region; Tema, the site of a modern deep-water port and sister-city of Accra; Sekondi-Takoradi, actually two adjoining cities that grew from Takoradi's location as the first major deep-water harbor in the Gold Coast and Sekondi's status as the capital of the Western Region; and Cape Coast, the pre-1877 colonial capital and present capital of the Central Region.

Urban residence has many benefits that continue to attract new immigrants. The potential to earn money is the most common element drawing young immigrants to cities, but there is also the attraction of urban life. The urban environment is cosmopolitan in character and urban culture offers an array of varied and dynamic influences. Links between the rural and urban areas continue to increase. Many rural residents hope to sell their wares in the city and rely on money remitted by family members working there. The spread of culture is another important factor in exchanges between the rural and urban areas. Just as new cultural patterns are created elsewhere and imported into the cities, so too the cultural stimuli in the city are transported via various means to the rest of the country.

The movement of population to the cities, however, has led to a significant decline in agricultural productivity since the 1960s. It has also contributed to growing urban social problems. Many people are removed from their relatives and sometimes even their immediate families. Many urban residents still see the rural areas from where they came as their home and have plans to return there after retirement. Overcrowding and the associated problems of traffic congestion, housing shortages, and pollution are also common, especially in Accra and Kumase.

Ghanaian cities offer a unique kaleidoscope of modern life. It is not un-common to drive down a narrow street in James Town, Accra, filled with people following a traditional priest. On the side of the street stand piles of wood, still the dominant cooking fuel in many areas, and children bathing with buckets of water. A short distance away, in the Airport Residential area, two and three story walled-in houses are common. The streets are wider and rarely congested with pedestrians, and virtually all of the houses use gas for cooking. It is a neighborhood as pleasant as any one might see in the world.

RESOURCES, OCCUPATIONS, AND ECONOMY

More than half of the Ghanaian labor force is involved in agriculture or fishing as the primary occupation. Farmers produce a variety of crops for domestic consumption and export. These include cocoa, yams, grains, palm oil, cotton, sugar cane, rubber, coffee, kola nuts, and timber. Recently, the export of pineapples, papaya, and bananas has increased. Some farmers also raise cattle. Fishing is an important occupation for many who reside along the coast and at the edges of Lake Volta. The industry increased three-fold between the late 1960s and 1990, but is now in a period of decline because of over-harvesting. Foreign vessels poaching in Ghana's coastal waters have accelerated this process of depletion. The government introduced regulations in 1992 to protect marine life and ensure future resources, but lack of funding is making the regulations difficult to enforce and the catch continues to decline. Small businesses operate in all areas of the country. Traders, usually women, sell agricultural and fishing surpluses in local markets. Many locally manufactured items can be found there as well, including tools, textiles, cookware, and a multitude of objects made from metal, wood, leather, raffia, and ceramics. Small businesses also form the bulk of the service industry,

A bicycle vendor selling cookies and frozen yogurt.

providing all types of repairs, hair styling, and anything necessary to keep society running smoothly. Retail sales, timber production, mining, and tourism are the other major sectors of the economy.

Timber

Timber is the fourth leading export earner, due in part to World Bank funding in 1986 for new logging equipment, but the industry is coming under increasing scrutiny. Most commercial forests are in the southern areas of Ghana and show signs of deforestation. A century ago, one half of the country was covered with forests of tropical hardwoods and other trees. Now, only about one-third of the forests remain and the densest areas of commercially valuable trees have been reduced even more. The government has taken measures to curtail this deforestation, banning the export of many species and imposing high duties on others. It has also promoted the export of wood products rather than logs. Though there are now a number of lumber processors, insufficient equipment, lack of infrastructure, and corruption have limited the growth of the industry.

Cocoa

Cocoa is the main cash crop and chief agricultural export of the country. Ghana is the second largest cocoa producer in the world, after Côte d'Ivoire. The cultivation of cocoa is not native to Ghana. European missionaries tried unsuccessfully to grow cocoa seedlings, but failed. Tetteh Quarshie, however, brought a single pod from Fernando Po in 1878, planted the seeds in his backyard, and changed the nature of the economy. Using the organization of kinship networks, cocoa cultivation spread quickly through the forested regions of southern Ghana. It provided a method of earning hard currency without abandoning farming. Even today, the majority of cocoa production is done on small farms in the central, forested regions. By 1885 it was being exported to Britain, and by the 1920s, it was the leading cash crop in the colony, accounting for more than half of the world's cocoa production.

Cocoa contributed to the budget surplus at independence and helped to finance many early improvement projects. Declining prices and production, however, resulted in two decades of weakening economic prospects. Aging trees, bushfires, widespread disease, bad weather, and low producer prices caused 1980 production levels to fall to one-third of those of 1960. The devaluation of the cedi, the national currency, contributed to the smuggling of crops through Togo and Côte d'Ivoire, where the currency provided more long-term security. Recent government intervention, however, has resulted in positive signs in the cocoa industry in Ghana. Replacement of old trees, new growing techniques, new and improved transportation networks, and higher prices paid to producers have helped to increase production significantly, resulting in Ghana's return to prominence in world cocoa production.

Mining

Mineral production matched the decline of cocoa exports, enhancing the long-term damage to the Ghanaian economy. Mining is an important industry, with gold being the largest export earner, and diamonds, manganese, bauxite, and iron ore bringing in much needed additional foreign exchange.

Gold has been important to the economy of the region for centuries. It was a vital element of the trans-Saharan trade during the era of the ancient Sudanese empires. The attraction of gold first brought the Portuguese to the coast in the fifteenth century. It was first found in the rivers or in the rocks under the surface, especially along the Offin River near Dunkwa. In 1874, the gold industry changed when the first gold mines opened in Wassa Fiase and Asante.

Gold mining is one of the oldest occupations in Ghana and gold was, and still is, a distinguishing feature of Asante royalty. The richest deposit in the world of high quality gold can be found in the Obuasi, Anyanfuri, and Bibiani mines, while the Tarkwa gold mine remains a significant producer as well. Although there are small-scale miners who work in groups in open pits and are registered with the government, most production demands large capital investment and is controlled by large corporations.

During the 1970s and much of the 1980s, gold, bauxite, manganese, and diamond exports fell dramatically. Aging equipment, the overvalued cedi, and widespread smuggling contributed to the economic crisis. The government has successfully encouraged renewed production by introducing new legislation and offering incentives to the mining industry. The export of gold, diamonds, manganese, and bauxite has increased. This, like the increase in timber and cocoa production, however, has marked a return to a neocolonial economy, dependent on raw materials and fluctuating world prices. In the last years of the 1990s, world prices for cocoa and gold plummeted and, coupled with rising oil prices, have led to massive shortfalls in the Ghanaian budget.

Tourism

Apart from the export of raw materials, Ghana has made huge advancements in other areas. Tourism recently usurped timber's place as the third highest export earner, offering a less destructive alternative for earning foreign exchange and creating thousands of new jobs. Government incentives, a rich cultural heritage, and a striking natural environment continue to attract more and more visitors. The Ghanaian government promotes festivals such as the Pan-African Historical Theatre Festival and Emancipation Day ceremonies to attract foreigners, especially Africans in the diaspora, to visit Ghana. Based on its current growth, the government expects tourism to become the number one export earner by 2010.

Manufacturing

Although the manufacturing industry in Ghana is having to recover from years of hardship, it is slowly gaining strength and now produces a wide variety of products. Early post-independence governments stressed manufacturing. A major aluminum smelter, timber and cocoa processing plants, breweries, cement factories, oil refineries, and textile factories commenced operations during this time. Devaluation, shortages of raw materials, and lack of foreign exchange, however, led to negative growth and many businesses ceased production. Only recently has renewed emphasis been placed on manufacturing and the slow process of recovery is beginning.

Economic Performance

The performance of the Ghanaian economy during the last twenty years has been mixed. Although serious strides have been made, the average citizen continues to suffer from low wages and high inflation. In 1983, Ghana accepted the recommendations of international funding agencies and introduced an economic recovery program, which promoted free-market forces and the development of local resources. The government reduced public budgets, privatized state enterprises, devalued the currency, and, with foreign assistance, began to rebuild the infrastructure of the country.

Between 1983 and 1986, the government increased payments to cocoa farmers, laid off 28,000 civil servants in one year alone, and removed price controls on most products. It also sold most state-run enterprises and renegotiated the one-sided electricity agreement with the American-owned Volta Aluminum Company. Major construction projects dotted the landscape, including new hotels, bridges, and roads. Ports were rebuilt and improved. The national electricity grid was expanded to cover a larger part of the country. Consumer goods, previously impossible to find, were again abundant in shops.

The price of structural adjustment, however, was high. Cocoa, gold, and timber exports did increase dramatically, reverting to the neocolonial economic structures that relied on exploiting some nonrenewable and even endangered resources at the expense of improving the industrial base. Inflation, increased foreign debt, reduced government revenue, and unemployment left the long-term success of structural adjustment in doubt. The economic prescriptions did not noticeably improve the everyday lives of most Ghanaians. Salaries remained low and the cost of many public services soared, leaving the average citizen to bear the negative effects of "economic recovery."

The export market still drives the production of raw materials in Ghana. Gold, cocoa, timber, and diamonds are shipped mainly to Germany, Britain, the United States, and Japan. Export trade moves through the two main harbors at Tema and Takoradi or through the main international airport in Accra. Since Ghana lacks significant oil reserves, the need for oil comprises a significant part of import needs and demands large outlays of foreign exchange.

GOVERNMENT

At independence, Ghana adopted a parliamentary system based on that of the British. Since that time, there have been alternating military and civilian governments. The 1992 Constitution of the Republic of Ghana returned the country to democratic rule. The Fourth Republic was instituted in January 1993 under the leadership of Jerry John Rawlings and the National Democratic Congress (NDC). Elections in December 2000 brought a peaceful transition from a group that had led the country for twenty years to the New Patriotic Party (NPP), under the leadership of J.A. Kufuor.

The constitution divides powers among the president, parliament, cabinet, Council of State, and an independent judiciary. The 200 members of parliament and the president are elected in separate elections by universal suffrage. Ghana is administratively divided into ten regions and 110 districts, each with its own district assembly. There are also a variety of councils, including area, zonal, and town councils. At the base of the administrative structure are the 16,000 unit committees.

The ten administrative regions are each headed by a regional secretary. The geographical boundaries, and in some cases even the names of these regions, are derived from those of the colonial administration, resulting in some geographic confusion: the Volta Region actually lies to the east of the Eastern Region; the Central Region is central only to the southern coast; and both the Upper East and Upper West Regions are further north than the Northern Region. Each of the regions has a regional coordinating council, consisting of a regional secretary, deputies, district secretaries, presiding members of the district assemblies, and at least two chiefs. The functions of the council are to implement regional projects and harmonize the programs of the district assemblies with national development policies.

Ghana's legal system is independent of all other branches of government. The court hierarchy includes the Supreme Court of Ghana, the Court of Appeal, and the High Court of Justice. At the town and village level, there are local and district courts. There are traditional courts, consisting of the National House of Chiefs, the regional houses of chiefs, and traditional councils. There are also quasi-judicial agencies and institutions, affiliated with personal or spiritual agencies, such as shrines, churches, or Muslim mallams.

The 1992 constitution protects the institution of chieftaincy and allows for the use of customary law and traditional councils. The National House of Chiefs has no executive or legislative power but does provide advice on all matters relating to chieftaincy and customary law. The constitution also protects fundamental human rights, forbids discrimination based on culture, gender, age, disability, or sickness, and guarantees freedom of the press and free speech.

The Republic of Ghana maintains a strong presence in world politics. It is a member of many international organizations, including the United Nations (UN), the Commonwealth of Nations, and the Organization of African Unity. It provides an abode and financial assistance for refugees from other African countries. Ghana has served an important role in conflict mediation and as a stabilizing influence in conflicts in Sierra Leone and Liberia, both through UN efforts and through the Economic Community of West African States. Ghanaian troops have participated in numerous UN peace keeping missions in Africa, Asia, the Middle East, and Europe. A Ghanaian, Kofi Annan, is the secretary general of the UN and has served in that position since January 1997. He was the recipient of the 2001 Nobel Peace Prize.

HISTORY

Early History

As early as the thirteenth century, trade and travel created economic and cultural exchanges with the ancient Sudanese kingdoms, especially for people in the central and northern areas of modern Ghana. Gold was in high demand and was in abundance in what was later called the Gold Coast. The trade promoted the development of larger villages, centered on agriculture, domesticated animals, and gold. The trans-Saharan trade also stimulated the development of early states in modern Ghana, including the Mole-Dagbani states of Mamprusi, Dagomba, and Gonja and the main Akan states of the Fante and Asante. Islamic influences, spread by the activities of merchants and clerics, also grew during this era, especially in the north. Although Islam by no means supplanted indigenous beliefs and practices, people did incorporate many aspects of Islam into their own religions. After the demise of Songhai in the sixteenth century, long-distance exchanges with peoples to the north decreased and attention turned to the south, to the coastal regions and the Europeans, whose commercial interest in gold, ivory, and pepper quickly changed to an interest in the more lucrative slave trade. The Asante Empire, already in formation, capitalized on this changing focus and, by the beginning of the eighteenth century, established the most influential state in modern Ghana.

The Asante Empire

As the trans-Atlantic trade developed, the Asante desired to gain a direct trading outlet on the coast. Under the leadership of Osei Tutu (d. 1712 or 1717), the Asante expanded their influence and became the most powerful force in modern Ghana. Osei Tutu created the Asante Union and was the first to hold the Golden Stool, the symbol of Asante nationhood and cultural unity. Stools existed previously as traditional symbols of chieftaincy, but the Golden Stool represented the larger confederacy of the Asante Union. According to tradition, the high priest, Anokye, initiated the descent of a stool of gold from the sky and gave legitimacy to Asante rule. Kumase became the Asante capital. It was one of the finest and most advanced cities in West

Africa, and the Asante state employed a few Europeans as advisors. The Asante kingdom was renowned for its wealth in gold, the regal displays of its royalty, and the nature of its political organization. The Asante converted gold into firearms through trade and used their power advantage to expand their influence. The Asante Empire developed a new constitution creating the titles of supreme ruler (*asantehene*), divisional rulers (*amanhene*), and Kumase chiefs. It also developed a complex and well-armed military force.

The success of Asante was due to its methods of administrative and military subjugation. Osei Tutu allowed the people who became part of the confederation to retain much of their own administration and customs. Local chiefs retained power over local affairs, and they were given seats on the Asante state council. The political structure and military prowess of the Asante resulted in continued expansion throughout much of the eighteenth century. Osei Tutu's successor, Asantehene Opoku Ware (d. 1750), expanded the empire to the north, while subsequent rulers continued the expansion southward. The latter conquests brought them into contact with the Fante and the Ga peoples, and into closer proximity to European merchants on the coast.

By the mid-nineteenth century, Asante political and military structures began to show weaknesses. The British, interested in curtailing the slave trade and restricting Asante influence along the coast, began to supply arms and advice to other coastal states, while engaging the Asante in frequent conflict. The first confrontation between the Asante and the British occurred in 1824, resulting in an Asante victory and the death of the British governor. An 1863 war between the two ended in a stalemate, while subsequent wars in 1824, 1874, and 1896 were won by the British; on the latter occasion they entered Kumase and burnt much of the city. They also deposed King Prempe, exiling him, members of his family, and several important chiefs to the Seychelles, and declared a British protectorate over Asante. The Asante people, however, were not yet defeated. The British governor, Sir Frederick Hodgson, demanded that, since the British were now the effective rulers of the kingdom, the Asante must hand over the Golden Stool. Insulted, the Asante, led by the Queen Mother of Ejisu, Yaa Asantewaa, attacked the British fort in Kumase. In the end, however, the firepower of the British was too powerful and they extended their formal authority over Asante and into the protectorate of the Northern Territories.

Early Europeans

The British were not the first Europeans to arrive. The Portuguese came to the coast of Ghana in the late fifteenth century. They were attracted by stories of lavish wealth in gold transported via the trans-Saharan trade routes. In 1471, they visited the gold producing region along the coast and, wishing to protect their interests in the area from other Europeans, built the Castle of St. George in Elmina eleven years later. The French arrived and named the area "Côte d'Or," or "Gold Coast," a name the British later adopted for their colonial possession. The Portuguese began to ship gold, ivory, and pepper to Europe, but slaves soon became the most valuable export commodity.

Early in the seventeenth century the insatiable demand for slaves in the New World produced a new economic order along the Guinea coast. The lucrative nature of the gold and slave trade brought into the area other Europeans who, like the Portuguese before them, built fortifications to serve as headquarters for their enterprises. During the height of the slave trade, there were thirty-two European fortresses along the Ghanaian coast. Built by the Portuguese, Dutch, Danish, and British, many still exist today and reflect four centuries of European trade in ivory, gold, and slaves. They have become prominent historical symbols and, especially in the case of the Cape Coast and Elmina Castles, popular tourist destinations as well. Christiansborg Castle in Accra serves as the present-day seat of Ghanaian government. After the Danish withdrawal from the Gold Coast in the latter half of the nineteenth century, the British became the dominant European power in the region and continued the transition from the trade in humans to what has been called "legitimate trade" in palm oil, timber, gold, and other resources needed in the industrial revolution.

The Colonial Era

The present-day borders of the Republic of Ghana began to take shape only in 1874, when the British changed the status of the Gold Coast from a protectorate to a crown colony, incorporating the coastal areas and extending north to the borders of Asante. After the Anglo-Asante war of 1896, the British proclaimed a protectorate over Asante, and the protectorate of the Northern Territories followed in 1902. The last remaining portion of modern Ghana was delineated somewhat later. The area to the east of the Volta River, previously part of German Togoland, was mandated to the British by the League of Nations following the German defeat in the First World War and, after a pre-independence plebiscite, it became part of modern Ghana in 1957.

Colonial contact with Europeans and Christians brought many changes in indigenous customs, institutions, and values. One of the administrative mechanisms employed to rule over a vast area without large financial expenditure and without subjecting large numbers of British men and women to the diseases of the hinterland was indirect rule. It was cost effective because it promoted local, direct administration by what the British called "traditional" or "native" chiefs, and by doing so, the British claimed, it was less intrusive in the everyday lives of the people. In many cases, however, the type of power given to the local rulers was not the same power that they had previously wielded. Rather than being a means to manage local affairs, chieftaincy often became an agency through which the people received colonial laws regarding taxation and bureaucratic procedures. Increasingly, local rulers came under the influence of colonial police and district commissioners. Instead of aspiring to please the people in their constituency, chiefs were ultimately responsible to the colonial authorities and their standing was often diminished within their own societies. Although it was intended to maintain power at the local level, indirect rule helped transfer that power to another sector of society.

As the power of the chiefs was associated with colonial rule, the educated elite, products of Western-style education, came to the forefront. Educated young men served in the colonial government and sometimes functioned as intermediaries between the people and the colonial administration. Combating the colonial mentality of the "uncivilized African," the educated elite often adopted the language, dress, and manners of the British. The educated elite formed an important element in colonial society. They worked as doctors, lawyers, and civil servants and ultimately led the drive toward independence. They developed new forms of social institutions and began to see themselves as the rightful heirs to the leadership of the country, in sharp contrast to the former powers of the chiefs. A distinctive class system developed, with Europeans on top, the African elite below them, and the masses at the bottom.

The aim of British colonial rule was to become financially self-sustaining through the extraction of resources. Effective exploitation of Ghana's natural resources, however, also demanded improvements in transportation and communication networks. Under colonial rule, railroads, an artificial harbor, airports, and telecommunication and postal services were introduced. New crops and export commodities were also initiated. Cocoa, timber, and gold brought great wealth to the British, who in turn used a small percentage of that revenue to finance improvements in infrastructure, education, and health care. The export of natural resources to Europe brought foreign consumer goods in return. It became fashionable to own European clothes or other imported items that denoted status, and local production of similar products often declined.

Independence Movements

Educated Ghanaians have a long history of constructive movements against colonial domination. Groups such as the Aborigines' Rights Protection Society, the National Congress of British West Africa, and the West African Students' Union protested over issues such as land tenure and elected representation from the late nineteenth century through the 1930s. In the mid-1940s, however, the development of a new Ghanaian nationalism emerged and the independence movement gained force.

The end of the Second World War brought new calls for greater African representation in government and eventual independence. Thousands of Ghanaian veterans returned to a colony suffering severe financial hardships. Shortages in goods, high costs of living, and unemployment spurred increasing discontent among the veterans and many other urban dwellers. Cocoa farmers, too, were unhappy because of measures used to combat the surge in swollen shoot disease, which involved the destruction of many of their trees. The turning point came in February 1948 when a group of soldiers planned a march to the Christiansborg Castle in Accra to protest their condition. When they neared the governor's residence, police opened fire, killing three and injuring five others. This incident caused an outbreak of rioting and looting in the already tense city. The riots of 1948 reflected the widespread dissatisfaction that had permeated all levels of Ghanaian society.

Following the war, the British introduced the 1946 Burns Constitution, granting Ghanaians additional seats in the Legislative Council and giving elected members a majority. Still, the Burns Constitution could not overcome the rising tide of discontent over political and economic subjugation. Founded in August 1947 by educated Ghanaians, the United Gold Coast Convention (UGCC) was the first true political party with an outspoken demand for self-government. Kwame Nkrumah, after attending Lincoln University in the United States of America and spending time in London, was summoned home to take on the position of UGCC general secretary. Despite its stated opposition to the colonial administration, the UGCC could not satisfy more revolutionary desires for immediate change, choosing instead to retain its slogan of self-government "in the shortest possible time." Nkrumah soon left the UGCC because he saw the members as too intellectual and too conservative in their timeline for independence. He wanted to forge a broader appeal to youth and to ordinary Ghanaians. In June 1949, Nkrumah formed the Convention People's Party (CPP), with its goal of immediate self-government represented by the slogan, "Self-Government Now."

The CPP, unsatisfied by British attempts to placate Ghanaians, developed new ways to achieve its aims. In early 1950, it embarked on the "positive action" campaign of inducing widespread strikes and employing other non-violent forms of resistance. The colonial administration reacted by promptly arresting Nkrumah and other prominent CPP leaders and charging them with sedition. The success of "positive action" and his arrest enhanced Nkrumah's status. After the riots of 1948 and a follow-up investigation by the British, a new constitution was introduced in 1951. Ghanaians gained appointments on the Executive Council and greater countrywide representation in the Legislative Council, but the new constitution did not grant full self-government and the British still retained executive power. Nkrumah and his CPP swept to victory in the general elections of February 1951; he was released from prison and became the first African prime minister of the Gold Coast colony. The government, based on the 1951 Constitution, which allowed the British power over key aspects, gradually evolved into a full parliamentary system. Another constitution was enacted in 1954, granting effective control over all internal affairs of the colony to Ghanaians, but conflict over the nature of the independent government and the question of British Togoland delayed independence until 1957.

Independence and the First Republic, 1957–66

On March 6, 1957, Ghana became an independent country, the first sub-Saharan African country to shed the chains of European colonialism. Amidst great hope for the country and the continent, Kwame Nkrumah became the first prime minister of independent Ghana. Nkrumah's years in office, however, produced only mixed results. Nkrumah wanted to develop an industrial base for Ghana and promote the liberation of the entire continent from colonial rule. He embarked on projects that called for extraordinary spending, quickly depleting the country's coffers and sending the economy into chaos. A sharp fall in world cocoa prices and widespread government corruption exacerbated the situation. Despite having ten times more foreign reserves than foreign debt at the time of independence, within ten years Ghana accumulated a foreign debt of U.S.$1 billion. The CPP left a legacy of debt for Ghana that continues today.

Successes during the Nkrumah regime were also on a large scale, however. The building of a new deep-water port at Tema, the construction of the Akosombo Dam, and the renovation of major roadways contributed to the overall development of the country. Under Nkrumah's leadership, the education system saw huge increases in enrollment at every level. One could argue that his expenditures on other projects did not show as much foresight and ultimately brought the economy to a standstill. He spent a great deal of the financial reserves of the country on grand projects like Black Star Square to commemorate independence day. Attempting to promote African pride, Nkrumah built a headquarters for the Organization of African Unity, only to see it establish its base in Ethiopia instead. Although these projects detracted from direct economic gains, they served another purpose.

Nkrumah realized that a fledgling country, freshly removed from a long history of economic exploitation and colonial rule, a country without a strong basis for unity, needed symbols to bring diverse groups of people together. The name chosen for the country was that of ancient Ghana, a symbol of African empire and, like modern Ghana, famed for its wealth and trade in gold. Ghana adopted a flag with three horizontal stripes: red for the blood that was shed fighting for freedom; yellow for the gold and other mineral wealth; and green for the lush vegetation that covered much of the country. There is also a black star with a yellow stripe, representing the hope of independence for the rest of Africa.

Nkrumah saw himself not only as the liberator of the Gold Coast, but as the liberator of Africa as a whole. Ghana became the home of African nationalism and Pan-Africanism. Nkrumah's ideologies led Pan-Africanist intellectuals such as George Padmore and W.E.B. Du Bois to immigrate to Ghana. Nkrumah was instrumental in the formation of the Organization of African Unity in 1963, and he promoted the policy of nonalignment between the Western and Communist power blocs, a policy sometimes detrimental to gaining Western financial support. Some argue that his attention to continental issues detracted from his leadership; that he ignored important areas of the economy such as agriculture and mining in favor of promoting his wider continental goals.

Such criticism caused Nkrumah to experience an increasing fear of a revolt and take strict measures to prevent such a revolt from occurring. Within a few years after independence, Ghana had become a *de facto* one party state. Nkrumah introduced the Deportation Act of 1957 and the Preventive Detention Act of 1958, the latter giving the government the power to imprison its opponents for up to five years without trial or appeal. The CPP administration used these acts to silence thousands of its opponents. By the time Ghana became a republic in July 1960, Kwame Nkrumah and the CPP were the only lawful rulers and Nkrumah was proclaimed president for life. Nkrumah's misuse of power and the deteriorating economic climate ultimately led to a coup.

On the day of the coup, a statue of Nkrumah was toppled and broken, leaving it armless. After sitting in storage for many years, that statue now stands outside the national museum. So too, Nkrumah's image suffered after his downfall only to be revived in later years. A government proclamation in the early 1970s made it illegal even to speak his name, but like the statue, Nkrumah's legacy as one of the founding fathers of Ghana has been restored.

National Liberation Council, 1966–69

On 24 February 1966, while Nkrumah was on his way to a conference in Asia, the Ghana Armed Forces and the Police Service took control of the government in a bloodless coup. They formed the National Liberation Council (NLC), banned the CPP, and suspended the constitution. In recognition of the abuses perpetrated under the Preventive Detention Act they freed political prisoners and opened the borders for others to return. The military leadership appointed civil servants to cabinet positions and promised to hold elections as soon as possible. Still, the problems that had built up over the last decade were not easily alleviated. The neglected economy needed much attention. The rapid development needed to satisfy the electorate was unattainable. Fears of centralized authority were prevalent. The NLC held elections in August 1969 and the Progress Party of Kofi A. Busia, who had fled the country in fear of political persecution during the Nkrumah years, won the popular vote.

The Second Republic, 1969–72

The Second Republic was inaugurated on 1 October 1969 with the victory of the Progress Party in the National Assembly elections. After more than three years of military rule, Ghanaians were optimistic that Busia and the many intellectual parliamentarians would attend to the economic and political problems of the country. High unemployment led the Busia government to introduce popular measures that led to the deportation of many foreigners, such as Lebanese, Asians, and Nigerians involved in the retail sector. The severity of the economic problems, however, led to the introduction of less popular measures as well. Students grew unruly over the introduction of university fees and an accompanying student loan program. A massive devaluation of the cedi, although much needed at the time, also led to resistance from the populace. Increasing economic woes, driven by a huge foreign debt and continuing troubles in cocoa production, led to austerity measures which drained resources from farmers, workers, the middle class, and most importantly, the army. After only twenty-seven months in office the Second Republic fell in another bloodless coup.

The National Redemption Council and the Supreme Military Council, 1972–79

Lieutenant Colonel Ignatius Kutu Acheampong used force to, in his words, "redeem" the country in 1972. He dissolved the elected parliament and took a number of painless and popular economic measures. Acheampong's National Redemption Council (NRC) revalued the cedi by 44 percent, hardly a long-term answer to an economic crisis in which the currency was already extremely overvalued. The council also introduced price supports for basic food imports, rescheduled foreign debts, and nationalized foreign-owned companies. As the government printed more and more money to make up for the declining value of the cedi, annual inflation reached more than 140 percent. The declining purchasing power of the national currency, in turn, led to the increased smuggling of cocoa to neighboring Togo and Côte d'Ivoire, decreasing government revenue even more.

From its inception, the NRC made no mention of a timetable for a return to democratic rule. The council justified the removal of the elected government by making allegations of corruption. In an attempt to strengthen the stature of the military government, the NRC members reorganized themselves into the Supreme Military Council (SMC) in 1975. Participation in government was largely restricted to a small group of military men. The SMC believed that military organization was the only way to begin the process of healing the country's economic woes. Continued economic decline, increasing censorship, and growing accusations of corruption led to rising discontent at all levels of Ghanaian society and the demand for a return to civilian rule. The SMC finally made plans for a union-type government that would incorporate a mixture of elected civilian and appointed military leaders. The leadership of the SMC replaced Acheampong with Lieutenant General Frederick W.K. Akuffo and scheduled elections for July 1979.

The Armed Forces Revolutionary Council and the Third Republic, 1979–81

However, on 4 June 1979, two weeks before the proposed elections, Flight Lt. Jerry John Rawlings staged a coup and toppled the SMC. First and foremost, he promised to stick to the election plan. Rawlings formed the Armed Forces Revolutionary Council (AFRC) and "cleaned house" by executing three former heads of state for embezzlement and eliminating senior officers in the military who had been accused of corruption. After three months, Rawlings, as promised, handed over power to the popularly elected People's National Party (PNP) and its leader, Hilla Limann, but not before a stern warning that the new political leaders would be held accountable to the people.

With only a one seat legislative majority, and under the watchful eye of former members of the AFRC now organized into the June 4 Movement, Limann's effectiveness was limited. Economic problems led to work stoppages and, after the dismissal of striking public workers, to the erosion of support that had always been tenuous.

The Provisional National Defence Council, 1981–92

On 31 December 1981, Rawlings again stepped to the forefront of Ghanaian politics, toppling Limann's government and establishing the Provisional National Defence Council (PNDC) in its place. The PNDC merited mixed reviews on the economic front. Inflation rates of more than 200 percent, the arrival of more than a million Ghanaians who had been deported from Nigeria, and a sharp decline in cocoa, gold, diamond, and timber exports made the economy the most pressing issue during the early PNDC years. An Economic Recovery Program went into effect and saw some success by the end of the 1980s. Inflation dropped, the economy grew, especially in the export area, and new construction projects were initiated. Still, for the average Ghanaian, financial stability was no closer.

Rawlings and the PNDC created various mechanisms that were designed to enhance the idea of universal inclusion in the economic and political institutions of the country. Members of "People's Defence Committees," "Committees for the Defence of the Revolution," and later district assemblies were involved in decisions and projects based in the community. In addition, members of these committees and assemblies were expected to expose those working against the common good. In each case, opponents voiced allegations of over-aggressiveness and the use of these mechanisms as tools to eliminate political opposition and postpone the transition to civilian rule. While local committees silenced some members of the opposition, others were forced into exile. After rerouting some of the national political power to the local level and reviving some of the key sectors of the economy, the PNDC appointed a committee to write a new constitution and return Ghana to democratic rule.

The Fourth Republic

In 1992, Ghanaians passed a referendum approving a new constitution. Political parties were again allowed to operate. The first parliamentary elections came quickly, however, and, without enough time to organize and campaign effectively, the opposition boycotted them. Rawlings reformed the PNDC into the National Democratic Congress (NDC) and won by a large margin. Elections in 1996 again put the NDC in control, but this time the opposition did take 65 seats in the 200-member parliament.

Economic challenges continued to demand attention during the Fourth Republic. The Economic Recovery Program remained in effect and many of the positive and negative aspects of that program were still evident. Sharp falls in the late 1990s in cocoa and gold prices, coupled with rising crude prices, have resulted in high inflation once again.

The 1992 constitution mandated that a president could serve no more than two four-year terms of office. Thus, Rawlings could not run again in the 2000 elections. His appointed successor and vice president, Professor John E. Atta-Mills, could not overcome people's perception of nepotism, corruption and economic mismanagement within the NDC. Ghanaians demanded a change. The New Patriotic Party took control of parliament, and its candidate, John Agyekum Kufuor, an Oxford-trained lawyer and businessman, became the new president in January 2001. The elections were widely considered free and fair and Rawlings, as he did in 1979, stepped down without resistance.

CULTURAL ISSUES

Though one can talk of the many cultures and customs of Ghana, Ghanaians have also developed a national identity based on their rich historical traditions of indigenous, Islamic, British colonial, and Western influences. The subsequent chapters reveal that these influences permeate virtually every aspect of Ghanaian religion, philosophy, literature, art, cuisine, dress, marriage, family relations, music, and dance. The many influences have been absorbed into a strong, dynamic culture that is firmly rooted in the past, but one that is also vibrant and able to adapt to present conditions.

Development favors the people residing in the southern half of the country. A larger population, more urban centers, higher reserves of natural resources, and sometimes political nepotism have resulted in a disparity in governmental distribution of national funds. Clean water, electricity, and health care are more readily available in the southern half of the country. Better transport and media structures, banking networks, employment options, and availability of imported goods in the southern half of the country also expose this discrepancy.

Although there are economic and cultural differences between geographic and administrative regions, as well as rural and urban areas, Ghanaians share traits that reflect particular aspects of indigenous culture. People emphasize closely knit kinship systems that affect interpersonal relationships, legal rights to property, and social roles and obligations. Many marriages today, for example, include both customary and Christian or Islamic rites.) Other rites and ceremonies are also important mechanisms to maintain ties between individuals, kinship groups, and the wider community. In Ghana, many people emigrate from the town or village in which they were born for better jobs or to experience a new environment, but almost always they retain a strong attachment to that town or village. Various rites performed during childhood and adolescence reinforce the sense of kinship and community. This attachment is strengthened through the occurrence of annual festivals that entice people to come together and celebrate the idea of community with their extended family. Every festival promotes traditional culture and customs through music, dance, storytelling, and art, processions of chiefs, tributes to ancestors, and purification rites.

Islamic influence is also pervasive, especially in the northern areas and in some pockets of urban centers. Islam did not attempt to supplant indigenous culture, but instead was adapted to fit current systems. Islamic influences are evident in many aspects of life. They are found in architecture, the arts, education, and, of course, religious rites and ceremonies.

Colonial and missionary influence also had a great impact on Ghanaian culture and customs, particularly in the southern and central regions. Missionary proselytizing, colonial education, Western technology, and changing economic activities were designed to subvert African culture in favor of colonial and Christian customs. They were, however, rarely successful in this endeavor. English is the official language, but it certainly has not detracted from the use of local languages. Christianity is a prominent religion, but many people adhere to traditional beliefs as well. Colonial education tried to disparage African culture, to eliminate the African past, and to teach students that all things African were uncivilized while those of the West were characteristic of a genuine culture. Classical music was promoted, but African music did not disappear. Western education provided knowledge of the Western world while ignoring the existence of an African past, but as Ghanaians became educated in Western ways, they also began to reclaim the African past and recreate their own worldview.

Since the time of independence, Ghana has sought to cultivate the philosophy of an "African personality," to revive, maintain, and promote Ghanaian cultural practices and integrate them into contemporary political and social institutions.[1] The very name of the country was chosen as a symbolic expression of a great African empire. Monuments and architectural endeavors were designed to promote the ideology of a Ghanaian identity. Government and the private sector offer their support to traditional festivals, while also promoting other forms of artistic expression. Government promotes culture on a national level through such festivals as the National Festival of Arts and Culture, which incorporates art exhibitions, a craft bazaar, and music and dance shows and aims to encourage communal support for development.

Globalization has made a strong impact on Ghanaian culture, giving people a strong cross-cultural appreciation. The art, architecture, dress, music, and dance reveal the impact of the Western world. It is difficult to listen to the radio and not hear music from the United States. Likewise, youth idols include Michael Jordan, Janet Jackson, and, increasingly, some U.S. hip-hop stars. Nevertheless, globalization has not driven out indigenous cultural elements. It has been blended into indigenous music and dance, and incorporated into traditional celebrations. American hip-hop music, for example, has evolved into Ghanaian hiplife music, drawing on the influence of Ghana's long-standing popular musical genre, highlife, and imported hip-hop.

While claiming their ethnic and national identities, Ghanaians also recognize their relationship to Africa and to the rest of the world. As a nation, Ghanaians strive to improve their everyday life by developing infrastructure, utilizing technology, and distributing resources more equally. They have accepted aid and support from outside sources, but believe that ultimately development must come from within, from the desire to make the most of the natural and human resources of the country to enhance all aspects of society. Culture plays an essential role in this development. Art, literature, music, and dance promote the Ghanaian national identity, both inside and outside the country. Ghanaian governments support cultural endeavors. Through the National Theatre, the National Archives, the National Museum, and regional cultural centers, they cultivate a single Ghanaian culture, while also recognizing the multiplicity of beliefs, ideas, and customs that exist.

NOTE

1. Ministry of Education and Culture, *Cultural Policy in Ghana* (Paris: UNESCO Press, 1975), 9.

2

Religion and Worldview

RELIGION is inseparable from virtually every aspect of Ghanaian life and is important in the determination of worldview. Religion commands a central place in the organization of social, political, and cultural life, and regulates the relationship between people and their physical and spiritual environment. Many different forms of religion exist in Ghana and tolerance of religious differences is very high. The constitution guarantees the right to religious expression, and the government makes visible efforts to support that right. Although people take their own faith very seriously, they also allow others to do the same, regardless of which God they hold highest. Personal and public displays of religion are frequent. People even preach on public busses and many of the passengers join in to what quickly becomes a call-and-response prayer session. Atheists are very rare and one who professes no faith in a higher being is looked at with great skepticism.

Ghanaians honor the religious holy days of other faiths. The national government recognizes both Islamic and Christian religious celebrations. Muslims throughout the country observe the Muslim month of fasting, Ramadan, but the end of Ramadan, *Eid-el-Fitr*, as well as *Eid-el-Adha*, are recognized as national holidays, as are the Christian celebrations of Christmas and Easter. During these times most businesses are closed and few people perform their regular work. The various traditional religious events also attract great interest regardless of faith. Islamic, Christian, and traditional religious holidays and festivals are social occasions when family and friends come together and celebrate.

Ghanaian religion and worldview are shaped by a variety of religious practices and belief systems from Africa and the outside world. The three main forms of religious practice in Ghana include indigenous religions, Christianity, and Islam. Christianity predominates in the southern half of Ghana, while Islam is most prominent in the northern regions and large urban centers. There is no sharp geographical differential in the followers of traditional religions, which maintain a presence throughout the country.

In general, the number of people professing Christianity as their primary religion has continued to rise since the first days of missionary activity, and especially during the last four decades. In the first post-independence population census, Christians numbered about 41 percent of the population, while today they are estimated to account for more than 60 percent. The number of people professing to indigenous religious faiths has decreased from 38 percent to 22 percent, while the number of Muslims has risen from 12 percent to about 15 percent during the same era. Many other religions attract some followers as well, including Hinduism, Buddhism, and Judaism.

Although the population census suggests a decline in indigenous religious practices, few people have dismissed traditional beliefs entirely. Christians and Muslims more often reconcile some indigenous beliefs and practices with their Christian and Islamic views.

WORLDVIEW

Ghanaian worldview is shaped by a variety of religious and secular beliefs. Worldview involves the way in which people explain their personal condition and their relationship with the physical and spiritual world around them. It describes the origins of heaven and earth and provides signs to decipher the future. Worldview also encompasses a means to understand the relationship of individuals to other segments of society, including individual and group identities within the world system. Many Ghanaian customs revolve around and incorporate religious ideas.

Regardless of religious faith, many people still subscribe to a traditional worldview. For Ghanaians, life is a process of renewal that begins at birth and continues after death. When children are born, there is a one-week period when they are not given names because it is believed that they are caught in-between the land of the living and the spirit world, and could return to the latter world at any point. After surviving this first week, the child is named and welcomed into the family and the community. Puberty celebrates a child's transition into adulthood, and marriage marks a time of increased responsibilities, including the task of bringing children into the world. These stages differ little, at least in the basic concept, from Western ideas of the life-cycle. The view of death and the image of the dead, however, are less similar. Death is viewed as a transition to another life, not necessarily just the end of an earthly one. The spirit of the deceased lives on and is believed to play an active role in human life. When people die, others seek to understand the cause of death. A natural death in old age is celebrated, but an untimely death is attributed to witchcraft. Immoral conduct or failure to appease the ancestors can also lead to premature death. In cases with suspicious circumstances, certain actions may be taken to determine responsibility. An Akan ritual (*funusoa*), for example, involves carrying the corpse around town, until the spirit directs the carriers to the house of the killer.

The foundation of the Ghanaian worldview lies in the belief that a Supreme God created the world, and that God is the source of all good and evil things. The way in which Ghanaians see the spiritual nature of the human body relates directly to the way that they relate to other people and the environment around them. Ghanaian worldview is shaped by the belief in two separate but connected worlds: the world of spirits and the world of the living. The spirit world contains a hierarchy of powers that includes the Supreme God, lesser gods, ancestors, witchcraft, and magic. This hierarchy reflects on how people view the composition of personal nature.

The Akan, for example, see individuals as a combination of four components that stress the importance of a Supreme God, the spiritual world, and the father and the mother. The Ga and Ewe have a similar approach to the makeup of an individual, but it also varies because of the different emphasis on matrilineal and patrilineal kinship.

In the Akan view, the first component of human nature is the soul (*okra*, or sometimes just *kra*). The *okra* is the spiritual part of humans that predates birth and survives after death. It is received from the Supreme God and links people to the Creator. The soul helps people make moral decisions and sustain their life powers. After death, it is believed that the *okra* returns to the Supreme God to account for its time on earth. Every *okra* has a name associated with the day of the week on which a child is born. A male child born on Friday, for example, is called "Kofi," and a female child is "Afua" (or in Fante, "Efua"). Each name corresponds to a specific spirit who watches over their human namesake, providing positive, and sometimes negative, guidance. Each name also is believed to contribute certain characteristics to the person. Friday-born children for example, are seen as *okyini*, or having a wandering spirit.

The second component of an individual is the *sunsum*, which helps determine individual character, intelligence, and personality. The *sunsum* can reveal itself in dreams or leave the body during sleep, and is also outwardly expressed on a regular basis. The *sunsum* is the spiritual part that can bring physical ailments, as well as leave the individual vulnerable to witchcraft and other evil spirits. A strong *sunsum*, however, can also help protect someone against attack by witchcraft.

The third element in the Akan idea of personal nature is the *ntoro*, which is believed to be inherited from the father through his semen. The father provides elements of his character, especially his moral qualities, to his children until they reach puberty, the age when their own *ntoro* begins to play a more prominent role. The recognition of a common *ntoro* forms an important bond between Akan children and their fathers, a bond which is sometimes transferred to the mother's brothers as the children get older. Like the *okra*, every *ntoro* is associated with specific personality characteristics and has a specific day of the week connected to it.

The last component is the *mogya*, or blood. It is provided by the mother during pregnancy and childbirth to support the family and lineage lines. In matrilineal societies, the *mogya* gives children their lineage status and ties them into the responsibilities that correspond to that membership. This relationship, based in the symbolism of blood, binds the children to the matriclan. At death, the *mogya* becomes a person's ghost (*saman*) and continues to live in that bodily form.

Other Ghanaian groups have similar ideas of personal nature. The Ga concept, for example, contains two unseen, distinct spiritual entities, the *susuma* and the *kla*. The *susuma* is the unconscious mind of a person that maintains the physical and psychological continuity of an individual between life and death. It is what makes individuals unique. The *kla* is best described as a non-physical entity, a personal spirit, and the life force of an individual. The Dangme also believe that the physical body must have a spiritual component to be alive. They believe that the *mumi* (spirit) is given to people by the Supreme God. The *mumi* provides the force that gives the physical body life.

Another aspect of Ghanaian worldview is the belief that everyone has a destiny given to them by the Supreme God, and only God has the power to decide peoples' fates. The Akan expression, *nkrabea mu nni kwatibea* ("you cannot avoid the destiny that God has assigned"), emphasizes this point.[1] In general, destinies are given to the spiritual components of people before their birth. For the Akan, destiny is decreed by God to the *okra*, and for the Ga it is delivered to the *kla*. Destiny, however, does not predetermine every step along life's path. People have control over the way their lives unfold, and fulfilling one's destiny is one of the most important goals of life. Through consultation with elders and diviners, people can help to prevent moral mistakes and imprudent acts. People must live moral lives and take responsibility for their deeds, and ultimately these actions will allow a person to reach their destiny handed down from the Supreme God.

An important component of traditional worldview is the belief in the existence of evil forces that can affect individual and group destiny. The need to fulfill one's destiny helps regulate social behavior, but supernatural forces can influence one's actions and limit success. Spiritual contamination, through the use of witchcraft or the failure to heed social and cultural taboos, can infect an entire community. People must take actions to protect themselves against harming others, including divination, purification, and making offerings to certain spirits.

Ghanaian worldview, then, is associated with how people see themselves as individuals, as part of a community, and in their relationship to the spiritual and physical world around them. Increasingly, Ghanaian worldview also takes into account the idea of Ghana as a nation. Ghanaians seek to understand their place in the international political, economic, and cultural environment. The development of a national consciousness did not begin to sprout until the mid-twentieth century when independence became a clear possibility. By the beginning of the 1950s, the idea of a Ghanaian nation began to spread throughout all levels of the population. The movement toward independence, the pan-African ideas championed by Nkrumah, and the increasing pride of Ghanaian culture and heritage following independence remain important components of the Ghanaian worldview. Ghanaians are proud that they became the first country to earn their independence from colonialism in sub-Saharan Africa.

Ghanaians also seek to enhance their worldly presence, through economic activities, politics, and sports. Ghanaian gold and cocoa have a significant impact on the international economy. Many Africans from the continent and throughout the diaspora wear Ghanaian textiles, especially *kente* cloth (a brightly colored cloth once associated with African royalty). Ghanaians hold high office in world organizations, with Kofi Annan serving his second term as the secretary general of the United Nations. Success in the World Cup, international boxing, and track and field also brings great pride, uplifts the spirit of the entire country, and contributes to the idea of a Ghanaian national identity.

Although many Ghanaians subscribe to some or all of the physical and spiritual components of the worldview discussed above, the way people look at themselves and the way they see the world around them continue to change with increasing urbanization and the availability of external cultural resources. Although most people still live in rural areas and observe many indigenous religious customs and practices, the expansion of outside influences has changed patterns of social behavior and beliefs. Urbanization and the cosmopolitan culture associated with urban centers have increased the availability of outside cultural stimuli. These influences also find their way into even the most remote villages. Ghanaians have traveled abroad for work, education, and leisure since the early days of colonialism, but the frequency of contact with other cultures continues to grow due to increasing participation in international peace-keeping missions, involvement in international business ventures, and changes in the rapidity and ease of travel anywhere in the world. Media forms, such as television, cinema, newspapers, magazines, and radio also bring outside cultural influences into everyday Ghanaian life and help to shape worldview.

Lastly, the expansion of education and the increasing presence of outside religious influences have had an impact on the changing Ghanaian worldview. Education creates a more diverse knowledge of the world, making outside scientific, philosophical, and cultural influences more salient on a day-to-day basis. Evolution may offer a more rational scientific explanation for the beginning of humanity than the various creation myths. Modern medicine may provide more plausible diagnoses and treatments for various sicknesses than traditional medicine. In both cases, however, one belief does not always invalidate the other, but simply offers another way to look at the world. More often than not, Ghanaians adopt foreign aspects into their worldview, but they first adapt them to fit into their ideas on the nature of their physical and spiritual environments. Modern medicine, for example, is recognized for its effectiveness against certain diseases, but it is considered useless against illnesses caused by spiritual forces. There is, thus, a need to grant importance to each in belief and practice.

Christianity and Islam first established formal institutions of education in Ghana and promoted wholesale conversion. Christianity, in particular, asked converts to dismiss many beliefs and practices of indigenous religion, and thus worldview, as improper. Still, traditional religion, Islam, and Christianity also share many similar characteristics. These include the belief in a Supreme God, the prescribed treatment of others, and the importance of community participation. Many converts maintain essential traditional beliefs that form the Ghanaian worldview. The belief in the existence of a hierarchy of spiritual powers, for example, still plays a significant role in determining one's social behavior and overall approach to life. Praying to a Supreme God, seeking redemption through a holy spirit, and acknowledging one's ancestors are easily incorporated into many of the external religions as well.

INDIGENOUS RELIGIONS

Indigenous religions incorporate a system of beliefs and practices that play a fundamental role in interpersonal interactions and explain the origins and development of the physical and spiritual environment. Unlike the declining importance of religion in most Western societies, indigenous religions continue to form a core of Ghanaian cultural and ritual life. Religion explains good and ill-fortune and provides a means to comprehend the unknown through its belief in supernatural phenomenon invoked by ancestors and witches.

In traditional religions, there are no literary documents, such as the Christian Bible or the Muslim Qur'an, which tell stories about gods or prophets. There are no written rules, rituals, doctrines, or practices. Such beliefs and practices are recorded, however, in various forms of oral history and literature. Myths, folk tales, songs, and proverbs pay respect to important gods and ancestors, and call on them for protection and good-will. Indigenous religion manifests itself in everyday life through its belief in the spirit world, its principles of morality, and in special ceremonies of worship.

Although the number of people who actually proclaim their adherence to traditional religion is declining, this does not reflect on its importance to society. Despite the impact of Christianity and Islam, traditional religion continues to have influence in social and political life because of individual commitment to the well-being of the family, lineage, and community. Whether people see themselves as Christian or Muslim, many continue to maintain indigenous religious beliefs about the existence of supernatural forces and follow certain traditional religious practices that accompany these beliefs.

The belief and practice of traditional religion varies from one ethnic group to the next. Even within an ethnic group there may be variances based on familial practices and beliefs. Though there are as many different types of traditional religions in Ghana as there are ethnic groups, there are also basic similarities. The most fundamental trait to all Ghanaian traditional religions is the belief in a hierarchy of spiritual beings that are responsible for the human condition. At the top of the hierarchy is the Supreme God, followed by lesser gods, ancestors, witches, diviners, and other spiritual powers, some of which are life-enhancing and others which are life-damaging.

Supreme God

Every Ghanaian ethnic group believes in the existence of a Supreme God. Just as Christians throughout the world use the English word "God" and

Muslims pray to Allah, indigenous religions also have their own names. *Onyame* (Akan), *Nyonmo* (Ga), *Mawu* (Ewe), *Eboore* (Gonja), and *Nwuni* (Mamprusi) are a few of the names used for the Supreme God in indigenous religions. Regardless of the language employed, the characteristics of the Supreme God are very similar in every case. God is considered the creator of all things and the source of all powers, both good and evil, which affect worldly life. The Akan proverb, "It is God who drives away flies from a tailless animal," supports this assertion. God is considered understanding and merciful, but capable of calling punishment on those who do not live according to society's rules.

Although responsible for creation, the Supreme Being is thought to be too powerful and too distant from the world of humans to be directly worshiped in daily religious life. There are no priesthoods or shrines devoted to the Supreme Being. The name of the Supreme God, however, is invoked during libation or sacrifice to other gods or ancestors. Individuals also pray to God frequently for help and protection, or to give thanks for their well-being, much the same as Christians and Muslims do in daily prayers.

Lesser Gods

All Ghanaian ethnic groups share similar stories describing God's departure from the earthly world to heaven and the delegation of spiritual relations with humans to lesser gods. The numerous *abosom* (Akan), *trowo* (Ewe), and *wodzi* (Ga) serve as intermediaries between the Supreme Being and people on earth.

The lesser gods are usually associated with elements of nature, such as rivers, bodies of water, trees, and mountains. The Supreme God created everything, including the heavens, the earth, and the sea, and each has a lesser god connected to it. The most important of these gods in Ga society, for example, is *nai*, the sea god, reflecting the society's emphasis on fishing. The Ga have a shrine dedicated to *nai* near the ocean. It is headed by a priest and associated with certain rituals designed to show honor and respect for the sea god. No fishing takes place on Tuesday, the holy day dedicated to *nai*. The priest pours libations and offers gifts of food on this day. If the god is pleased, the people will be assured of prosperity. If the harvest of fish begins to decline, then the people know that the sea god must be displeased and additional actions must be taken to seek atonement.

Some of the lesser deities are linked with specific objects or actions. The *nyigbla* of the Anlo-Ewe, for example, is a war god who provides protection and courage during battle, while other gods are responsible for rain, thunder, or farming activities. Even farming can have different gods linked to different crops. For the Ga, cultivation of millet is associated with the *kpele* gods, while yam, a more difficult crop to grow and harvest, is linked to the *otu* gods, as well as objects of leadership, such as stools and drums.

Like *nai*, many of the lesser gods have priests and priestesses attached to them. A shrine serves as the residence for their spirit and acts as a place of worship for their followers. The traditional priests and priestesses are seen as mediators who are given instructions from their corresponding gods. Unlike the Supreme God, lesser gods frequently receive structured worship, but it is always led by the priests, priestesses, and other trained members of the shrines. Priests and priestesses receive extensive training in divination and receive frequent requests for consultation from clients. They remain important members of society today, heading some of the religious festivals and offering their services to those who are physically or spiritually troubled.

Religious festivals and individual rites are held to purify the community and offer sacrifices to the lesser gods. These actions recognize the influence and power of these deities and help to ensure peace and prosperity. When people offend any of the gods, some actions must be taken to mollify them. The breaking of a societal taboo or failure to follow through on an action promised to gods can bring their anger and lead to the introduction of evil spirits into the lives of the offenders and their families. The first step for an offender is to admit guilt, followed by the presentation of various sacrifices at the shrine of the god. The amount of sacrifice is determined by the magnitude of the offense. Sacrifices may include liquor, kola nuts, chickens and goats, or anything of value.

The majority of lesser gods are part of a community's belief structure and have existed within a particular traditional religion for as long as there have been followers of that religion. Some of them, however, are individually owned by wealthy and powerful individuals. These are usually more recent creations and are associated with particular objects used in witchcraft. They gained power through the establishment of a priesthood cult and frequently have a shrine devoted to them.

Ancestors

The Supreme God and the lesser gods are revered, but the ancestors receive the most visible veneration on a regular basis. All Ghanaian traditional religions believe that the spirits of ancestors can affect the lives of those on earth. Ancestors can manifest themselves in many forms, including human bodies, in dreams, or through possession. Ancestors provide the foundation for moral life and societal stability through the enforcement of customs and taboos that regulate group behavior. Ancestors are spiritual beings who have the power to bring good fortune and provide protection, but when dissatisfied with individual or group actions, they can also bring punishment, ill-fortune, and sickness. Paying proper tribute to ancestors can help assure an abundant harvest, good health, and a large family.

Ancestors are believed to be the most accessible link to the spiritual world. They are dead forebears of a family who have contributed to the well-being and prestige of a lineage and the community. It is believed that, as parents, grandparents, chiefs, and priests, ancestors continue to exercise authority over their living descendants and maintain an active interest in their affairs. In most Ghanaian societies, only those who have lived long lives and died honorably move into the ancestral world. In Akan society, for example, people who die prematurely because of an accident or unexplained circumstance cannot join the ancestral world. Their spirits exist on earth until they can be born again into a new body to finish their life and fulfill their destinies.

The belief and veneration of ancestors can be seen in various aspects of Ghanaian life. One of the most common practices is pouring the first few drops of a beverage or dropping a few bits of food on the ground, thus providing sustenance to the ancestors and acknowledging their presence. In many societies, the spirits of ancestors exist in sacred stools. Some groups have special rooms, shrines, or stool houses, watched over by priests, priestesses, or other religious specialists. Some of the most important symbols of ancestral authority are blackened stools, believed to carry the spirit of their chiefly owners. Upon death, the white stool of a leader is blackened with soot and egg yolk and placed in a special room with other blackened stools and is brought out for occasional tribute.

The political and religious functions of chiefs and elders are reinforced during religious festivals when people participate in rituals that emphasize the relationship between the living and the ancestral world. The current chief, whose power is derived from the ancestral chiefs, usually oversees ceremonies that pay tribute to ancestors. During the *odwira* festival of the Akan, for example, the chief makes offerings of food and drink to the spirit of the ancestors by putting small amounts on the blackened stools. Likewise, during the *homowo* festival of the Ga, the family elders and chiefs sprinkle some of the ceremonial meal of *kpekpei* around the house and neighborhoods to pay tribute to the ancestors.

The belief in, and reverence for, ancestors relates directly to Ghanaian's view of the relationship between the land of the living and the land of the dead. Death is not the end of life, but marks the transfer of the soul from the earthly world to that of the ancestors. The Ewe, for example, see life and death as having an intimate relationship. The Ewe word for death, *ku,* is also the word for seed, suggesting that death is the seed, or the beginning, of life.

The importance of ancestors lends great importance to funerals as a social and ritual event. Without the proper ceremony, the soul of the deceased cannot become an ancestral spirit. The nature of the funeral rites depends on the status of the deceased. There are specific rites for chiefs, musicians, hunters, fishermen, and farmers. Items are included in the coffin of the deceased according to their standing in life. Chiefs, for example, are buried with some of their regalia, while everyone is provided at least some food and clothes for their journey to the other world.

Witchcraft

The spirit world not only links the living and their ancestors, but it can also provide power to witches. Most Ghanaian societies acknowledge the earthly presence of other spiritual entities and recognize the effect that the power of magic can have on human life. The Akan call witchcraft *bayie*, the Ga refer to it as *aye*, and the Ewe as *adze*. Car accidents, miscarriages, and any unexplained circumstances could be blamed on the intervention of evil spirits or witchcraft. Upon death, people pass from the physical world to the spiritual world, but whereas ancestors are the spirits of those who have lived long and respected lives, witches and ghosts contain the spirits of those who have died prematurely or dishonorably. Their souls have been rejected in the spirit world and they roam the earth, having the power to create havoc for the living. There are also good ghosts who exist in the human world and visit at night to try to put things right. They are the images of people who died a natural death.

Witchcraft is used to refer to a variety of magical powers that cannot be comprehended in the human realm. Witches, however, are living people, both male and female, who can use the powers of the supernatural for evil deeds. Just as priests and priestesses serve as the intermediaries with the spiritual power of lesser gods, witches are believed to also have the means to access a different type of spiritual power. People accused of being witches are usually those who exhibit some variance of anti-social behaviors. Loners who do not partake in community duties, wealthy people who do not share their money with others, or the extremely poor who may be impelled to seek witchcraft to enhance their status may be looked at as witches. Physical traits, too, can lend themselves to identification of witches. People with certain physical defects, such as red eyes, are sometimes accused of being witches.

The powers of witchcraft can be used in various ways. They may be used to eliminate an opponent in a sporting match, a political campaign, or a court case. Tactics may include delaying the arrival of opponents, triggering a sickness to make them forfeit, or even causing them to die. In a recent election, for example, one observer reported that a candidate was struck in the face by a crow and complained that people were using witchcraft to diminish his success. Soon after, the candidate felt dizzy and died later on his way to the hospital.[2]

It is believed that witchcraft can strike anyone at any time and, thus, great effort and time can be spent trying to purge evil spirits and seek help from good spirits. During unexplained misfortunes, people seek to find out the supernatural cause of their problem from traditional priests or diviners. Once the cause is determined, remedies can range from protective charms and amulets, to ritual bathing and sacrifice.

Divination is another popular method of dealing with powers of witchcraft. Divination involves the use of certain objects to predict future events. It can be used to locate lost objects, determine the cause of a sickness, or any other type of information helpful to the client. The Anlo Ewe have an organized and elaborate system of divination (*afa*) associated with a particular deity. The system of divination is divided into priests (*bokowo*) and ordinary members (*bokoviwo*). The *bokowo* are men who have knowledge of divination techniques, while ordinary members, men, women, and children, do not. The *afa* divination technique is an elaborate procedure. The diviners throw four halves of palm kernels onto a mat or piece of wood and read the kernels by determining their order, assessing whether they are face-up or face-down. Each of the many combinations is associated with a short saying that is believed to contain information about the issue being presented. It takes a great deal of training to learn all of the possible outcomes. A simpler way to perform the divination ceremony is to use four cowrie shells or pieces of kola nut. They are thrown in the same way as the kernels, but they can be used for "yes" or "no" type questions only.

Indigenous Religion and Change

Indigenous religious beliefs and practices are dynamic and continue to change with the needs of society, the development of new ideas, and the introduction of new objects. Although based on long-standing beliefs developed during the many centuries of their existence, numerous encounters with Muslims and Christians, the appearances of new religious leaders, and the incorporation of new technology has influenced those beliefs and altered the practice of them.

New objects are sometimes acquired and can assume religious significance. The Akan *kuduo*, for example, is a metal urn first introduced by Muslim traders in the fourteenth or fifteenth century. These urns are now important symbols of wealth and religious power. They are sometimes found in Akan religious shrines where they are believed to represent the heart and essence of the deity.

The practice of many rituals also undergo changes that can be recorded and justified in the oral tradition. In the annual *aboakyer* festival of the Effutu people in Winneba, the object of sacrifice was originally a live leopard caught with the bare hands of a Fante warrior. Over time, too many men were killed and many more sustained serious injuries. The people appealed to Penkye Otu, the god of the festival, who reportedly suggested a live deer instead, the animal that is still used in the festival today. In this case, oral tradition upholds the story and justifies the use of the deer in the festival by attributing the decision to the god.

In other cases, the introduction of new items made those previously used less desirable. In many religious rituals, for example, chiefs, elders, and priests once poured libations with palm wine or water. It is now more common to use locally brewed or imported liquor, because it is believed that many gods prefer it and it has a higher prestige factor.

The success of Christianity and Islam on a national level does not mean that the importance of indigenous religion is waning. It continues to influence the way in which people see the world and their place within it. Almost all Ghanaians, regardless of class or education, are affected by indigenous religion, consciously and unconsciously. People maintain a strong belief in the power of the Supreme God and the existence of lesser gods. Most Ghanaians continue to honor their ancestors and have at least a minimal belief in supernatural powers. Whether the powers attributed to the lesser gods, ancestors, and witches actually exist or not is irrelevant. The beliefs alone can be a factor in shaping social behavior. People avoid actions or objects that might lead them to be associated with witchcraft and limit those behaviors that might bring the wrath of spiritual powers and invite the presence of evil forces.

The desire to maintain many of the important indigenous beliefs and practices is evident in the recent success of some Christian churches who are more willing to incorporate local customs. Many of the most important beliefs and values of Ghanaian indigenous religions correspond with those of Pentecostal and Charismatic churches, thus contributing to their rapidly increasing popularity. These features are discussed more below.

CHRISTIANITY

Christianity is the dominant faith in the southern and central parts of Ghana and commands the most followers overall. Christianity arrived in Ghana in distinct phases. The early phase lasted from the arrival of the

Europeans in the late fifteenth century until the expansion of British influence in the mid-nineteenth century. The early influence was largely confined to the coastal regions and saw only limited and scattered conversions to Christianity. The Portuguese held the first public mass in 1482 at the Elmina castle, the site of European trading activity. European traders had little interest in Christianizing the population, but they were accompanied by missionaries of all faiths who sought out converts and built makeshift churches.

Christianity began to see greater success in the early nineteenth century when various religious faiths established more formal bases. The Basel Mission (Presbyterian), the Methodist Church, and the Bremen Mission (Evangelical Presbyterian) were founded in Ghana between 1829 and 1847. The Roman Catholics followed when the French established a mission at Elmina in 1880. By 1906, Catholicism had established a mission in the northern area of Navrongo. Other Christian religions began to make some inroads as well, including denominations from the United States, such as the AME Zion Church, which was established in Keta around 1896, and various Pentecostal faiths in the early twentieth century.

A key component to the early Christian missionary activity was the creation of missionary schools. Churches attempted to attract converts by offering formal education, with the belief that once able to read, people would understand the Bible and accept Christianity. Although resistant and wary of Western religion at first, many families eventually began to see the benefits of education and sent their children to the schools. The early success was most profound amongst a developing Ghanaian elite, who saw conversion as a way into employment with the colonial administration or a step toward obtaining professional degrees. Missionary schools were the only available outlet for formal education for much of the colonial period. Since the Education Act of 1960, however, the national government has assumed financial responsibility for the majority of schools.

Many of the Christian missions focused their evangelization in specific areas. The presence of the various Christian religions today generally relates to the geographical emphasis on early missionary activity. Evangelical Presbyterians attract the largest following among the Ewe in the Volta Region, Presbyterians among the Akwapim, and the Methodists among the Fante. The Roman Catholic Church has followers throughout the country. All of the major Christian faiths are represented in major cities.

Today, Ghana has the highest percentage of Christians in West Africa. In every Ghanaian town Catholic and Protestant (including Methodist and Anglican) churches can be found everywhere. It is difficult to walk anywhere in the southern half of the country and not see or hear a Christian slogan marketing every imaginable product and recommending advice to the viewers

One of the first theaters in Ghana, the Palladium, is now a Pentecostal church.

and listeners. Christian music consumes a substantial part of radio air time, many businesses have religious names, such as the "In God's Time" hair salon and the "Clap for Jesus" barber shop, and posters frequently advertise Christian crusades soon to be passing through town offering salvation to those willing to commit themselves to Jesus.

In the past few decades, Ghana has entered into a third phase of Christianity. Independent African Churches, Pentecostal, and Charismatic faiths have increased their membership rapidly during the last twenty years, reflecting the success of religious faiths that adapt their practices and doctrines to suit local beliefs. Some people have estimated that there are more than 3,000 different sects of these Christian churches in the country. Some of these include the Lighthouse Chapel International, the International Charismatic Church, the Apostolic Church, the Christ Apostolic Church, the Assemblies of God, and the Church of Pentecost. The Church of Pentecost is the largest Protestant church in Ghana with an estimated 920,000 followers. Many of them are local branches of Apostolic or Pentecostal churches in Europe or the United States, while others are local creations. The thousands of local churches bear names such as the Brotherhood of the Cross and the Divine

Life Power Ministries. They exist in any open space or shelter, from the inside of elaborate buildings to the yards of small residences. Many of the sects are focused around a single charismatic leader. Some of them have their own television and radio programs.

Ghanaian independent churches include the Musama Disco Christo Church, which broke away from the Methodist Church of Ghana, the Apostle's Revelation Society, and the Kristo Asafo Christ Reformed Mission. The Kristo Asafo church was established in Accra in 1971 and later established branches in Kumase and several other towns in southern Ghana. The Ghanaian spiritual churches emphasized healing and exorcism in their services and quickly gained popularity. Many of them broke up, however, due in part to disorganization, and opened the door for the rise of the Pentecostal and Charismatic churches.

The independent African churches and the Pentecostal and Charismatic faiths have grown because of their incorporation of many beliefs from indigenous religions into the Christian framework. These churches are less rigid than the orthodox Christian churches. They emphasize faith healing, prophecy, and express a strong belief in signs and miracles. Dynamic and forceful orators lead the services, which are filled with lively music and dance and often feature spiritual possessions that lead people to speak in tongues. They rely on the power of the Holy Spirit to bring about miracles and inspire spirit possession. They incorporate many more local cultural influences into their practices and are very appealing to those disenchanted with the staid ceremony of the orthodox churches.

There are also a few foreign branches of proselytizing Christianity in Ghana. These include the Seventh-day Adventists, who have a large presence and an active press in Accra; Jehovah's Witnesses, who have their Kingdom Halls in many major cities; the Church of Jesus Christ of Latter-day Saints, who send selected followers on missions abroad during their education; and the Christian Scientists.

Effects of Christianity

Christianity introduced many changes into Ghanaian societies. Some early converts, eager to please the missionaries and the colonial administration, disavowed their traditional beliefs, changed their mode of dress, and adopted European names. Educational achievement, rather than age and lineage, became determinants of status, altering the traditional authority structure. Orthodox Christianity was opposed to the elemental indigenous religious beliefs in lesser gods, ancestral veneration, and the practices associated with witchcraft. The Christian faith considered these beliefs and practices to be pagan and "savage." As we have seen, however, these beliefs, and the religious ceremonies associated with them, were important in establishing social and cultural values, and were instrumental in maintaining social organization.

Disavowing everything associated with indigenous religion and wholesale acceptance of Christian practices and beliefs was an unacceptable option for most Ghanaians. During its early presence in Ghana, however, Christian missionaries tried to achieve just that. Christians were once forbidden from attending traditional religious festivals. Church leaders forbade attendance because of the emphasis on paying homage to lesser gods, ancestral tribute, and use of ritual objects. Neither did traditional leaders want Christians partaking in the ceremonial rites because it was believed that they would contaminate them and reduce their ritual effectiveness. These festivals were much more than religious events however. They helped to maintain the unity of society and remembered individual lineages, and nonparticipation by a few members detracted from the celebration. The festivals also reinforced the structure of society by recognizing the specific powers of ancestors, elders, and chiefs. The importance of family and community took precedence in the end as church leaders and traditional authorities removed their resistance to participation.

Missionaries set out to establish the orthodox practices of their church. These practices opposed many traditional customs. Puberty rites, bridewealth, and polygyny contradicted Christian beliefs and teachings and were considered "uncivilized." Some converts shunned these traditional customs. Some managed to justify them with their Christian beliefs. While the majority recognized the sharp differences between the two religious systems, many people also saw the benefits of maintaining some presence in both.

The early missionaries made positive contributions to Ghanaian societies in the areas of education and medicine. The most important was the introduction of formal education. Missionaries established all of the early schools in Ghana. Education offered a means for socioeconomic advancement. The ability to read and write could earn a graduate employment in the colonial administration, or perhaps a trip abroad to further their education. An educated Ghanaian elite came out of these early missionary schools. They became doctors, lawyers, and accountants. The educated elite disrupted social order by reducing the power of the elders and chiefs. The educated elite, however, were also the most important group in the drive toward independence in 1957, and have continued to fulfill prominent social and political roles during the independence era.

Along with schools, some of the churches established health clinics and hospitals in rural areas. They also taught various farming techniques and encouraged women to become active in certain occupations. Medical work and occupational instruction contributed to societal development, but they were also meant to promote missionary work by attracting converts.

With almost two-thirds of Ghanaians professing faith in Christianity today, the effects are obviously pervasive. Yet, the importance of traditional religion to overall social organization is evident in the fact that Christianity was never able to replace it completely. Even for those who profess Christianity or Islam, many continue to practice traditional beliefs and customs. People may subscribe to Christian beliefs, but in certain situations, such as sickness, mishap, or other ill-fortune, it is common to turn to a traditional diviner or priest in search of a cure. Today, it is not uncommon for people to participate in a traditional ceremony one day and attend a Christian church the next. Many Christian funeral practices, for example, have not displaced traditional funeral rites, but have been added to them.

The growing popularity of Pentecostal and Charismatic churches demonstrates the viability of Christian religions that are compatible with certain indigenous religious beliefs and are able to adapt to local cultural practices. The belief in witchcraft and divination, and the dynamic and expressive nature of the services, contribute to their attractiveness. Orthodox Christian churches, realizing the popularity of the Pentecostal variant of Christian worship, have also begun to adopt some of these practices. Some now have healing sessions and prayer groups, and most incorporate local music, features designed to attract new followers and keep their current ones.

Music and dance, important aspects of traditional religion, were generally not allowed in the orthodox Christian churches. Western-style church services had no connection to the traditional Ghanaian celebration of religion. There were a few pioneers, such as Ephraim Amu, who attempted to wear African dress on the pulpit and adapt the Western-style hymns to Ghanaian choral styles, but most churches resisted and were slow to change their long-established traditions. The growth of the Pentecostal churches has forced orthodox faiths to make adjustments in their religious services. Today, even the Catholic Church allows drumming, dancing, and singing during religious services. Many churches also sponsor social activities, including drumming and singing groups, which are very popular with young people.

The increasing expressiveness of Christian services has created conflicts with local religious customs. During the Ga annual festival of *homowo*, for example, there is a one-month ban on drumming and general loud noise. Everyone in the Ga traditional areas, regardless of ethnicity, is supposed to abide by the ban. It is feared that loud noises during the drum-ban could detract from the ritual purification of the period. Most leaders of other religious faiths respect traditional customs. Recently, Ga traditional leaders, representatives from various Christian faiths, and the Ahmadiyya Muslim

Mission called for respect for the ban. Some of the independent churches, however, have refused to reduce their volume, inciting some Ga youth to take physical actions to enforce the ban.

While some people participate in religious practices with the hope of salvation and the desire for community participation, others do so with the hope of earning some money. Many new churches, especially the Pentecostal and Charismatic types that rely on a single, dynamic leader, open each year, but some of their founders do so with the hope of making a profit. They operate from the backyard of their residential homes or in rented buildings and see the church as a money-making venture. A few chairs, a microphone and speaker, and, of course, a collection basket are all that is needed to start a church. In the late 1980s, the government attempted to regulate these start-up churches, but the act summoned resistance from Christian groups and it was later repealed.

The majority of churches, however, are legitimate and make valuable physical and spiritual contributions to personal and community development. The various Christian faiths have banded together to organize themselves and, occasionally, to comment on the overall management of the country. The Ghana Christian Council, representing most of the major orthodox Christian churches, was founded in 1929. The Christian Council links Ghanaian churches with the World Council of Churches. Catholics are united under the National Catholic Secretariat, established in 1960. Though they generally focus on the concerns of their congregations, church leaders have used the national organizations to make political statements as well. In 1991, for example, both Christian umbrella organizations called for the military government to begin the process of returning the country to constitutional rule.

ISLAM

Islam has a longer history in Ghana than Christianity, but does not attract as large a following. In fact, compared to other West African countries, the proportion of Muslims is quite low, limited mainly to the northern half of the country and urban centers. Ghanaian Muslims came from a variety of places in West Africa. Islam first came into West Africa via the trans-Saharan trade routes, as early as the eighth century, during the ancient empire of Ghana. The leaders of the subsequent Western Sudanese empires of Mali and Songhai adopted Islam and hastened its spread into the northern regions of modern Ghana around the fourteenth century. Islam was brought into this area of Ghana by Mande and Wangara traders and clerics. Muslim traders later brought Islam into contact with Asante chiefs and kings. During the nineteenth-century jihad of Uthman dan Fodio, many Muslims escaped the violence in Nigeria by moving into the northeastern region of Ghana. Many Muslims from neighboring countries, especially Nigeria, continue to migrate to Ghana today.

When religious clerics first arrived in northern Ghana, they had some influence with northern chiefs, but there was little wholesale conversion. Even today, Islam in northern Ghana is more profound in the cities and towns, rather than in the rural areas, where more people subscribe to indigenous religious beliefs. In Tamale, the largest city in the northern region, there are three distinct types of Muslims divided by economic class, age, and Islamic sect. The first, the educated, elite, government workers, and wealthy business people, form a small class of power brokers who are generally more main-stream Muslims. The second and largest group is made up of young people, usually males, who have migrated from the rural areas to the city in search of economic success. The third main group in Tamale consists of more rad-ical, Shiite-inspired Muslims who demand a greater role for Islamic law.

Since arriving in Ghana, many Muslims have migrated southward, usually to urban centers. Almost every city has at least a small percentage of Muslims, but Accra and Kumase have by far the largest populations. Many come from the northern regions as traders or on other types of business. Except for the economically well-off, Muslims often gather in a specific area or areas of a city, called a Zongo. In Accra, for example, the community of Nima is the home to many Muslims, although many other groups live there as well.

The fundamental ideology of Islam is based on the text of the Qur'an, which is believed to be the word of God revealed to Muslims through the Prophet Mohammed during the seventh century. It recounts his life, from the Arabian town of Mecca, where he received his first revelation around A.D. 610, and his trek to Medina (formerly called Yathrib) in 622, where he began to attract many followers. This trek from Mecca to Medina, about 200 miles to the north, is known as the *hijra*, and is one of most important tenets of Islam. The Qur'an was produced in 645, fifteen years after his death.

Other books were introduced as well. One of these was the Sharia, or the "canon law" of Islam. All of the writings form the *sunna*, the beliefs and practices as told by Prophet Mohammed, which all Muslims must follow. The most important of these practices form the five essential tenets of Islam. The Five Pillars of Islam are: (1) the *shahada*, the belief that "There is no God but God (Allah), and Mohammed is the Prophet of God"; (2) *salat*, the performance of ritual prayer five times per day; (3) *saum*, the fasting from dawn until sunset during the month of Ramadan; (4) *zakat*, the giving of alms to the poor; and (5) *hajj*, the pilgrimage to Mecca if one is physically and financially able.

Most Muslims in Ghana belong to the Sunni sect, the largest and most traditional form of Islam. Sufism, a less orthodox type of Islam that places greater importance on mysticism, is represented by the Tijaniyya and Qadariyya brotherhoods. The Qadiani faction of the Ahmadiyya movement is found along the coast, especially around the city of Saltpond in the Central Region. The sect, originating in nineteenth-century India, is considerably more radical than mainstream Islam and is known for espousing strong anti-Christian views. The Ahmadis (followers of the Ahmadiyya movement), however, also strongly emphasize formal education and vocational training, as well as the construction and management of hospitals, all of which have done much to promote religious education and well-being of Muslims.

Islamic activities in Ghana continue to change as influences from outside are introduced. Since 1970, The Islamic Reformation and Research Centre, with financing from Saudi Arabia, supports the education of Ghanaian students in Arab universities, the construction of schools, and other social services in Ghana. They also undertake missionary activities to help spread Islam to new areas. The Nation of Islam and its leader, Louis Farrakhan held a national convention in Ghana in 1996, but its organization within the country is limited and it has attracted few followers.

Effects of Islam

In general, Islam was more easily adapted to traditional religious beliefs and practices than Christianity. Important features of Islam, such as festivals, religious offices, and rites of passage, blended easily with traditional customs. Islam, for example, allows a man to marry up to four wives, while polygyny (one man having multiple wives) has always been an important part of traditional society. In other cases, traditional and Muslim festivals, such as the *damba* festival, were combined, utilizing aspects of Islam (Mohammed's birthday) and traditional society (pouring libations and celebrating community unity). Some Islamic clerics, when approached for help with a spiritual sickness, have also been known to utilize a combination of traditional healing techniques, such as charms and amulets, and beliefs derived from the Qur'an.

The religious identity of Muslims is more easily ascertained by their outward appearance and actions than that of Christians. Their dress, such as the *agbada* robes, represents part of the traditional dress of northerners, but is also similar to the dress of other Muslims throughout West Africa. Public prayers and rituals also identify a practicing Muslim. Required to pray five times per day, Muslims can be seen frequently gathered together in a mosque or a makeshift prayer ground kneeling down and facing Mecca. During Ramadan, one can identify Muslims by the dawn-to-dusk fasting, and the large meal that is consumed following sunset. The architecture of northern Ghana, especially that of some mosques, is derived from the Islamic architecture of the Western Sudan. Another important aspect of Islam is the *hajj*, the trip to Mecca that all Muslims should make during their lifetimes if they are able. Upon returning from the *hajj*, men and women are outwardly identified as Muslims by their assumption of the prestigious titles of Alhaji and Alhajia, respectively.

The Hausa from Nigeria, a predominantly Islamic group, have had an impact on the development of northern Ghanaian society. Hausa and Muslim identity are closely linked in the minds of many Ghanaians. Many Muslim customs and actions are associated with the Hausa. The Hausa language spread throughout the West African region during the trans-Saharan trade and is still commonly used in northern Ghanaian Islamic schools. Many non-Muslim Ghanaians refer to northerners, regardless of ethnicity or religion, using the generic term, "Hausa."

Muslims have created national groups to represent their interests. Like the umbrella Christian organizations, the Muslim Representative Council of Ghana manages religious, social, and economic conflicts that affect their religious brethren. Together with the Christian groups, they have worked to maintain a harmonious relationship between followers of the two religions. The Council also arranges the pilgrimages to Mecca each year. Despite these activities, however, the Council has done little to increase the quality of education for Muslims in the north, a deficiency that is largely responsible for its low economic and technological development when compared to the southern and central areas. The Ahmadiyya movement, mentioned above, is an exception.

When Islam was first introduced to northern Ghana, it brought with it a system of writing, a new language, and institutions of formal education. At least a basic comprehension of Arabic, the language of the Qur'an, is still required of Muslims everywhere. Islamic education in northern Ghana, however, has received little assistance from the national government, nor enough attention from Muslim societies. Many young Muslims in Ghana today have to look elsewhere to receive an Islamic education, especially at the advanced levels. Growing contacts with the rest of the Islamic world have opened up new opportunities for young Ghanaians. Increasing numbers of students have been receiving full scholarships to go to Islamic countries in North Africa or the Middle East to attain their university education. In addition to university scholarships, Islamic countries have also supported the construction of schools and mosques and sponsored development projects in northern Ghana. Some of the completed projects, however, exclude all non-Muslims from using them. Such policies are representative of a more fundamentalist type of Islam, emphasizing Islamic unity over family and lineage connections.

Unlike countries such as Nigeria where the percentage of Muslims is significantly higher, there have seldom been instances of conflict or animosity between Christians and Muslims on a national level in Ghana. Christianity is continuing to find some converts in the north, while north-south migration continues to increase the population of Muslims in Ghanaian cities and fosters more everyday interaction between the two religious groups. Since the most recent elections, national political power is shared at the highest level of office, with a Christian president and Muslim vice president. Muslim and Christian leaders frequently come together to make statements about national issues. As tensions were rising during the 1992 elections, the Christian Council, the National Catholic Secretariat, the Ghana Pentecostal Council, and the Ahmadiyya Muslim Mission called upon all political candidates and parties to help quell the volatile situation.

Most Ghanaians make very little of the religious differences between Muslims and Christians, with members of the same family sometimes belonging to different faiths. If a friend or relative of a different faith is getting married or holding a naming ceremony for a newborn, it is not uncommon to attend, regardless of one's own faith. Christmas, Easter, *Eid-el-Fitr* (the end of Ramadan), and *Eid-el-Adha* (the commemoration of Abraham's sacrifice of his son) are times for everyone to greet family, friends, and neighbors, despite the religious symbolism associated with each.

Although amiable, relations between Muslims and Christians have been changing during the last few decades as both the Christian and Islamic presence in northern areas continues to grow. During the last two decades, Christian missionaries have been taking a greater interest in evangelizing in the northern regions. Although the number of Christians in the north remains low, the visible presence of Christian schools, medical clinics, and community groups is influencing some people to convert. Some groups focus only on converting Muslims to Christianity. Members of one such group, the Converted Muslims' Christian Association, publicly condemn Islamic beliefs and embellish stories of those who have converted to Christianity to disparage Islam even more. Such outward displays of religious fervor have resulted in scattered violence between Muslims and Christians. During recent clashes across the northern regions, for example, Muslims burned and looted a Christian mission and threatened the lives of some missionaries. The violence was widespread, but people on both sides of the quarrel also shielded others from harm. Muslim leaders, for example, helped protect the lives of Christians, while Christian missions offered sanctuary to Muslims. Ghanaians have looked at the frequent eruptions of religious violence in Nigeria with great interest. Although many people perceive a growing rift between Christians and Muslims in the northern regions, Ghanaians are cautious to avoid the same fate.

There have also been instances of tension and unrest between Islamic groups. Ghanaian Muslims sometimes clash with other West African Muslims living in Ghana over leadership roles. There have been a few instances of physical skirmishes at the Mosque during prayers, and subsequent closures of mosques by the government. In other cases, Ahmadis have clashed with mainstream Muslims. In general, there is little cooperation between the two groups, and it is common for one group to leave a conference table if the other is present. Some of the youth who return from university education in Arab countries also incite conflicts with traditional Ghanaian Muslims. One of these groups, *Ahl ul-Sunna,* is a missionary-oriented group of Muslims trained largely in Saudi Arabia. Educated in what they see as a more pure form of Islam in the Arab-Muslim world, they return to Ghana and condemn practices such as the use of charms or amulets. These cases, however, are infrequent in Ghana and people of all religions generally live together without conflict based on religious ideology.

Ghanaians participate in many different ritual systems, some based on indigenous religions, and others based on various forms of Christianity and Islam. The rituals and religious beliefs of each reveal similarities and differences. The religious practices of many Muslims and Christians overlap with those of indigenous religions. Ghanaians are able to adapt to one without dismissing the other, thus satisfying multiple spiritual, psychological, and social needs. New religious leaders have not eliminated the power of the lesser gods and the ancestors, nor have they replaced traditional priests and diviners. It is not uncommon for people to attend a Muslim mosque or a Christian church, and then engage a diviner or traditional priest when they are experiencing physical or spiritual problems. Christians and Muslims still pour libations to the ancestors and lesser gods, and retain the belief that the spirit world can provide an explanation for misdeeds, sicknesses, and periods of bad luck.

Some of the rituals and practices of traditional religion are on the decline, but it continues to play a major role in Ghanaian life. Religion, more so than any other aspect of Ghanaian culture, plays a fundamental role in determining the nature of social interactions, family and lineage organization, personal appearance, traditional arts, and music and dance. In short, religion is fundamental to understanding the culture and customs of Ghana.

NOTES

1. K.A. Opoku, "The Destiny of Man in Akan Religious Thought," in J.M. Assimeng (ed.), *Traditional Life, Culture and Literature in Ghana* (New York: Conch Magazine Ltd., 1976), 22.

2. George Ayittey, "How Ghana Was Saved," *Ghana Review International,* 77 (2001), 17–19.

3

Literature and Media

> I have fulfilled my mission. I came into the world with song. No
> one can sing with my voice. But I have nothing, neither children
> nor wealth. My reward is beyond, and here in the words I leave
> with you the youth. My songs are gifts from the creator himself.
> —Hesino Akpalu, Ewe Poet[1]

LITERATURE is found in many areas of Ghanaian life. There are few formal
or informal occasions which do not incorporate various aspects of the Ghanaian literary tradition, including oral literature, written literature, and performance literature or drama. These are not distinct genres, however, because
written literature and drama incorporate elements from oral tradition. Within
the various types there are different styles, including poems, proverbs, narratives, and novels, as well as formal and popular styles. A discussion of
Ghanaian literature and dramatic performance cannot be isolated from the
development of media forms, which have drawn from, and contributed to,
creative literature.

ORAL LITERATURE

Many different types of oral literature help preserve and shape the history
and worldview of Ghanaian communities. These are by far the oldest of the
literature forms. Proverbs, poetry, songs, and oral narratives are used to communicate complex messages or simple morals, to praise or criticize others,
and to tell stories about the creation of the world, describe the nature of

divine power, or recall important historical events. They are a means of handing down traditions and customs to new generations. Above all, oral literature provides an outlet for social criticism and commentary and contributes to social cohesion. Western education and urbanization have lessened the importance of oral literature, but it continues to thrive in many communities because of a lack of printed material and because of its prominent role in maintaining traditional culture.

Oral literature is a powerful performance medium because, by definition, it is dependent on performers, who accentuate their words and meanings with gestures, facial expressions, intonation, and mimicry. It is deeply tied into the social context in which it is performed. The actions of the performers are, in part, determined by active and passive audience participation. Performers change their presentation, from the type of story to the complexity of words and images, depending on who is in the audience. Performers also respond to verbal and nonverbal suggestions, perhaps cutting a story short or using repetition to emphasize a point. Oral literature is improvisational, especially in the narrative form. The performers vary the script and continuously update it or make it more topical and relevant.

Proverbs

Proverbs are one of the most common forms of oral expression. Ghanaian societies have thousands of proverbs that express the wisdom of communities and provide a means to understand life in the past and present. Public speakers and linguists are expected to have a wealth of proverbs available to them in order to communicate effectively. An Akan expression reiterates this: "We speak to a wise man in proverbs, not in plain speech." Proverbs can be used to address a subject or criticize an individual who, because of social or political restrictions, cannot be named directly. They may be used, for example, to comment on government neglect or wrongdoing by an elder without explicitly naming the problem or the person, yet the listeners know what or who is being addressed.

A proverb is usually a short saying, well-known by society or particular groups within society, that expresses a truth, offers a guide to good conduct, and warns against foolish acts. A particular proverb can function in different ways according to the context. The Adangbe proverb, *yi hi si ne nakutso buo pee* ("the knee does not wear the hat when the head is available"), for example, may be used in court to maintain the hierarchy, but it may also be used in everyday life as a caution against the arrogance of youth. Another, *Adeo kake loko adeo enyo,* expresses the fundamental idea that we must count one before counting two. Proverbs relating directly to human behavior often use a negative proposition to accomplish their goal: *ke otui obofu munyu wui tso puomi o tso ba be buanyaa* (Adangbe: "if you do not utter insulting words into a hole in a tree, the leaves of the tree will not shake"). This proverb deals with the nature of gossip and insults. It asks the listener not to speak ill of anyone so that no one will be offended by another's words.[2]

Proverbs include similes: *Nyamesom tsede asordan tokura mu ahwehwe; igyina ekyir hwe a, oye wo kusuwu; se ehen mu a na ihu ne few* (Akan: "Religion is like a stained glass window which is dark when one views it from the outside. One will appreciate its beauty only from inside the church").[3] Many proverbs are metaphorical and make a philosophical statement. These fall into two categories: those with animal themes and those referring to humans. Certain animals are used to illustrate particular traits: *Edzifo dzepe ntsi na oma adowa ka bodambo mu* (Akan: "It is the gluttonous bee that gets itself stuck in the palm wine bottle"). The meaning, gluttony will get one into trouble, is obvious to the listener, but its expression in a proverb shows wisdom and is less likely to insult its intended target.

Some proverbs are represented by symbols on Akan gold weights, in patterns of cloth, and in the language of drums. The symbol of the wisdom knot, for example, brings to mind the proverb, "The knot tied by a wiseman cannot be undone by a fool." It is usually found on objects of art associated with leadership and affirms that leaders have the right to their position because of their great wisdom. The Kente pattern, *tikoro nko agyina* ("one head does not go into council"), says that it is better for two people to make a decision rather than one. The Republic of Ghana gave a carving bearing this symbol to the United Nations and it now hangs in the United Nations building in New York City.

Poetry and Songs

There are many different poetic forms, many of them closely associated with songs. These include dirges, praise poetry, and abuse poetry. Some poetry is tied to particular occupations such as Ewe fishing communities, or to warrior groups such as the *asafo* companies of the Fante. Poetry is used to praise gods and ancestors. Like proverbs, poetry sometimes uses drum sounds as a medium of communication or to emphasize the message. Poems can be performed by professionals, semi-professionals, or amateurs. All Ghanaian societies use various forms of poetry, ranging from informal lyrics and songs sung by friends, to complex court and praise poetry.

Professional poets are attached to chiefs and royalty in Akan, Guan, and Ga-Adangbe societies, although today the attachment is less formal than it used to be. These orators perform panegyric and libation poetry praising ancestors and chiefs. Within an Akan royal court, there are various types of performers, including poets and musicians. Both, however, perform a similar function, praising the deeds of past rulers at all important state occasions, such as the installation of a new chief, a state funeral, or a national festival. Some Akan drummers are poets too. In drum poetry, the drum sounds represent the words of the poem, producing language tones and patterns that are recognizable. Drum poetry can incorporate riddles and proverbs:

> The path has crossed the river.
> The river has crossed the path.
> Which is elder?
> We made the path and found the river.
> The river is from long ago,
> From the ancient creator of the universe.[4]

Elegiac poems, or dirges, are also commonly performed at many Ghanaian funerals and memorials. All Akan females, for example, are expected to participate in this highly creative aspect of mourning. Developing the necessary skills is important to a child's education, as one expert remarks: "A woman must wail and wail in words, in coherent and expressive utterances provided by tradition."[5] If a female is not trained properly, her mother and father will suffer when their daughter is unable to properly mourn them at their funerals. Akan dirges are solo performances without musical accompaniment. Of course, the words are important. They might praise the ancestors, the deceased, or their village, reflect on past deeds, or send a meaning. Still, the mourners use more than words to express their message, relying on voice tones, expressions, emotional releases, and body movements to improve their performance style. Here is part of a dirge sung by a mother for her dead son:

> Grandsire Gyina with a slim but generous arm,
> Fount of satisfaction
> My friend Adu on whom I depend,
> I depend on you for everything, even for drinking water.[6]

At a funeral, many females take turns presenting dirges, each one creating an expression of her emotions based on her relationship to the deceased.

Oral poetry is a dynamic style that adapts to contemporary situations. Politicians, for example, incorporate it into their rhetoric, just as they do other forms of traditional culture. Nkrumah had a traditional poet attached to him just as the Asante court poets served Asante royalty. His job was to perform praise poetry before Nkrumah gave a speech in public, on the radio, or in parliament. The poet recited praise songs to enhance Nkrumah's national mystique and to promote the idea of a Ghanaian nation. Most panegyric poems to Nkrumah included appellations such as "Shaker of the brave, Shaker of the mighty, Shaker of the brave, Kwame, The Ever-Ready All-Embracing Protective Hyde."[7] Nkrumah's opponents also used poems to criticize his government, without publicly naming anyone or identifying specific problems.

One of the most interesting forms of poetry, *halo*, is found among the Ewe.[8] *Halo* poetry is used to settle disputes or reduce hostilities within a community. As it is not appropriate to criticize people directly, *halo* offers a means to reduce aggression and provide social sanction. When two people agree to settle a dispute through *halo* songs, the poets begin to construct their strategy, often digging into family history or other matters for stories, true or fictional, that can be used against their opponent. Exaggeration is a key element of the performance competition. On a given day, one of the poets begins to perform the first *halo*. This is followed, sometimes days or weeks later, by a response from the other. The people of the community serve as the judges and decide the winner after a number of performances. One such competition went on for five years. *Halo* is, above all, an entertainment form. The performances attract large crowds, and the poets use humorous satire and exaggeration to garner laughs. One author relates a description of an elder who was ridiculed in a *halo* song for "having ears so large that whenever he took the canoe, the boatmen had no need of sails."[9] Although *halo* can get quite aggressive (a British representative in the area even banned it at one point), the poets always walk away as friends. *Halo* does not enjoy the same popularity as it once did, but remnants of it remain in other forms of Ewe poetry.

Narratives

Storytelling forms an important basis for social cohesiveness and is a favorite recreational pastime appreciated by Ghanaians of all ages. Oral narratives allow the people of the community to come together and relax after a hard day's work. Most stories are performed in the evenings, usually by a family member or by community elders. Anyone can tell stories, but the skill is associated with knowledge and wisdom so the best storytellers are usually older women and men. In a typical storytelling session, the audience gathers in a circle around the narrator. The story line depends on skills of the individual storyteller. Folktales often use animal imagery to provide answers to questions about the natural or mythical world or impart a moral lesson.

They might also raise themes of economic hardship, migration, and other subjects relevant to the contemporary socioeconomic environment.

The performance context is crucial to oral narratives. The setting, situation, and actions of narrators are as important as their words, audience movement, and the facial expressions that they evoke. The audience also plays an important role. There is a close rapport between the narrator and the audience. The narrator looks to the audience for inspiration. The unfolding of the story is often decided by the audience's reaction to the storyteller. Some narrations call for musical accompaniment, which members of the audience can provide through singing or clapping. The audience also has an active call-and-response relationship with the storyteller. Many stories cannot begin until the audience has answered an opening call from the storyteller. During the story the audience will, through comments, body movements, and facial expressions, help provide the storyteller with new twists in the plot.

Introductions to stories employ well-known phrases to get the audience's attention and signal to them that the story is ready to begin. These differ from one society to another but usually rely on some repeated phrase. Some Akan say, for example, "Abraa! Abraa!" ("Listen! Listen!") and the audience responds with "Yon! Yon!" ("We are listening! We are listening!"). The storyteller might then ask a question having to do with the story's main message: "Do you know why the moon is in the sky?" When the audience responds, "No, why?" the story can begin. The conclusion is also a formal utterance that brings the story to a close and creates a link to the next storyteller. The storyteller may ask a question and the first respondent in the audience becomes the next to perform.

Ghanaian folktales frequently employ animal characters with human characteristics. The animals exhibit greed, jealousy, honesty, or loneliness to amuse the audience and sometimes to teach a moral lesson. The animals include the hare, the tortoise, the deer, the rat, and many others. Kwaku Ananse, the spider, is the most ubiquitous trickster figure in Ghanaian folk tales. The popularity of Ananse stories is evident in the Akan word for all folktales dealing with animals, *anansesem* (ananse, or spider, stories). Ananse the spider assumes a variety of character traits in the stories. He might be clever, foolish, funny, gluttonous, or lazy. Most Ananse tales contain a lesson. A common Ananse story explains how wisdom spread from one man to everyone in the world: Ananse possessed all the wisdom in the world and, being selfish, he put it into a large pot and tried to hide it in a tall tree. He tied one end of a rope around the pot and the other around his neck. He attempted to climb the tree with the dangling pot resting on his stomach, but it was too cumbersome and he was unable to scale the tree. As he pondered how to get to the top, he heard laughter and his son's voice behind him suggesting that if he carried the pot on his back he would find it much easier to climb the tree. Angered by the perceived arrogance of his son, Ananse threw the pot to the ground, breaking it and scattering wisdom all over the world. The obvious moral is that no one person can have a monopoly of wisdom. The story also, however, teaches general lessons about gluttony and about respect, pointing out that one cannot expect a son to show the proper respect for his father if the father does not share his resources with his family.

Ananse stories are found in many societies of West Africa and, through the spread of African culture during the era of the slave trade, in many parts of the Caribbean as well. The stories were carried by word of mouth, and the spelling of the name has changed in some places, while in others it is totally different, but the characteristics of the spider remain the same. In Jamaica, the spider role is played by Anancy, while in Haiti, the character is called Ti Malice. Such tales are also found in the United States. The Gullah of South Carolina and Georgia, for example, tell "Aunt Nancy" stories that closely resemble the original Ananse tales.

WRITTEN LITERATURE

Written literary traditions arose with the trans-Saharan trade and grew with the coming of the Europeans. Today, the literature of northern Ghana still shows Islamic influences, while that of the south reflects the influence of Christian missionaries. Ghanaian written literature, however, has evolved into an original style, incorporating elements of oral tradition into the written form in a dynamic and symbiotic manner.

Indigenous Language

Written literature in vernacular languages in Ghana varied according to region. In the south, it began with the advent of Christian missionaries. The first forms of written literature in indigenous languages were translations of the Bible, hymns, and popular prayers such as *A Pilgrim's Prayer*. By the beginning of the 1950s, only a few works of fiction had been produced, including a few books of poetry and short stories. The best known of the early writers was Ferdinand Kwasi Fiawoo, a Western-educated Ewe, who composed three plays that were popular with local audiences. One of them, *Toko Atolia* (The Fifth Landing Stage), was published in 1937. The play discusses Ewe traditional customs, instructs youth, and teaches moral lessons. Unlike the rigid language used in translations of the Bible, Fiawoo employs a verbal style that relates more closely to the flow of spoken Ewe. Other significant works of literature have been produced in various Ghanaian languages including Twi, Akwapim, and Fante, as well as Ewe, Dagbane, and Ga.

English Language

Poetry

Before the colonial era, poetry was not a distinct type of written literature; it was associated with the oral performance tradition. One exception may be that of Umar ibn Abu Bakr ibn Uthman al-Kabbawi al-Kanawi (1858–1934), who lived in northern Ghana in the nineteenth century, and is thought to have written 1,200 poems in Arabic and Hausa. The evidence, however, is scanty.

In general, recent written English language poetry has maintained ties to the oral tradition, linking traditional forms and elite written literature by drawing on styles such as dirges and praise poetry. In the 1970s, Atukwei Okai spurred new developments in Ghanaian poetry with attempts to enact stage dramas using a poem as the script. The performances reintegrated the audience into the poetry genre and strengthened its standing within Ghanaian literary arts. Poetry takes many forms in Ghana. Some writers have transcribed traditional poetry into the written form, some have espoused patriotic poetry, as in Michael Dei-Anang's three volumes published between 1959 and 1965, and others have investigated the Ghanaian identity and the struggle to survive in competing cultural realms.

In *Rediscovery and Other Poems* (1964) and *Petals of Blood* (1971), Kofi Awoonor uses dirge techniques that he learned from his mother to explore the conflicts between traditional and Western culture and between informal and formal education, as well as the harmful effects of Western imperialism. Other well-known Ghanaian poets include Frank Kobina Parkes, Joseph Abruquah, and Ama Ata Aidoo, as well as the "new generation" of poets, Kofi Anyidoho, Vincent Odamtten, and Eugene Opoku-Agyemang.

Novels

Although pre-independence novels were few, Ghana has a long history of publishing literature in English. Many early writers came from elite families and also worked as journalists. Their position in society gave them unique insights into British and colonial culture, at least from the perspective of the African elite, and many writers used this position to comment on the colonial condition. Most Ghanaian novelists, past and present, were educated in the West and have published their major books abroad, but their novels, although written in the English language, employ styles and themes that are characteristically Ghanaian.

In 1911, the first West African novel, *Ethiopia Unbound*, by a Ghanaian lawyer and journalist, J.E. Casely-Hayford (1866–1930), was published in London. Like many Ghanaian novels, *Ethiopia Unbound* provided a critical commentary on the colonial system, addressing the economic and racial motivations that lay behind the European division of the continent. Another piece of written literature from the same era is a play, *The Blinkards*, by Kobina Sekyi (1892–1956). First performed in 1915, the play parodies the life of the African elite in the Cape Coast, their rejection of Ghanaian cultural values and their affinity for all things European, even their names. Although first performed in 1915 it was not published until 1974.

Many plays were written during the colonial era, but the second Ghanaian novel was published only in 1943. The novel *Eighteenpence*, by R.E. Obeng (1868–1951), also expressed strong anticolonial sentiment and showed concern for the moral well-being of a man within traditional society. Since the early works by Casely-Hayford, Sekyi, and Obeng, almost all Ghanaian writers have focused on similar issues of personal morality, identity, and the culture of politics.

After *Eighteenpence* very few novels were produced in Ghana until the overthrow of Nkrumah in 1966. Press censorship and the threat of detention hindered literary activity during the Nkrumah era. In 1966, however, the publication of Ghanaian novels reached a turning point. Many earlier writers who had published works in the Ghanaian literary magazine, *Okyeame*, were now able to publish their novels without fear of persecution from the government. The quantity and quality of Ghanaian writing grew exponentially in the next decade. Numerous novels were published, many of them portraying the contemporary period and exploring self-identity in a society undergoing rapid social change, but they provided little political commentary. These included Abruquah's *The Catechist* (1965), Asare Konadu's *A Woman in Her Prime* (1967), Francis Selormey's *The Narrow Path* (1966), and many others. Three writers, however, stand out because they reflect a sharp change in style and message.

Ayi Kwei Armah's *The Beautyful Ones Are Not Yet Born* (1968) and Kofi Awoonor's *This Earth My Brother* (1971) are the two most important novels of the post-Nkrumah era. Rather than following straight chronological order, they employed symbolic structure and surrounded their writing with myth and ritual. They were much more political than others and did not hesitate to criticize post-independence governments for corruption, nepotism, and general mismanagement.

Ayi Kwei Armah (b. 1939) is the best known Ghanaian writer. *The Beau-*

tyful Ones Are Not Yet Born (1968) depicts the life of an office worker struggling to survive within a crumbling world. It indirectly criticizes Nkrumah's government by portraying rampant corruption in society and one worker's fight to remain outside of it, even though his family pressures him to fit into the system and take bribes so that all can enjoy a better life. Armah sees not just Ghana but all of Africa as cursed by its leaders. Armah's views arise out of experiences living, writing, and teaching in North America, Europe, and all over Africa. In the 1960s, Armah began to publish poems and short stories in the Ghanaian literary magazine *Okyeame*, as well as in Western journals such as *Harper's* and *The Atlantic Monthly*. His experiences are transferred into his writing. In his short stories and novels he explores themes of conflict between African and Western lifestyles, examines colonial oppression, and revitalizes the history and culture of great African empires. Armah merges the African past, present, and future into a single image that provides a commentary on contemporary Ghanaian life. One passage from *Why Are We So Blest?* (1972) reveals the nature of his commentary: "What was there to talk about anyway? Revolution. Commitment. Justice. The only thing I was aware of these days was despair, and it was not a thing I wanted to sit and talk about, not in this place.[10] Armah's other novels include *Fragments* (1970), *Two Thousand Seasons* (1973), *The Healers* (1979), and *Osiris Rising* (1995).

Kofi Awoonor (b. 1935), a poet, novelist, and literary critic, has also used images of traditional life, myth, and culture to criticize the cultural and political policies initiated by Christian missionaries, the colonizers, and Ghanaian governments. His best known book, *This Earth My Brother* (1971), focuses on the everyday life of an educated lawyer and the difficult development of the new nation forming around him. Awoonor was closely associated with Nkrumah and went into exile soon after the coup that toppled the president. When he returned in 1975, he was jailed and wrote a book of poetry, *The House By the Sea* (1978), that relates to his detention.

Ama Ata Aidoo (b. 1942), a poet, playwright, and novelist, is one of Africa's greatest female writers. She is most famous for her collections of short stories, such as *No Sweetness Here* (1970), which depict life in postcolonial Africa. The stories in *No Sweetness Here* describe the difficulties of creating a new nation in the early years of independence. Like Armah and Awoonor, Aidoo tackles government corruption, but her writing style is very different. She started her career writing plays, staging her first, *The Dilemma of a Ghost*, in 1965. She soon began to write short stories. Her early training as a playwright is evident in all of her works. Her writing is brilliant in the way it describes the stage scene and employs written dialogue, much as a playwright would do. Her style blends oral and literary traditions. Like the other popular novelists, she explores postcolonial life and self-identity, but her themes also include the effects of social conflict on the consciousness of Ghanaian women. Aidoo's novel, *Changes*, which explores the lives of professional working women and their conflicts with the cultural assumptions of men, won the Commonwealth Writers Prize in 1993. Her most recent work is a collection of short stories, *The Girl Who Can and Other Stories* (1997).

Popular Literature

There is another type of written literature that does not fit into the categories of poetry and novels. Popular literature is the most recent form of written literature in Ghana. It began in the 1940s, but began to flourish with the increased literacy of the Nkrumah era and the expansion of the Ghanaian publishing infrastructure in the mid-1960s. It is defined by its widespread appeal and local publication, compared to the more elite literature which is usually published abroad. It transcends ethnicity, class, generations, and gender and attracts an audience from both literate and semi-literate sections of the population. Oral literature, in contrast, is usually limited to a particular ethnic group. Popular literature is disseminated through locally published pamphlets or chapbooks, and appears in serials in newspapers and magazines. It is usually written in English and most works explore themes of romance, everyday life, and urban living. Pamphlet and chapbooks are inexpensive compared to imported novels and are easily obtained in any major Ghanaian city. They are usually written in uncomplicated language, which also contributes to their widespread appeal. The best known Ghanaian popular writers are J. Benibengor Blay, Asare Konadu, and Akosua Gyamfuaa-Fofie.

DRAMA AND POPULAR THEATER

Modern dramatic performances in Ghana have evolved under the influence of both oral and written literature and are capable of reaching a wide-ranging audience. There are two distinct types of modern drama. The first, more closely related to written literature, is often called "institutional drama." It features performers from theater groups or schools, and usually attracts educated audiences. This type of drama is most often scripted and utilizes a stage setting, complete with managers, technicians, and producers. It originally drew on Western models such as Shakespeare. This type of theater, with elevated stages, written scripts, and audience-actor separation, first came to Ghana with European performances in Elmina and Cape Coast during the early colonial era. The colonial government targeted an audience of educated Africans through formal educational institutions, patronage, and production support. Some success was achieved, but the majority of plays did not have any relevance to Ghanaian life, failed to integrate African performance elements like music and dance, and made little impact on their intended audience.

Increasingly, Ghanaian playwrights began to incorporate Ghanaian dramatic influences and attract a larger following. The person most instrumental in this development was Efua Sutherland (1924–96). Sutherland attended the School of Oriental and African Studies in London and studied English, linguistics, African languages, and drama. She returned to Ghana in 1950 and began to write, first producing poetry and short stories. She believed that cultural education was important to national development. She helped form the Ghana Association of Writers and the literary magazine *Okyeame*. The latter was the first completely Ghanaian journal of writers and served as an outlet for virtually all aspiring Ghanaian authors of the 1960s.

Sutherland wanted to give artists another medium to show their works to the general population and so she started the Ghana Experimental Theatre Project. The experimental troupe first performed Ananse stories and achieved quick popularity. The success of the venture led to its expansion into the Ghana Drama Studio. Its new site, opened in 1961, featured a round stage patterned after a traditional Ghanaian courtyard to eliminate the division between the actors and the audience that characterized Western theater. The first presentation was *Odansam*, a play abut a young man who was confronted with death before his time. Sutherland's plays often featured elements that drew their creative form from traditional storytelling. When Sutherland became a research associate in the Institute of African Studies at the University of Ghana, Legon, she created a drama syllabus that emphasized the connections between oral tradition and contemporary life. To further this aim, she encouraged students to go into communities and collect materials.

One of Sutherland's most successful projects was the creation of community theater for development. She helped construct a replica of the Ghana Drama Studio, Kodzidan (House of Stories), in the town of Atwia to enhance the potential of its people's already established oral traditions. Sutherland created a full-time drama company, Kusum Agoromba, and used the stage to promote the development of drama in Ghana, both at the national and community levels, by incorporating vernacular languages into the performance. She attempted to link the more formal theater movement with popular theater by presenting Ghanaian folktales in a modern theater setting.

Sutherland's crowning achievement was the development of Ghana's biggest international festival, the Pan African Historical Theatre Festival (PANAFEST). She wrote a paper in 1980, "Proposal for Historical Drama Festival in Cape Coast," which called for a platform to expose new talents and served as the basis for the realization of PANAFEST in December 1992. The first festival was held in Cape Coast and Accra with the theme "The Re-Emergence of African Civilization." It is now recognized as an international cultural event dedicated to the ideals of Pan-Africanism and African development and has been held biennially since 1992. It uses the arts to promote continental culture and the unity of Africans throughout the world.

In the early 1990s, Ghana built an impressive National Theatre building. Constructed on the original site of Sutherland's Ghana Drama Studio, it hosts a variety of music, speeches, and literary and popular drama. The theater can seat several thousand people comfortably, with a large stage that is impressive even by Western standards. Due to economic constraints and lack of support, however, Ghanaian theater has also suffered many setbacks during the last few decades, but it continues to further the adaptation of oral performance to the contemporary stage.

During the 1980s, many playwrights and leaders of acting groups infused their work with greater influences from Ghanaian performance style to, as one expert writes, "assert the view that contemporary reality and [the] colonial legacy will have to make sense only in terms of the African past. It is not the other way round."[11] The Ghana Dance Ensemble began to perform dance dramas that combined mime, dance movements, music, and song with theatrical elements like props, costume, make-up, and special effects. The performances incorporate story lines that draw on Ghanaian artistic forms and translate them to the contemporary stage. Many theater groups today select scripts that incorporate the resources of oral and written performance literature, combining poetry, dance, and dramatic effects to produce performances that reflect contemporary realities. Drama has also found new popularity on television and provides a further outlet for actors. A popular show, *TV Theatre*, features drama scripts written by established Ghanaian writers and often employs actors from the Legon School of Performing Arts.

The other major type of drama in Ghana is the "concert party," sometimes called "comic opera." Resembling the improvisational, impromptu style of oral literature, the concert party is a form of traveling popular theater that combines the traditions of Ghanaian storytelling, song, dance, and drama with cultural influences from American movies, Latin music, and African American performance. This type of performance began in the 1920s and is popular throughout the country, especially in the rural areas. The concert party tradition emerged out of various factors, including colonial and mission education, American artists and films, and the developing music and dance styles. Mission schools frequently performed cantatas, or morality plays, that gave aspiring actors valuable experience at an early age. Vaudeville and new films from the time of the First World War, particularly those that showed

Charlie Chaplin and Al Jolson, also influenced the development of the concert party tradition.

Concert parties appeal to the average Ghanaian, the transport drivers, traders, mechanics, seamstresses, street vendors, and farmers. The thematic content, focusing on the stories, themes, and language of their everyday lives transposed into fiction, gives the members of the audience something that they frequently cannot find in films, videos, television, or more formal literary drama. Concert party performances use comical characters from traditional lore to impart contemporary messages about topical subjects and social and moral issues. They employ vernacular languages and rely on highlife and traditional music to accompany the acts. Performances take place anywhere that is available, in nightclubs, cinemas, house compounds, sports fields, or town squares.

Most groups have three central characters: the Joker, the Gentleman, and the Lady Impersonator. The Joker, in particular, melds the imported black-face minstrel with the Ananse spider figure, an important character that Africanizes the performance. The central characters don fancy dress, wigs, mustaches, and make-up. Typical shows once began with brass bands that marched around town to stir up support, but are now more likely to feature masked bell-ringers because of the expense of hiring full bands. The shows feature dancing and singing, comedy, and the main dramatic part of the performance, the "Scene."

"Bob" Ishmael Johnson (1904–85) is credited with creating the modern concert party genre. He was influenced by earlier versions created by Teacher Yalley, and learned from a visiting African American vaudeville team, Glass and Grant, who toured in Ghana in 1924–26. Johnson got his nickname, "Bob," from African American sailors and the name has become synonymous with the Joker character to this day. He formed his first group in the 1920s and turned professional in 1930. His many groups, the most famous of them being the Axim Trio, toured extensively throughout West Africa and led to the proliferation of concert party groups in the 1940s and 1950s throughout the region. Another performer who deserves mention is "Bob" Cole (1925–93), who was influenced by Johnson's group and modeled his Happy Trio after his predecessor. Cole also composed highlife songs and performed with the Uhuru Band.

Concert party performances remain popular throughout Ghana today. They have been made into films, such as *I Told You So*, starring Bob Cole, they feature regularly at the national theater as well as on television shows, and they have had their plays transformed into formal and comic literature.

NEWSPAPERS AND MAGAZINES

The media, too, developed during the colonial era. It is much more than a means to broadcast news and provide entertainment. In an environment where technological facilities are limited, especially in the rural areas, television, radio, and the print media are used to educate, inform, and disseminate information about local topics in English and vernacular language.

Ghana has a long history of newspaper publication. Most of the early editors came from families of the African elite in Cape Coast and Accra. Newspapers were important in spreading local and international news, but they were also instrumental in promoting ideas of independence during the colonial era. Since 1957, Ghanaian governments have feared the use of the press as a revolutionary tool and have sought to control it through censorship and intimidation.

Most early press activity was in Cape Coast, the capital of the colony before 1877. Charles MacCarthy, the first crown governor of the Gold Coast, launched the hand-written *Royal Gold Coast Gazette and Commercial Intelligencer* in April 1822. The Cape Coast paper lasted only until December of the following year, just a month before its founder was killed in the conflict between the Asante and the British.

There was a long break before Charles Bannerman set up the *Accra Herald* (later named the *West African Herald*) in 1857. Charles Bannerman was the son of a prominent figure in Ghana, James Bannerman, who was the son of a Scottish officer and his Ghanaian wife. With his brother Edmund's help, the Bannerman's *Herald* became the first African-owned newspaper in Ghana. Every publication carried the statement: "THIS JOURNAL is edited, printed and published entirely by Natives of The West Coast Of Africa." The newspaper was published in a number of different places, including Accra, Cape Coast, and Freetown, Sierra Leone. It continued to be published until 1874.

There were also a number of missionary publications that can be classified as newspapers. The Wesleyan mission sponsored two journals, the *Christian Reporter* and the *Christian Messenger and Examiner* in English, and the Basel Mission established the vernacular paper, *Sika Nsona Sanegbalo* (Ga: "Gold Coast Storytellers"). Very little evidence, however, remains of these papers today.

Ghanaian journalism took a big step forward in 1874 when James Hutton Brew established the *Gold Coast Times*. Also located in Cape Coast, it was produced every two weeks and ran from March 1874 to November 1885. In its first editorial, Brew delineated the policies of the paper: "In instances where the rights and interests of the people are disregarded, and attempts are made to tamper with them . . . we shall be found at our post, prepared to perform our duty fearlessly and independently, regardless of the frowns of King or Kaiser."[12] The *Times* commented on contemporary social issues in its editorials and it also published the views of English papers on the British presence in the Gold Coast. This is not to say that the *Times* was an organ for the expression of nationalist opinions, for it was more concerned with material improvements and, despite the promise to expose slights against the "people," it worried more about protecting the coast from Asante influence.

Brew followed this venture with another paper, the *Western Echo*, that began production in the same month that saw the end of the *Times*. The *Echo* lasted only a little more than two years, but its influence was profound. It revealed a dramatic shift from the opinions espoused in the earlier Brew publication. Whereas the *Times* was politically mild, the *Echo* was more direct and confrontational in its approach. It introduced the first local newspaper column, "The Owl." Using various pseudonyms, the author of this column commented on supposedly restricted government matters, satirized colonial officials, and professed the desire for self-government. An editorial in the 9 December 1885 issue stated: "This colony above all others on the West Coast of Africa is entitled to representation in the administration of government." Taking an even stronger position, it asked the questions: "Are the people here not anxious for independence, it may be asked? Are they going to remain forever in the background and to lag behind in the great struggle? What are they going to do?" Brew also hired a sub-editor, his nephew, J.E. Casely-Hayford, a man that would later be recognized as one of the preeminent Ghanaian lawyers, political leaders, and journalists of his generation.

Between 1885 and the turn of the century many newspapers were established only to cease publication a few years later; some lasted no longer than a single issue. By the turn of the century, other newspapers began to espouse antigovernment ideas. Originally a mission paper, the *Gold Coast Methodist Times* (est. 1886) became an important antigovernment voice when Rev. M. Attoh Ahuma became the editor in 1894. One writer described the paper under Attoh Ahuma as "a nationalist tract, full of passages burning with patriotic zeal and anti-colonial passion."[13] Attoh Ahuma, fired after three years for his political views, associated himself with the Aborigines' Rights Protection Society and, with another nationalist clergyman, established the weekly *Gold Coast Aborigines* (1898), which later became the *Gold Coast Nation and Aborigines*. Another weekly newspaper, *The Gold Coast Leader*, was established in 1902 and continued to be published until the early 1930s. The *Leader* was recognized as the paper with the highest quality among the newspapers that existed in the Gold Coast during the first thirty years of the twentieth century. The man most closely identified with the paper was Casely-Hayford.

Following the demise of the *Leader*, two new personalities emerged and changed the Ghanaian newspaper scene. J.B. Danquah established the *West African Times* in 1931, and Nnamdi Azikwe, who later became the first president of Nigeria, edited the *African Morning Post* from 1934 until his return to Nigeria in 1937. Mabel Dove Danquah wrote for the *Times* and, before becoming a member of Parliament in 1954, was the first female journalist of notoriety in Ghana. Both Danquah and Azikwe used their editorial positions to agitate for political change within the colonial system. Azikwe left Ghana after being cleared of a charge of sedition by the West African Court of Appeal.

As the nature of national politics began to change after the Second World War, so too did the types of newspapers. Upon his return to Ghana in 1947 and his break from the United Gold Coast Convention (UGCC), Kwame Nkrumah established three papers: the *Ghana Evening News*, the *Morning Telegraph*, and the *Daily Mail*. With the Convention People's Party (CPP) sponsoring or editorially controling these, the opposition sought outlets to express their views, founding the *National Times, Talking Drums*, and *Ghana Statesman*.

In 1950, the West African Graphic Company opened for business in Ghana. With foreign ownership and outside sources of funding, it provided a stable publication basis that changed the dynamics of Ghanaian journalism. Over the next decade, the company introduced three new papers, including the *Daily Graphic* and the *Sunday Mirror*, hired many of the best Ghanaian editors, journalists, and technicians for higher wages, and offered a better working environment than they would have received elsewhere. Production, too, improved with new machines and increased capital resources. Journalists began to acquire a professional status that they had not previously held.

From 1960 until recent times, freedom of the press was limited by fear of government oppression and retaliation. By 1960, there were fourteen publications sponsored by the government in various languages. Government control meant one-sided news for the most part. In the early years, the government rationalized this by arguing that there was a need to create unity within the new nation of Ghana and that publicizing alternative opinions would hamper that endeavor. During the past few decades, no explanation was offered except that the government did not like to be criticized. Foreign institutions owned a few papers, but rarely did they delve into oppositional politics for fear of deportation or closure. Journalists expressed fear and hesitated to write anything against the government. The exception to this was the *Ashanti Pioneer*, based in Kumase.

When Rawlings came to power, he repealed the 1973 Newspaper Licensing Law and gave power to the free press. The government, however, soon grew tired of critical editorials and forced some newspapers to close down. For the next decade, the independent press was restricted through intimidation, a policy that initiated the era known as the "culture of silence."

With freedom of the press written into the new constitution, many government and independent newspapers, espousing a wide variety of opinions and topics, have been established since 1992. There are two national daily papers published in Accra, the *Daily Graphic* and the *Ghanaian Times*. Nondaily papers include the *Chronicle*, the *Accra Mail*, the *Independent*, the *Echo*, the *Voice*, and the *Business Weekly*. There are also a number of weekly entertainment, sports, and tabloid publications. These include the *Mirror*, the *Weekly Spectator, Graphic Sports, Graphic Showbiz*, and *P & P*. The *Pioneer* is published in Kumase, but most weeklies come from Accra and are distributed nationally on a limited basis. Vernacular newspapers continue to exist and new ones arise from time to time, the latest being a monthly Ewe paper, *Midim Ne Miase Nyatepe La* ("search for me to hear the truth").

Newspapers are very popular in Ghanaian urban centers. Vendors crowd busy intersections, selling to waiting motorists. Others sell from stands, posting numerous newspapers around the front and sides of kiosks. It is common to walk by one of these stands and see a crowd of people reading the different papers for the latest headlines and interesting stories. Newspapers publish news and announcements from government and private sources. They also frequently contain columns and offer space to poets, writers, and cartoonists, which helps to promote the arts in Ghana.

The independence era has seen a proliferation of magazines and journals about Ghanaian political, economic, and cultural life. Many were produced monthly and were owned by churches, specialized groups, or government, but most have ceased production or are produced only infrequently. Some of these included *Drum* (Ghana edition), the *Radio Review and TV Times*, *Talking Drums, What's on in Ghana*, and *The Ghanaian*. There are also various academic journals, such as the *Bulletin of the Ghana Geographical Association, Universitas*, and the *Legon Observer*, which focus on Ghanaian and African issues. Readers patronize foreign magazines dealing with regional and continental issues, such as *Africa, West Africa*, and *New Africa*, as well as other international publications like *Newsweek, Time*, and *The Economist*.

RADIO AND TELEVISION

Radio broadcasting is an important means of disseminating information in Ghana. During the colonial era, radio provided entertainment, but it was also used to promote colonial political and cultural policies. Since independence, governments have controlled broadcasting in a similar way, aiming to publicize their views while restricting those of others. During the last decade, however, independent stations have proliferated throughout Ghana. In many rural areas, where printed media are unavailable or literacy is low, radio informs the people about national and international issues that contribute to the overall development of the country. Radio is the most widespread broadcasting medium in Ghana because personal radios are inexpensive and widely available. It is estimated that one in three Ghanaians has a radio set. Television, too, could have a similar impact, but reception does not extend to many areas and the cost of a television is prohibitive.

Radio

The Ghana Broadcasting System began airing news and music in 1935 under the name Station ZOY. With a small replay set in an Accra house, it served about 300 subscribers in the city and relayed news, entertainment, and music from the BBC as well as broadcasting shows in local languages. During the early days, crowds of people gathered around a single rediffusion box or at the central public venue at the Palladium Cinema in Accra to listen to the broadcasts. Soon afterward, rediffusion stations opened in Cape Coast, Sekondi, Kumase, and Koforidua. By 1939, the Gold Coast had installed a more powerful transmitter and Station ZOY could now be heard through much of the country as well as in neighboring countries.

When the Second World War began, Station ZOY became a means to promote the British war effort. The number of relay stations increased to sixteen and news programs were aired in Twi, Fanti, Ga, Ewe, and Hausa. The British controlled the content of radio shows, especially toward the end of the war as calls for independence intensified. They restricted songs that they deemed seditious. Records such as "Proceed with Caution" and "Obide Aba, Obide Nam Kwanso" ("Today it is my turn, tomorrow it will be yours") were censored and never heard on the radio during the colonial era. As independence loomed, however, the number of programs produced in Ghana increased, broadcasts were extended to schools, and a Ghanaian news division was established.

At independence in 1957, Station ZOY became known as the Ghana Broadcasting Corporation, or more popularly, Radio Ghana. In 1961, the External Service was launched. The "Voice of Ghana" broadcast news and opinions in English, French, Swahili, Portuguese, Hausa, and Arabic to all of Africa. Kwame Nkrumah wanted to spread independence fervor and African pride throughout the continent. Radio Ghana aired programs like the

Africa Scene, Cultural Heritage, One Continent One People, and *For Freedom Fighters.* Due to aging equipment and lack of funding, however, the range and quality of the External Service has been severely curtailed.

After independence, the Ghana Broadcasting Corporation (GBC) established two channels, Radio 1 and Radio 2. The former broadcast programs in Ghanaian languages, aired news and translated newspaper editorials, and provided information about regional events and topics and special programs for women and youth. Radio 1 also dedicated significant time to music and entertainment programs, such as *Listeners' Choice* and *Variety Entertainment,* as well as discussions of matters important to rural listeners. Radio 2 had three components: a commercial service, English language programs, and broadcasts to schools. The commercial service aired announcements from local businesses as well as social and funeral notices. The English language section produced talk shows, features, interviews, discussions, and drama catering to an urban audience. It included a quiz show, *What Do You Know?,* a cultural show, *Our Cultural Frontiers,* and a program on local and international affairs, *Focus.* The school service aired programs designed to educate the listener. These included lessons on English pronunciation, French, music, and storytelling.

Radio 1 still exists today and enjoys a sizable audience, especially in the rural areas. New programming has added to its success. A phone-in show brings news of Ghanaians abroad to their families and friends at home. During the election in 2000, candidates broadcast their views on Radio 1, stating their campaign promises and answering calls from listeners. News, education, sports, and entertainment appear in the regular schedule as well, featuring interviews with local sport stars and all types of Ghanaian music.

Beginning in the late 1960s, the infrastructure of Ghanaian radio deteriorated, decreasing from as many as fifteen transmitters to only two by 1983. The government of Jerry Rawlings undertook the Radio and Television Rehabilitation Programme to improve the technical situation and the quality of broadcasts.

Until recently, the government, fearing the use of radio by opposition groups, closely controlled broadcasting by continually deferring the granting of licenses for independent radio stations. The 1994 pirate radio broadcasts of Radio Eye in Accra led the Frequency Registration and Control Board to grant the first FM license to a small college radio station, Radio Universe, at the University of Ghana. By the end of 1995, numerous independent FM radio stations had arisen, carrying a wide range of news, music, drama, educational information, public announcements, religious material, sports, and talk and education shows. There are now more than twenty-five private FM stations in Ghana, located in all the major urban areas. Whereas people formerly relied on shortwave radio to listen to the BBC and the Voice of America, these can now be found on local FM stations.

Television

In July, 1965, the Ghana Broadcasting Corporation started a television service (GBC-TV) with transmitting stations near Accra, Cape Coast, Kumase, and Tamale. Government sought to use television to supplement educational programs, to showcase the fine arts of Ghana, and show historical dramas. Much of the actual programming was quite different, however, with foreign films sometimes accounting for as much as 50 percent of airtime.

A number of Ghanaian programs did meet the goals of the government. *Ghana Builds*, for example, promoted made-in-Ghana goods and attempted to do away with the misconception that foreign goods were superior. Public health programs, such as *Doctor in the House* and *U and Your Health*, increased public awareness of bilharzia, smallpox, guinea worm, and onchocerciasis, and encouraged the vaccination of children. More recent programs cosponsored by UNICEF focused on immunization, breast feeding, growth charts, and oral rehydration.

Cultural programming helped promote national unity. *Our Heritage* discussed chieftaincy, arts and crafts, and showcased traditional festivals like *homowo, afahye,* and *aboakyir.* Other programs revolved around topics dealing with religion, the law, and social obligations. Entertainment programs, too, have promoted Ghanaian culture. *Osofo Dadzie* and *Obra* brought concert parties to television, while others, like *Musical Rendezvous, Come Listen Awhile, Guitar Bandstand,* and *Music in Country Style,* have featured Ghanaian musicians and dancers. *Osofo Dadzie,* a satirical series in Twi, portrayed the nature of contemporary Ghanaian society. It ran for a decade and was very popular throughout Ghana.

Until 1996, all television in Ghana was controlled by the state, and the government in power used the medium to promote itself. Under Rawlings, shows like *3 Years of Self Reliance, Looking Back,* and *He Is Back* praised the achievements of the PNDC, commemorated its third anniversary in power, and told the story of Rawling's two coups. When the Ghana Frequency Registration and Control Board finally assigned new frequencies for private TV stations, TV 3 and Metro TV acted quickly and now attract a large number of viewers. The South African MNET and Channel O provide satellite TV access as well. The new television stations show mostly foreign productions, but there are also a number of locally produced shows. The problem lies in their duration, often due to difficulties meeting the necessary production expenses. While producing films locally can be quite expensive, it is far less costly for networks to acquire foreign films, especially older ones. Recent weekly series produced locally include *Taxi Driver* and *Build Your Ark*. *Taxi Driver* is based on the day-to-day to life of a taxi driver in Accra. It is a comedy that mixes English, Pidgin, Ga, Twi, and occasionally other Ghanaian languages found in Accra. *Taxi Driver* and *Build Your Ark* became big hits from their inception. Viewers were sure to set aside time to watch them and often discussed the shows with their friends at work or school. After their successful initial runs, however, these programs were taken off the air "temporarily" while the producers sought new funding.

Ghanaian TV today features a mix of Ghanaian, African, Indian, and Western productions. On a given evening, one could watch the *Oprah Winfrey Show*, a Nigerian or Ghanaian film, a European soccer match, or a live broadcast of the Pop Chain talent competition from the National Theatre. News shows are quite popular, with the local morning and evening news supplemented by CNN and the BBC. Foreign entertainment shows include soap operas and telenovellas like *The Bold and the Beautiful, Sunset Beach*, and *Esmeralda*, as well as dramas, movies, and children's shows such as *Sesame Street* and *Mighty Morphin' Power Rangers*. Most local television stations show Nigerian and Ghanaian movies at least once or twice a week. These movies often explore social commentary, as in the case of *House on Fire*, which deals with the suffering endured by a man who had promised to marry a young woman but did not follow through on his oath.

Religion and education consume a sizeable amount of broadcast time on Ghanaian television. On some channels, the broadcast day begins at noon with religious shows. Fridays feature *Quran Recitation* and *Islam in Focus*, while Sundays are dedicated to Christian programs from the Lighthouse or Solid Rock Chapels, and shows like *God's Miracle Power, Voices of Inspiration*, and *Gospel Trail*.

Traditional music and dance and local and national festivals are broadcast to encourage the development of Ghanaian culture in various forms of expression. Shows such as *Talking Drum, Gold Blast*, and *Akan Drama* also feature Ghanaian performance arts. There are a number of shows in vernacular languages. *Showcase* and *Adult Education* feature Ewe, Ga, and Dagbani, while Akan is spoken in *Cantata, Agoro, Concert Party*, and *Mmaa Nkomo*. One of the newest shows is *Life and Style*, which educates viewers on important matters that might otherwise be overlooked, such as preparing for an interview, etiquette, or dressing properly. It also covers local entertainment, fitness and health, and fashion news. Another popular show, *Odo Ne Asomdwee*, highlights topics of current interest, including clashes between traditional beliefs and legal codes, taxation of churches, compensation for victims of disasters, and birth control.

Although Ghanaian productions are still in the minority they have made huge strides over the last decade. Critics of media globalization find many Western programs too violent, sexually explicit, and generally culturally inappropriate for Ghanaian audiences. This contrasts sharply with the nature of much of the locally produced programming, which focuses on entertainment and on social, cultural, and educational themes that relate to Ghanaian life. Humor, for example, has a greater impact when it uses images relevant to Ghanaian culture and everyday life. Western media infiltration will not subside, but with sufficient resources it has already been proven that Ghanaian productions can attract a large audience share. In the meantime, Ghanaian radio and television will continue to play an important role in entertainment, education, and development at the individual and national levels.

NOTES

1. See Kofi Awoonor, *Guardians of the Sacred Word* (New York: Nok, 1974), 5.

2. S.S. Dseagu, "Proverbs and Folktales of Ghana," in J.M. Assimeng (ed.), *Traditional Life, Culture and Literature in Ghana* (New York: Conch Magazine, Ltd., 1976), 88.

3. Ibid., 85.

4. J.H. Nketia, *Drumming in Akan Communities* (London: Thomas Nelson & Sons, 1963), 47.

5. J.H. Nketia, *Funeral Dirges of the Akan People* (reprinted, New York: Negro Universities Press, 1969), 101.

6. Ibid., 195.

7. Kwesi Yankah, "The Making and Breaking of Kwame Nkrumah: The Role of Oral Poetry," in Richard Priebe (ed.), *Ghanaian Literatures* (Westport, CT: Greenwood Press, 1988), 49.

8. For a discussion of *halo* poetry see, Daniel K. Avorgbedor, "It's a Great Song! *Halo* Performance as Literary Production," *Research in African Literatures*, 32, 2 (2001), 17–43.

9. Kofi Awoonor, *Guardians of the Sacred Word* (New York: Nok, 1974), 7.

10. Ayi Kwei Armah, *Why Are We So Blest?* (London: Heinemann, 1974), 55.

11. K.E. Agovi, "New Directions in the Ghanaian Theatre of the Eighties," paper presented at the Institute of African Studies, University of Ghana, Legon, 31 August 1989.

12. *Gold Coast Times*, 1, 1 (1874).

13. K.A.B. Jones-Quartey, *A Summary History of the Ghana Press, 1821–1970* (Accra: Ghana Information Services Department, 1974).

4

Art and Architecture/Housing

Art expresses both the tradition and aspiration of a people, what they have experienced in the past and what they consider desirable for the present and the future.
—Ghanaian artist, Vincent Kofi[1]

GHANAIAN traditional art and architecture serve both aesthetic and functional purposes. An earthenware pot and a carved calabash, for example, are beautiful to look at but also play an important role in various ceremonial rites. Kings and chiefs wear expensive ornamentation and textiles to enhance their prestige within society, and funerals utilize numerous art objects to ensure the safe passage of the deceased to the world of the ancestors. Ghanaian art and architecture employ many layers of symbolism that reflect the social and cultural structure. A piece of Ghanaian art depicts the history and beliefs of not just the artist but the entire community from which it originated. Art and architecture are produced as outlets for the creative expressions of the artists, but they are also functional representations of the secular and spiritual lives of society and act as agents of communal and national unity. To appreciate artistic and architectural forms in their totality, it is necessary to look at them in their practical context.

ART

The Ghanaian concept of "art" differs from that of Western cultures in the emphasis on its importance to society. Traditional art, an integral part of social life, reflects the social, cultural, political, and philosophical values of a community. The symbolic and practical use of costumes, ornamentation, and religious objects enhances the presentation of the performing arts, augments political stature, and strengthens religious life. Whereas the Western world sees art as something that stirs emotions within the viewer because of its technical qualities, Ghanaian art focuses more on function and, by participation in that function, it creates spiritual beauty through an association with sacred and secular powers. The Ewe word for art, for example, is *adamu*, meaning a skill or value, which refers to a wide range of art works, objects, ornamentation, and even handwriting techniques.[2] Ghanaian art is essential to society and symbolizes value in every aspect of social and cultural life.

Traditional arts both predate and have been influenced by Islamic and European factors. For centuries, Ghanaians have had contacts with Muslim traders and holy men, European traders, and Christian missionaries. Outsiders brought new religious philosophies and introduced new materials and methods of production that influenced craftsmanship. Christianity, in particular, discouraged the use of traditional arts in schools and religious services, deeming these arts to be animistic and primitive. Since independence, however, government and educational institutions have led a revival of interest in Ghanaian traditional arts and many artists continue to produce beautiful works in a variety of media, including sculpture, painting, textile, metalwork, pottery, basketry, beads, and leatherwork. The fine arts cannot be separated from other forms of cultural expression because they are linked with musical, dance, and dramatic performances as well as other cultural forms such as literature and architecture.

Functions

Ghanaian traditional arts are, above all, functional. Most sculptures, paintings, and textiles are associated with particular performance or ceremonial contexts and are not meant to be viewed in seclusion or in a museum. The aesthetic qualities of the art are interrelated with its functional objectives. Artists emphasize functionality and create objects that exhibit spiritual symbolism, enhance status, and help organize social relations for individuals and the community as a whole.

Art plays a functional and aesthetic role in the various festivals that are held each year throughout Ghana. The ceremonies bring people together to strengthen the bonds between the community, the ancestors, and God. The cleansing acts utilize art forms. In the room where the state stools are kept, the chiefs and elders pour libations over the chief's stool and invoke the spirits of the ancestors for prosperity and protection. Following this, there is often a durbar in which the participants wear decorated textiles and display colorful umbrellas, swords, linguists' staffs, ornamented drums, and personal jewelry.

Art plays an important role in all of the rites of passage involving birth, puberty, marriage, and death. During pregnancy, women sometimes carry wooden symbols of fertility on their backs to ensure a safe pregnancy and a healthy child. At the time of the naming ceremony, children's arms and legs are adorned with precious beads and other jewelry. During the ceremony associated with initiation into adult life, young boys are given sculptures to hold or masks to wear to invoke the spirits of the ancestors to give them courage. Boys also learn to make textiles, leather and metal items, and wooden and clay sculptures during initiation to give them skills to thrive as adults. In the female initiation ceremony, girls adorn themselves with beads and gold ornaments in their hair and on their neck and wrists. After the ceremony is complete, the initiate is placed in front of her house on a traditional stool or paraded in the street, so that the community can see that she has made the transition from girlhood to adulthood.

From the type of cloth worn by mourners to the type of coffin used, funerary art also serves aesthetic and practical functions. Ghanaian funerals celebrate the beginning of a new spiritual life rather than dwelling on the end of the earthly one. Sympathizers wear special cloth stamped with traditional designs. Depending on the age of the deceased, the cloth may be russet-brown (for those who died in their prime) or white (for those who lived a long and happy life). The immediate family and close relatives, however, wear red cloth and headbands, although this is becoming less common with some groups. The deceased is dressed in the best cloth and adorned with expensive jewelry. Other items are put in the coffin to ensure that the deceased will have all of the necessary things on their long journey to the other world.

In Akan societies, terra-cotta portraiture is commonly used to commemorate the deceased, especially wealthy and powerful figures. Terra-cotta heads or full bodies are sometimes draped with expensive cloth and set on state chairs at royal funerals. Ceramicists, always female, create these terra-cotta works in the image of the deceased and as a symbol of continuity between life and death. Each work has individual traits, in hair style, facial hair, adornment, and scarification, that help family and friends recall the image of the deceased. These works are carried down the street in a procession, much like the deceased, but they are buried at a special site called *asensie* ("the place of pots").

Another form of funerary art has become popular only in the last few decades. Custom coffin production started in the 1970s with Kane Kwei, a carpenter who began to make coffins in a wide variety of shapes and styles. He designed coffins according to the profession or stature of the deceased. A fisherman might be buried in a giant fish-shaped coffin or a chief in a coffin shaped like a leopard, eagle, or elephant, all symbols of royal power. Over the years, others have started to produce them as well, in shapes that have included cocoa pods, onions, outboard motors, and even a Mercedes Benz.[3] These coffins are more expensive than others and are usually purchased by middle-class and wealthy families.

Art is also an important symbol of leadership. Creative art is used in the decoration of royal houses or compounds, as well as in religious shrines associated with leadership. Kings and chiefs differentiate themselves from the rest of society by the regalia that they wear or carry with them. Ghanaian chiefs might wear many rings, beaded bracelets, and necklaces. They drape themselves in beautiful cloth, and golden objects adorn their crowns and sandals. Individual and domestic ornamentation are used to enhance the social status and dignity of the ruler and to form a link to ancestral power. Jewelry, textiles, swords, and walking staffs identify other community leaders and demonstrate the level of wisdom, wealth, and power that they have attained.

The ownership of leadership art reflects its social value and communal functions. Among the Akan, chiefly regalia belong to the state; it is only loaned to those in power who must watch over it during their reign. The most famous piece of Akan regalia is the Golden Stool of the Asante, which symbolizes the unification of the Akan peoples under Asante rule. Oral tradition states that the Golden Stool descended from heaven and marked the unity of the Akan people. Carved wooden stools existed long before the Asante Empire, but their symbolism has been heightened over the last three centuries by their association with state power and royalty. Many are used as seats, but others, such as the Golden Stool are adorned with beautiful paintings, carvings, and metalwork which increase their symbolic importance. Throughout Akan societies, stools represent individual and state power. When an important person dies, it is believed that his soul is transferred to his personal stool. Carved from a single block of wood, stools usually have a rectangular base, with four corner posts connected to a saddle-shaped top piece.

Other symbols of royalty include decorated swords and staffs. Swords, like stools, had practical uses within society long before their association with spiritual and political institutions. Some Asante swords have specific histories, names, and appointed guardians. Whereas stools and swords predate the Asante Empire, staffs are a more recent introduction into Ghanaian societies. They likely became important symbols for linguists around the beginning of the twentieth century, after the British presented government staffs to chiefs authorizing them to be their people's intermediaries with the colonial government. Linguists carry wooden staffs adorned with gold that represent their high position within the king's court. At the top of the staff rests a sculptured image or symbol such as two people eating at a table, a cock, or a hand holding a sword. Each symbol carries a message, giving the staffs both visual and verbal powers. Previous to the staffs, totems of clans and clan heads were the more common symbol, reminding and recording important ancestral figures.

Textiles

Textiles are an important artistic expression of culture because, in their various forms, they utilize the entire range of symbolic images and can be seen in all aspects of Ghanaian life. Outside the country, textile art is the most famous Ghanaian art form. *Kente* and *adinkra* are popular African cloths and are worn by Africans throughout the continent and in the diaspora. *Kente* and *adinkra* patterns and symbols can be found in a variety of items produced for Western consumption, including oven mitts, book covers, sashes, hats, and holiday cards.

Akan symbolism uses several thousand motifs, each associated with particular meanings derived from proverbs, historical events, human attitudes, animal behaviors, plant life, and objects. The symbols present both a visual and a verbal message. The ladder motif, for example, when seen at a funeral, is associated with the saying "everyone climbs the ladder of death," which means that no one can cheat death forever.

Textile art is seen in everyday and ceremonial life. Specific cloths may be worn around the house, at the office, or to a soccer match. *Kente* cloth is a ceremonial cloth that comes in a variety of colors, sizes, and designs. Men usually wear a large piece of cloth in the style of a toga, draped around the body and over one shoulder. Women usually wear multiple pieces, one as a wrap-around skirt, another as a top cloth, and sometimes another small piece as a shawl. Different textiles are often worn for specific occasions or to identify certain social roles. The most elaborate and costly *kente* cloths were once reserved for kings, chiefs, or specific members of royal families, while lighter and less expensive versions could be worn by anyone who could afford them.

The Asante are the best-known producers of *kente* cloth, using a variety of checkerboard and diagonal patterns, but it is also produced by Ewe craftsmen. Ewe *kente* is not as brightly colored and is woven with more geometric patterns and figural motifs, sometimes including images of birds, drums, or human figures. *Kente* is hand made by men on a horizontal treadle loom by raising and lowering the harnesses with strings that are held between their toes. The loom is always used outdoors, and a heavy rock placed a long distance from the loom holds the tension on the threads. The fabric is woven in long, narrow strips about four inches wide which are then hand sewn together into larger pieces of cloth. As the thin strips of cloth begin to form, the rock moves closer to the weaver. The technique probably came from the Western Sudan, arriving sometime around the sixteenth century in the northern areas. During the seventeenth century, weaving was established in Bonwire, a village outside of Kumase that is still recognized as producing the finest *kente* cloth in Ghana. At first, raffia was used to make *kente*, then locally grown cotton became more common. It is believed that the name came from the first weavers who used raffia fibers to make cloths that resembled baskets, called *kenten* in Akan.

Individual *kente* designs have specific symbolic meanings derived from a variety of historical, religious, and sociocultural contexts. They also represent human characteristics, or public institutions. One of the most prestigious designs is *adwinasa* ("all motifs are used up"). The name came from a weaver who used all the known motifs to weave cloth that would please the Asante king. The tradition states that after completing the cloth, the weaver remarked that he had used up all of the motifs. *Adwinasa's* association with royalty and the creative use of every symbol determines its symbolic representation of elegance, wealth, creativity, and excellence in craftsmanship.

A *kente* design based on historical events is *toku kra toma* ("Toku's soul cloth"). The cloth commemorates the queen mother Toku, who was captured and killed in battle. It symbolizes courage and self-sacrifice. A more recent design reflects the changing political climate of Ghana after independence. *Obaakofo mmu man* ("one person does not rule a nation") signifies the traditional Asante system of rule that emphasized democratic principles. This design consists of nine squares, symbolizing nine tufts of hair, a type of haircut worn by some royal advisors. The cloth was once called *Fathia Fata Nkrumah* ("Fathia is a good wife for Nkrumah"), but after Nkrumah became an autocrat and was overthrown, that name was removed.

Other *kente* designs include *sika futuro* ("gold dust"), symbolizing spiritual and monetary wealth; *abusua ye dom* ("the family is an impregnable fortress"), representing the essential function of lineage in Asante society, and the importance of family unity, cooperation, and understanding among members; and *wofro dua pa a na yepia wo* ("if you do the right things, you gain communal support"), which expresses hope, sharing, and mutual benefits and is based on a proverb: "One who climbs a tree worth climbing gets the help he deserves."

Another popular Ghanaian hand-woven cloth is *adinkra*. Like *kente*, *ad-*

inkra is woven in long, narrow strips but it uses heavier cotton and less complex patterns and colors, sometimes having just a single colorful stripe on each narrow piece. Once the strips are sewn together symbolic designs are stamped onto the cloth. *Adinkra* printing, associated with the Asante, developed in the nineteenth century. Royalty and spiritual leaders first used the cloth at important ceremonies. Today, however, many Ghanaians use the cloth for special occasions, especially festivals, funerals, and all the rites of passage. *Adinkra* means "saying farewell" and is thus commonly worn for funerals and mourning ceremonies. The images are created with carved stamps and combs using a natural dye made from boiling a mixture of the bark of the *badie* tree and iron slag.

The numerous *adinkra* symbols have meanings associated with them. Oval shapes represent femininity and beauty, a half circle symbolizes fertility, a cross means piety, and an arrow signifies new life. Moon and star symbols are also common *adinkra* motifs, representing love, loyalty, and harmony. The two most famous *adinkra* symbols are *gye Nyame* ("except God") and *sankofa* ("go back and fetch it"). *Gye Nyame* is derived from a proverb that states that no one is alive today who saw the beginning of creation, "except God." *Sankofa*, a popular motif for Africans in the diaspora, is represented by a bird looking backward. It reminds people to remember the past and learn from it. Other *adinkra* symbols include *Nyame nwu na mawu* ("God, do not die to let me die too"), which represents the omnipotence of God and the afterlife of the human soul; and *dwenini aben*, ram's horns, symbolizing mental, spiritual, and physical strength. It is associated with the proverb "the ram may bully, not with its horns but with its heart."

Sculpture

Wood carvings and clay sculptures have a long history in Ghana and play important roles in traditional religious ceremonies and rites. Objects include stools, fertility dolls, decorative combs, and human and animal figures. Two of the most common objects are traditional stools and *akuaba* dolls.

Stools are important to the status and structure of most Ghanaian societies. Important people and family heads own stools, which provide their souls with a place to rest after death. Stools use various symbols that define their functions and meanings in society. The *adenkyem-dwa* stool, for example, depicts a crocodile with a fish in its mouth, representing power. It used to be found in religious shrines. Different stools are associated with specific roles. There are stools for kings, stools for queen mothers, stools for men and stools for women, and stools that can be used by anyone. Some stools reflect the history of Western influence, incorporating images such as gunpowder kegs and padlocks into the stool design.

Although masks are popular spiritual symbols throughout West African societies, their use is not as pervasive in Ghana as elsewhere. The spiritual powers and functions that are sometimes found in masks are more frequently observed in Ghanaian wooden and clay statues. These statues may be placed on altars in shrines or carried by women to ensure fertility. The *akuaba* ("Akua's child") dolls are among the most common wooden carvings in Ghana and are well-known internationally. Tradition states that a woman incapable of having children was instructed by a priest to care for a wooden figure and, after she became pregnant, other women started to carry the dolls around on their backs during pregnancy. Gender and shape are very important in all sculptures. The *akuaba* dolls, with flattened round or oval heads, cylindrical torsos, and exaggerated buttocks and breasts reveal the idealized Akan depiction of beauty. The *akuaba* dolls are usually adorned with beads and jewelry and are almost always female, reflecting Akan matrilineal values.

Sculptors, mostly men, also carve a variety of other items not intended for ceremonial or spiritual use. They craft items commonly used in homes and workplaces, such as chairs, canoes, drums, doors, mortars, pipes, and walking sticks. One of Ghana's most famous sculptors is Saka Acquaye (b. 1923). He is a multitalented individual who has excelled in music and drama, as well as sculpture. His works can be found throughout Ghana. One of his pieces, a statue of J.B. Danquah, stands in Osu, Accra, at a busy traffic circle named after the Ghanaian statesman. He has also produced a sculpture of Governor Guggisberg for the Korle Bu Teaching Hospital, the "Farmer" and the "Makola Market Woman" statues that stand in front of the Ghana Commercial Bank in Tema, and three busts of the founding fathers of Achimota College that are featured on the lawns of the school. Acquaye sees sculpture as a means to communicate history to subsequent generations and as a record of the people. His work has also reached international audiences. He has produced large carved wooden doors for buildings in the United States, including the Johnson Wax Conference Center in Racine, Wisconsin, and the African American Heritage Association Lecture Hall at Wayne State University in Detroit.

Metal Arts

Metalworking is popular throughout Ghana, but the Asante, in particular, excel in crafting metals because of an abundance of gold, the former military success of the Asante Empire, and contacts with Islamic artists and traders.

Gold was commonly used in metalworking because it was thought to contain magical powers. Golden objects were produced to provide protection for the deceased in their journey to the land of the ancestors and lend spiritual support to the image of the powerful Asante state.

The military success of the Asante Empire produced changes in craft production. When the Asante sought tribute from the peoples that they conquered, artists were sent to the capital and brought with them new metalworking styles, such as lost-wax casting and various hammering techniques. Artists molded brass and gold into a variety of objects such as goldweights, jewelry, individually cast beads, and urns. Originally a North African technique, lost-wax casting uses gold, brass, bronze, and copper to shape metal objects. The design is first pressed into wax and covered with clay. Once dry, the wax is melted away leaving the image pressed in the modeled cavity. The metal is heated and poured into the mold and, once cooled, the clay is chipped away, leaving only the metal object. It is a difficult technique because the casting process is hidden and imperfections are not evident until the hard clay is removed. In addition, no two products will be exactly alike because the process allows for only one casting to be made from each wax and clay model.

Ghanaian goldsmiths are known for their artistic skills. They design a wide variety of crowns, necklaces, rings, and other ornaments for the Ghanaian and international markets. The best known Ghanaian products of lost-wax casting, however, are copper alloy goldweights. Dating back to the trans-Saharan trade, the goldweights were used on scales to weigh gold dust, the metal that was used as currency in precolonial times. Today, artists produce goldweights in many different shapes, including animal, plant, and human forms. Though they are no longer actually used as weights, they are commonly worn as jewelry and are very popular with tourists.

Many of the earliest goldweights were small, made in geometrical or barrel shapes, some with punched designs or copper inlay. Later types began to employ elaborate figurative symbols, including groups of people or animals. Some of the early symbols derived from North African influence, while later ones, such as cannons, rifles, and ships, came from contact with Europeans. Many of them invoke visual and verbal symbolism. The image of two men eating at a table, for example, is sometimes found on the top of linguists' staffs and recalls a proverb: "Food is for its owner, not for the man who is hungry." In this case, food represents chieftaincy, which belongs to the heir, not to those who simply desire it. The popular *sankofa* symbol is also commonly found on Asante goldweights.

The *kuduo*, a metal urn used by the Akan, also deserves mention for its importance with regard to secular and religious power. Its origins date to the fourteenth or fifteenth centuries, and it was probably brought from the Western Sudan by Islamic traders. Produced using the lost-wax casting method, *kuduo* were owned by states, by wealthy individuals, and by powerful shrines. They are visual symbols of the *ntoro* kinships through which Akan families identify themselves. They come in different styles, but the most popular styles are based on those that originated in Mamluk Egypt. The originals were made of copper alloy and featured Arabic inscriptions. Some of them still exist within Akan shrines today, where they are considered the heart and essence of a deity.

Pottery, Basketry, Beads, and Leatherwork

Ghanaians are also known for their artistry in making pottery, basketry, beads, and leatherwork. Beautiful earthenware pottery is a principal item in everyday domestic life and in ceremonial rites. The pottery items used around the house are traditionally made by women, but men make the ceremonial pottery. First, the clay is obtained from pits around rivers or in wetlands. The clay is then cleaned and pounded with a mortar and pestle. Most pottery used to be made by hand and baked in a fire, but today it is common for artists to use pottery wheels. Once the shape is made, the pots are decorated with traditional patterns and symbols and other ornamentation. Pottery serves a functional purpose in the home, providing vessels for cooking, for storing water and palm wine, and for use as plates. It can be molded into sculptures, smoking pipes, and various ceremonial items.

Basketry also has both functional and aesthetic values. Ghanaian baskets range from practical and plain types to those which are elaborately woven with beautiful colors and intricate designs created with dyed fibers or painted images. Weaving materials include palm branches, raffia, cane, sisal, and other plant fibers. Everywhere in Ghana, baskets are used to carry fruits and vegetables, market wares, fish, and meats. Woven items are used as trays, sleeping or praying mats, and sieves. People use woven fans and adorn themselves with woven belts, handbags, and hats. Cane chairs are also popular.

Bead making is another common form of Ghanaian art that has existed for many years. Using shells, glass, clay, hard seeds, and stones, artists create beautiful beads utilized in jewelry, decorations for handbags, belts, hats, and sandals. The highest quality beads include *bota* and *aggrey*, which are often worn by elders and chiefs as a sign of status.

People in the northern regions raise cattle, sheep, and goats much more than those in the southern areas and, thus, leatherwork has become an important craft in those regions. Leather is dyed red and black and made into handbags, footwear, sheaths, wallets, briefcases, and many other items. In all areas of the country, the hides of domestic and wild animals also serve as the material for leather products including drum heads.

Traditional Artists

Traditional artists have a high standing in society because they provide the objects necessary for, and play a vital role in, social, religious, and cultural activities. The best artists are often closely associated with state and spiritual leaders. Traditional artists usually serve an apprenticeship before being allowed to strike out on their own. The spiritual nature of their crafts necessitates training that only an experienced artist can provide. Once the training is finished, the artist may join a traditional guild of artists working in the same medium.

The spiritual value of traditional art necessitates certain rituals when preparing the base materials from which the artists work. Wood for sculptures or drums, for example, must be prepared before carving can begin. The spirits that live in the wood must be propitiated. This is done by offering prayers and libations to ensure the safety of the artist as well as the spiritual power of the finished item. Potters offer similar prayers before digging for clay, and weavers never destroy an old loom for fear that it will bring bad luck.

Modern and Tourist Art

Like traditional artists, modern artists work with a variety of materials, including wood, bronze, clay, and paint, but their works display a greater combination of Ghanaian and Western styles. Their works, although based on traditional art, are usually meant for viewing, not for functional use. Most of the modern artists have received long training in formal institutions in Ghana and abroad and produce their works for both local and international consumption.

Modern art in Ghana began with the establishment of the first school of art at Achimota. The school promoted painting by emphasizing its role in national arts and culture and encouraging new work in sculpture, weaving, and ceramics. After graduating, many of the students began to teach art in other schools and lessons in traditional arts can now be found in schools throughout Ghana. During the late colonial era, the British Council began to take an active interest in traditional arts, sponsoring the first Ghanaian art exhibition in 1945. Today, there are a number of government and private institutions in Ghana that support the fine arts, both traditional and modern. These include the Accra Arts Centre, the Asante Cultural Centre in Kumase, and the Tamale Cultural Centre. Various schools, too, promote art education at advanced levels, offering vigorous training and degrees in the fine arts.

There are numerous modern artists in Ghana today. Vincent Kofi (1923–74), who studied at Achimota School, the Royal College of Art in London, and Columbia University, is probably the most famous Ghanaian sculptor. He has taught at various schools in Ghana and has attempted to bridge the gap between traditional and modern art through his work and his teachings. Other sculptors include El Anatsui (b. 1944), who has worked with concrete, wood, and clay and made lifesize sculptures for various sites in Ghana. A number of female artists have also excelled, including Elizabeth Ansah, a talented Ghanaian painter. Other well-known artists include Ablade Glover, Ato Delaquis, and Amon Kotei.

Still, the development of new modern art styles is slow. Modern artists receive little economic support, because tourists prefer to buy what they see as the more traditional "African" art. Nicholas Kowalski, a Ghanaian painter trained in Ghanaian schools, sees part of the problem as arising from art education: "Art schools in Ghana are killing initiatives among our young artists. They have stereotyped the teaching of art and have consequently been repeating the same things since the early 1960s."[4] Kowalski, like many modern artists, uses traditional themes and combines them with modern ideas. "Three to Four," for example, a painting of a vibrant market scene, employs abstract figures wearing fashionable clothes and vogue hats. Kofi Amoah does a similar thing in his "Kpanlogo Dancers," an acrylic painting that shows *kpanlogo* dancers in fancy clothing associated with Western fashion.

The pervasiveness of tourist art limits the development of modern art in Ghana. In economically challenging times, many artists prefer, or are forced, to focus at least part of their time on income-earning artistic forms such as tourist art. The image of Ghanaian art in international circles typically relates to Akan, especially Asante, art forms such as *kente* cloth, goldweights, *akuaba* dolls, and stools. Since these are the forms most frequently found in the country, this is not surprising, but Akan art forms also received additional help early in the independence era when all the world's eyes were watching. During this time, Nkrumah and the Convention People's Party made concerted efforts to promote Ghanaian cultural forms, incorporating Akan swords, musical instruments, and a golden chair into his inauguration as president. Nkrumah frequently wore *kente* cloth while he was in power.[5]

There are many creative and skilled artists, producing sculptures, paintings, textiles, metal and leather items, basketry, and beads, who have developed their skills as a means to obtain economic prosperity. The traditional art forms mentioned above are now produced in greater numbers than in the past, but sometimes without the previous quality or social and cultural significance. The "airport art" that is intended for unwary tourists does not demonstrate the training and knowledge that are features of Ghanaian traditional arts. Still, a trip to any of the best markets and shops will reveal that there are many quality craftspeople producing a wide selection of carvings, sculpture, goldweights, beads, and textiles available for anyone to purchase.

ARCHITECTURE AND HOUSING

Architecture must be seen as another aspect of the fine arts. Architecture follows the adage, "form follows function," by exhibiting both functional and aesthetic qualities that are adapted to particular environments. The nature of social structure and religious ideology, the available materials, the changing technology, and the range of economic activity determine architectural types. Historical influences also play a role, with the northern regions revealing more Islamic influence and the southern regions revealing more European influence. Traditional architecture and housing are elaborate in terms of function and building technology but they are also a reflection of social values and environmental conditions. Building designs and decoration reveal an individual's status within the community. The placement of houses within a compound reflects the various levels of hierarchy within a family and stresses the importance of social relations between family members and within the community as a whole. The pattern of movement associated with particular environments contributes to architectural styles as well. In warm climates, it is not only the architecture itself that must be considered, but the outside space that the physical structures define. A great deal of time is spent in the open air and the architectural styles help unite indoor and outdoor spaces.

Rural Architecture and Housing

The majority of Ghanaians live in long-established rural settlements. Although there are many different types of residential structures, the majority of people stay in some version of a residential compound within a large or a small village. A traditional residential compound consists of a number of structures that create an enclosure around an open courtyard. A typical compound contains a kitchen, bathroom, living areas, and sleeping rooms. Most compounds have a specific room, a veranda, or a place in the courtyard that is used to welcome guests, an important custom in Ghanaian societies. The courtyards host a variety of domestic activities.

A village is a collection of compounds, each housing an extended family. Status, family ties, religion, and occupation determine the organization of a village. The chief's house is the nucleus of the settlement, and each extended

Two views of the castle at Elmina, originally built in the late fifteenth century.

family occupies an area of the village called a ward. In established villages, a single ward is a smaller version of the entire village, usually consisting of one lineage group only. In many northern societies, there is also a Muslim ward which consists of the *mallam's* house, a central mosque, and a Qu'ranic school. Although most rural people practice agriculture, residence may also be determined by those who have specialized professions, such as butchers, blacksmiths, or drummers.

Within a single compound, the layout is determined by status and gender. In Dagomba society, a large antechamber for welcoming guests is nearest to the entrance. Next to that is the compound owner's room. Through the entrance is the open space, which hosts various activities, including weaving, dancing, playing, and storytelling. Furthest from the entrance are the women's houses and cooking areas.

Northern compounds may house a single family or numerous related families. The most common arrangement involves several related families sharing a compound with separate living areas but with a common enclosed yard where cattle or grain may be kept. Just inside the entrance to a compound, there are round thatch-roofed structures, which serve as shelters for animals, and tall mud brick grain silos. Many of the living quarters have flat roofs, which are used for drying grain and, because they are cool at night, for sleeping during the hot season. Most houses feature an entrance opening with a short semicircular wall around it to provide privacy and protection and keep out flood water. Outside the entrance and usually under a shade tree is a sitting area with a log bench and straw mat where family elders can rest and discuss matters with others.

Housing and architectural styles reinforce social organization and emphasize family unity. The compound in Akan societies consists of a central courtyard, which serves as the center of household activities, surrounded by a multi-room rectangular building. The style reflects the Akan concept of private and public space. The open courtyard is the public space within the compound walls. Small groups of guests are received on a porch, in a specific spot in the courtyard, or in a larger antechamber reserved for various activities such as wakes or settling family disputes. Within the compound, there are also a number of private rooms, including living areas, bedrooms, and a rainy season kitchen. The kitchen area usually extends into the courtyard. The interior is not used for cooking, except in inclement weather, as women prefer to cook over a fire in the courtyard or under a tree. In some large Akan compounds, there is a separate section for women, with its own courtyard, sleeping rooms, and kitchen.

Round houses are more common in the northern areas of Ghana, while rectangular ones are more common in the southern and central regions. In

Children preparing palm fronds that will make up one of the non-metal roofs in this village.

areas where the two shapes coexist, women generally reside in the circular buildings and men in the rectangular ones. Due to the colonial influence, rectangular buildings are seen as more modern and represent higher status, but circular walls are stronger and stand up to the weather much better.

Traditional houses use many different materials in their construction. The walls are often built with packed mud, earthen bricks, or cement blocks. The roofs are framed with rough timber or bamboo poles, and covered with mud, palm branches, or aluminum sheets. Mud is the most popular building material in traditional architecture. Its strength and pliability allow for a variety of shapes and styles. Some northern groups, such as the Konkomba and Tallensi, build curved-wall structures and elaborate granaries with "technical perfection . . . [that] evokes the same type of admiration as a meticulously wrought, well-proportioned piece of pottery."[6] Others prefer square-walled buildings and use wooden rafters as the main ceiling support, making use of mud only to completely seal the roof.

The materials used in the design of traditional homes help keep the houses cool in the high temperatures that are often experienced in Ghana. In northern Ghana, where the temperatures can vary significantly between day and night, there are few windows in buildings. During the day, when much of the time is spent outdoors, the rooms store heat, which becomes important when the temperature drops at night. In contrast, during the hot season, some people sleep on the mud-covered house roofs, which are comfortable and cool. Using mud or thatching for roofs also provides considerably more insulation against heat and cold than more modern aluminum sheets.

Weather considerations can also determine the best location for the house. In some northern societies, most houses are built on a west-to-east slope. The main entrance is at the highest point facing to the west because the harmattan winds and strong rains come from the east and northeast. Scored walls and the sloping structure help to reduce erosion and channel the flow of water to specific areas. The husband and his wife or wives usually live in separate buildings. The women's residence, at the low point of the compound, contains a living area, bedrooms, and outdoor and indoor cooking spaces. The residence of the husband has a bedroom and a larger living space for receiving guests.

Coastal architectural designs are also adapted to their environment. Using local materials, they utilize more rectangular shapes and provide numerous windows to take advantage of the cool breezes that blow off the ocean and the smaller variance between day and nighttime temperatures. These houses often have a sheltered veranda as well, and the open courtyards are used in the preparation of fish and repair of items such as fishing nets.

The environment also affects the building schedule. Construction, renovation, and repair of existing structures are usually carried out during the dry season. Without a protective surface, traditional adobe houses last only about five years and, during their lifespan, constant maintenance is required. Some groups treat the walls and floors with a protective coating made by breaking up shells found along river banks. Others use vegetable juices or cement and plaster, making the surfaces smoother and more resistant to deterioration caused by the temperature and humidity variations and the driving rain. Circular houses last much longer than their rectangular counterparts. Farming and religious activities determine at what point in the dry season the bulk of construction and renovation will take place. The cultivation and harvesting of crops demand great amounts of energy and time, and only after these activities are finished can people devote the necessary labor to other projects. Yam farmers begin construction projects in the middle of the season after harvesting the late yams, while societies that rely more on grain cultivation undertake these projects much earlier. This pattern is altered in Islamic communities if the month-long fast of Ramadan occurs during the dry season.

In most rural areas, construction is not a specialized profession. Building activities bring community members together and require participation by everyone that is able. The collective process promotes stylistic homogeneity within a village. Men perform most of the structural work on the house, while women take care of the finishing and decorations that give houses some diversity. In addition to treating the walls with a protective agent, some house owners also adorn entrances with pieces of pottery or decorative china. Decorations such as these are a sign of the owner's wealth and status.

Some houses are decorated with painted or engraved symbols using traditional motifs. Akan architecture uses a variety of symbols to convey messages about the family or the significance of the building itself. These symbols were originally limited to important public buildings, such as the houses of leaders and religious shrines, but they are now found in both public and private architecture. Architects of modern buildings also employ symbols to signify the nature of the building. The Children's Library complex in Accra, for example, bears the symbol *mmabunu benyini* ("the young shall grow"), while a hostel for medical students at one university has a wall that features the symbol *yen yiedie* ("our well-being"). Many modern churches, temples, and cultural centers also incorporate numerous symbols.

Religious structures are often the most striking buildings in a given area. Traditional shrines exist throughout rural Ghana. They are considered to be homes for powerful deities that protect communities, heal individuals, and help in dispute settlement. Many shrines are elaborate buildings with artwork and regalia adorning the walls, furniture, and floors. Some, such as the Akan *abosom*, are closely associated with rulers and have priests attached to them. One of the most elaborate shrines is the *posuban* of the Fante *asafo* companies, the former military units that are a feature of Akan societies. The *posuban* shrines, found in what are now urban areas in the central coastal regions, once contained arms and regalia and provided meeting points for particular *asafo* companies. Today, they hold the sacred drums and other symbols of the company and help distinguish one company from another. The land on which they stand is sacred and ancient, but the present concrete forms of the shrines reveal clear post-independence trends, drawing on Western influenced themes such as churches, coastal castles, and just about anything else. Some shrines are built to resemble warships, and others are shaped like airplanes or multistoried buildings.

In the northern areas, where Islam has a greater influence, mosques stand out in many communities for both their form and their color. The most impressive are those constructed in a style that developed during the days of the Western Sudanese empires and was carried south by traders and clerics. This design utilizes triangular clusters of mud pinnacles with protruding wooden spokes held together by horizontal wooden crosspieces. Urban Christian churches have also contributed to architectural styling in Ghana, although most rural churches are not elaborate structures.

Urban Architecture and Housing

The history of architecture in urban centers is very different from that in rural areas. Urban centers are generally characterized by a greater variety of social and cultural influences and tend to feature a more heterogeneous architectural environment than rural settlements. The architecture of most Ghanaian cities, for example, represents a combination of colonial, Western, and African styles. In the heyday of colonialism, merchants and other Europeans built pretentious houses that signified their perceived superiority over the African population. Their whitewashed houses stood out around the smaller mud and brick houses of most urban Ghanaians.

In urban areas, traditional and modern residence structures exist side by side. Spatial limitations restrict the expansion of compounds and enhance overcrowding, but there are also many similarities to rural patterns. An extended family may occupy a house or houses within a specific neighborhood. The concept of a shared open space remains relevant as does the physical separation of rooms for husbands and wives. Urban areas, on the other hand, have a greater percentage of residences designed for nuclear families, and not geographically located according to kinship ties. Urban residential patterns do not reflect the same reliance on kinship as their rural counterparts. Individuals rent sleeping quarters because of proximity to their work place or because the rent is within their budget. Some share a single room with a sibling or cousin to reduce the costs, which also contributes to overcrowding.

Accra, because of its position as the political and economic capital of the country, exhibits a wide range of architectural styles. It is an interesting mix of small houses within established residential patterns, usually in run-down or deteriorating areas, surrounded by impressive administrative and commercial buildings. Urban architecture includes nineteenth-century colonial style buildings, multilevel elegant mansions of the elite, with large porches, lush green gardens, and whitewashed walls, as well as modern glass and steel skyscrapers and apartment complexes. There are also more modest single and multistory brick and cement houses that have many amenities and provide a high standard of living for their inhabitants. Tucked away in particular areas of the city, very different conditions are found. In places like James Town, Ussher Town, and Nima, the streets are narrow and rimmed by open gutters, designed more for pedestrians than for vehicular traffic. The houses are rapidly deteriorating. They are a hodgepodge of cement, wood, and tin structures, some lacking even the most basic necessities of water or waste disposal facilities.

The architecture of Cape Coast and Accra reflects the long history of European residency and influence. The former European residential areas stand out for their location and architectural styles. Buildings such as the Customs House and General Post Office in Accra were built by the British in a renaissance style, with symmetrical Roman arches, while others like the Parliament Building exhibit the influence of British colonial architecture.

Around the time of independence, the capital city began to feature structures that enhanced the image of the Convention People's Party and emphasized the ideal of the Ghanaian nation and pan-African unity. In 1956, for example, a large bronze statue of CPP leader Kwame Nkrumah was placed in front of the Ghanaian Parliament Building. The statue was designed by an Italian and is reminiscent more of Greek heroic monuments than of any Ghanaian traditional art designs. On the base of the statue are carved three of Nkrumah's well-known utterances: "We prefer self-government with danger to servitude in tranquility," "Seek ye first the political kingdom and all other things shall be added unto it," and "To me the liberation of Ghana will be meaningless unless it is linked up with the total liberation of Africa."

Other independence era constructions, commissioned mostly from American and British architects, include Black Star Square, the National Museum, the Accra Community Centre, the Organization of African Unity meeting hall, and a number of commercial buildings. The area around Black Star Square is one of the most impressive in Accra. The square consists of a large assembly ground with covered seating and a striking presidential stand. Near the square is Independence Arch, with the words "Freedom and Justice" inscribed in large letters celebrating the liberation of the country from colonial rule. The large Roman-style victory arch ushered in the era of Ghanaian independence. This area was important to the development of nationalist ideas in the early independence era, and today it is the site of major processions celebrating independence day and other national holidays.[7] Even the seat of Ghanaian government represents both continuity with, and a break from, the past. It is located in Christiansborg Castle (now called just "the Castle"), a former European trading fort and symbol of European exploitation and colonial power.

The architecture of Kumase, the capital of the Ashanti Region, exhibits more homogeneity than Accra. The pride of the Asante people is evident at the main traffic circle, which contains a large Asante stool. Though it is a large, sprawling city, Kumase is really a collection of Asante quarters. Except for the commercial center, Kumase architecture reflects more traditional influence, but the residential patterns are similar to those of Accra, with a large percentage of the population renting rooms from private landlords. About half of Kumase's residents live in traditional, one-story compound houses, while some occupy similar but multilevel compounds. The city center is more densely packed than that of Accra and has seen far less construction during the last four decades. It features some nineteenth-century multilevel buildings that reflect the colonial presence, but none of the majestic buildings and monuments associated with a national capital. The residence of the *asantehene*, the Asante Cultural Centre, the Okomfo Anokye hospital, and the sports stadium are the most prominent buildings in the city. The central area is congested and features an impressive and sprawling market, the largest in Ghana, where one can buy almost anything, from clothing and shoes to pots, pans, radios, and a variety of tools.

Because of its environment and lower population density, Tamale, the capital of the Northern Region, is very different from both Kumase and Accra. Tamale is flat, and it is dusty much of the year. There are few paved streets in the city, which does not exhibit the same architectural variety as larger cities along the coast and in the Ashanti Region. The main part of the city consists of one or two story mud and concrete buildings. Behind the main street, the buildings progressively begin to reflect more and more traditional architectural styles and, in many ways, an agricultural community. Although Tamale has not received its fair share of development revenue to date, the Ghanaian government has made a pledge to devote more resources to the northern regions in general and raise their development to the level of the rest of the country. A new University of Development Studies was recently opened in Tamale as part of that plan.

Notes

1. Vincent Kofi, *Sculpture in Ghana* (Accra: Ghana Information Services, 1964). Quoted in Lawrence Grobel, "Ghana's Vincent Kofi," *African Arts*, 3, 4 (1970), 68.

2. Monica Blackmun Visona et al., *A History of Art in Africa* (New York: Harry N. Abrams, Inc., 2001), 22.

3. For an excellent discussion and numerous photos of these coffins, see Thierry Secretan, *Going into Darkness: Fantastic Coffins from Africa* (London: Thames and Hudson, 1995).

4. John Owoo, "Nicholas Kowalski," *Graphic Showbiz*, 26 April 2000, 12.

5. See Janet Hess, "Exhibiting Ghana: Display, Documentary, and 'National Art' in the Nkrumah Era," *African Studies Review*, 4, 1 (2001), 59–77.

6. Labelle Prussin, *Architecture in Northern Ghana* (Berkeley: University of California Press, 1969), 114.

7. For more on nationalist ideas in architecture, see Janet Hess, "Imagining Architecture: The Structure of Nationalism in Accra, Ghana," *Africa Today,* 47, 2 (2000), 35–58.

5

Cuisine and Traditional Dress

CUISINE and dress are two of the most visible signs of any social group's material culture. Ghanaian food and drink go far beyond their nutritional value. Certain types of ceremonies demand specific types of customary food or a particular style of dress. The many different varieties of food, drink, and dress reflect the availability of local materials and their connection with religious and social values. The types of dress, in particular, help affirm individual and group identities, and reinforce aspects of age and class status.

CUISINE

Ghanaians are known throughout West Africa for the variety and quality of their cuisine. Traditional cuisine features indigenous plants and animals, as well as those introduced from elsewhere during centuries of trade and cultural contact. Today, one can find a variety of traditional and international foods in Ghana. In Accra, roadside stands selling every type of local food sit between American-type fast food restaurants, complete with drive-through facilities, and Indian restaurants. A Japanese sushi restaurant and a restaurant serving fine Italian cuisine are located only a few blocks away. In other urban areas, Chinese and European cuisine are common. For most Ghanaians, however, traditional foods remain an important part of their diets, and they consider foreign foods, although fine to eat, as nothing more than snacks.

Patterns of Consumption

Ghanaian diets consist mainly of starchy foods such as yams, cassava (a starchy root), millet, maize (corn), and rice. Plantain is also consumed regularly by some groups. These staples are served with soups or stews and portions of meat or fish. Hot and spicy foods are common, with most Ghanaians believing that the pepper cools the body and cleanses it of impurities. Ghanaians supplement their diet with a variety of fruits, nuts, and breads. The traditional Ghanaian diet is high in carbohydrates but low in protein because meat is prohibitively expensive and only small portions are served with most meals.

There are codes of etiquette that surround Ghanaian eating habits. Food is eaten with the fingers, but it should never be touched with the left hand, which is considered dirty. It is common for members of a family, a single generation, or a group of siblings or friends to sit around a table and share one large bowl of food. Before eating, the host passes a bowl of water around and all the people present wash their hands. With the fingers of their right hand, they take a small piece of the staple food, usually *fufu, kenkey, banku,* or rice, form it into a small ball, and dip it into the soup or stew. The eldest male gets the best meat but is required to leave a portion for the children to eat later. Although there are variations between ethnic groups, it is also common to leave a small piece of food in the bowl for the cook.

There are different kitchen styles in Ghanaian homes, but they all perform the necessary cooking tasks. Cooking equipment includes modern gas ranges and ovens, portable kerosene stoves, and three-stone fires, fueled by charcoal or wood, that securely hold the cooking pots. Aluminum pots and utensils are common today, but much food is still prepared and served in earthenware pots, wooden bowls, and calabash shells.

Most Ghanaians prefer to eat at home. From a young age, women are trained by their mothers to cook, a skill that men look for in a potential wife. Traditionally, Ghanaian recipes were not written. They were passed along orally and to write them down was a sign of inadequate training. If a woman was seen looking at a recipe book, everyone would assume that she did not know how to cook. The only way to learn the recipes is by experience because the recipes do not use exact measurements or cooking times.

It is rare to see Ghanaians eating in public and it is considered improper to eat in front of someone else without inviting them to partake of the food. Visitors are invited to join in a meal, even if they arrive just before the meal is served. Ghanaian families must always prepare extra food because of the frequency of such occurrences. Guests thank the host and often show appreciation at a later date.

Single and working men who do not have regular access to home-cooked foods frequent the ubiquitous "chop bars" that are essential to the everyday life of society, especially in the urban areas. Usually located in the open air, chop bars have benches and tables and sell a variety of inexpensive local soups and stews that have been prepared in advance. At the chop bars, one can see businessmen in suits, blue collar workers, students, and elderly men eating good food and enjoying lively conversation. It is rare to see women eating at these places because that would give the impression that they do not know how to cook.

Also at the side of the roads, but different from the chop bars, are stands that sell snack foods. People snack on *kelewele*, plantain fried with ginger and hot pepper, or *kyinkyinga*, local kebabs that are coated with hot pepper and often sold around drinking "spots," or beer bars. There is also a popular snack called "Kofi broke man," a dish of roasted plantains and groundnuts. It is meant to satiate an individual during a time when he has very little money.

There are many regional and ethnic differences in Ghanaian cooking that largely reflect the types of crops produced. People in the northern regions grow more sorghum, grains, and rice than those in the central and southern regions. They also practice pastoralism and other forms of animal husbandry and eat more river fish. People in the Ashanti Region eat more plantains and vegetables such as spinach. Coastal people such as the Ga eat more ocean fish and other seafood, while the Ewe of the Volta basin eat lake fish and corn products.

Eating habits vary. Most Ghanaians eat three meals a day, but some choose to have one large meal early in the morning and eat smaller amounts later. If asked, they will say that they have eaten one meal because only the staple foods are considered "real" food. There are many different types of foods that can be served throughout the day. For most people, the evening meal is the largest. It is usually eaten early to allow time for the food to digest and the individual to enjoy other evening activities. Evening meals will always include one of the staple starches in the Ghanaian diet. Soups and starches are commonly eaten at midday or in the evening, but in some regions they are also eaten early in the morning to provide energy for the long day ahead.

Although there are a wide variety of agricultural products found throughout Ghana, yams, corn, cassava, and millet are the favorites that are integral to many different types of meals. Traditional societies rely daily on only a few different types of foods. In urban areas, most people enjoy foods from all over the country, but they still seek the specific staple food associated with their group. The Ga are associated with *kenkey*, the Asante and many other groups with *fufu*, northern groups with *tuo zaafi*, and the Ewe with *banku*. Other common staples include rice, yams, cassava, and plantains.

The most typical Asante dish is *fufu*, a combination of plantains, cassava, and yams. Popular throughout much of West Africa, *fufu* is pounded with a wooden mortar and pestle into a dough-like substance. Preparing *fufu* is usually a two-person job. While one person is pounding, the other gradually adds the ingredients along with water, and turns the food inside the mortar. Sometimes, two people work pestles in opposing strokes. People who have never seen it done before often cringe at each downstroke, fearing that the turner's fingers are about to be smashed by the pestle, but each time they pull their hand away just in time. *Fufu* is prepared in different ways according to the region. In northern Ghana, *fufu* is made from yams, while in southern Ghana it is made from cassava, cocoyam, and plantains. It can be topped with hot sauce, served in a soup, or as the accompaniment to a main dish.

Maize is the staple of the coastal Ga. It forms the main ingredient of their favorite food, *kenkey*, while other coastal groups transform maize into *banku*. *Kenkey* is made from corn meal pounded into a dough. The dough is wrapped in dried corn husks or plantain leaves and steamed, in a process similar to the preparation of tamales. It is most often eaten with fresh fish and hot pepper sauce. *Kenkey* has become popular throughout Ghana, but it varies from region to region. In northern Ghana, sorghum is sometimes used instead of maize for preparation of the dough. Similar to *kenkey, banku* is prepared from a mixture of corn meal and cassava, but it is fermented for up to three days before cooking.

In the northern areas, *tuo zaafi* (usually shortened to T.Z., and pronounced "Tee Zed") and rice are the most popular staple foods. *Tuo zaafi* is a boiled and thickened porridge ball made from millet or corn flour and served with a "slippery" okra stew. The average northern family eats *tuo zaafi* often, as much as twice a day. Rice is becoming more common throughout Ghana today because it takes far less time to prepare than the other starches. Quick preparation is especially important for women who have demanding jobs and cannot spend much time cooking but are still expected to perform all of the cooking duties. Rice can be served plain with any of the soups and stews, or as *omo tuo*, large rice balls that are commonly served early on Sundays with palm or groundnut soup. Other rice dishes include *jollof* rice, a tomato and rice dish made in a single pot, and *waakye*, rice and beans mixed together with a little fried meat.

Yams, cocoyam, plantains, and beans are important in many foods and, prepared in a variety of ways, can be substituted for the other staple foods.

Yams and plantains can be boiled, fried, roasted, or grilled and eaten with any of the stews. Plantains, in particular, are rich in iron and potassium. Beans are popular with rice in *waakye* and many other dishes. They provide protein where meat is scarce. Black-eyed peas are cooked with fried onions, tomatoes, and dried fish to make *aduafrol* stew. Another popular dish is "red red," which pairs black-eyed peas cooked in palm oil with fried plantains.

Soups and stews are found in the majority of Ghanaian dishes and are eaten with any of the carbohydrates. There are many different types. The most popular are light soup, made from a light broth and served with *fufu*, pepper soup, a spicy soup that is believed to be a good remedy for sicknesses such as colds and the flu, and palm nut soup, made from palm nuts and peppers. Groundnut or peanut soup, is probably the best known Ghanaian dish outside of Ghana. Other soups are made from salted beef, fresh fish, snails, or other types of seafood.

Stews are thicker than soups and usually contain additional ingredients. The basic sauce for many stews is made from tomatoes, onions, and various herbs, sautéed in oil. Three popular varieties of stew include okra stew, *abom* eggplant stew, and *kontomire*, a stew made from spinach. *Palaver* sauce is similar to *kontomire* but also includes *egusi* seeds, a seed that resembles a melon seed.

Almost all of the soups and stews are served with meat or fish. The most popular meats are beef, chicken, goat, guinea fowl, and mutton. Meat is seen as an important part of the dish and the quantity and quality of meat served are indications of status and wealth. Sheep, goats, and poultry are raised throughout Ghana, even in urban centers, but the savanna environment of the northern regions favors larger cattle ranches. Guinea fowl meat is a popular snack any time of the day. Originating in the north, it can now be found throughout Ghana, especially in places like Accra and Kumase. Wild animals are also caught and consumed, including different types of deer (Akan: *wansan*), antelope (Akan: *otwe*), and *akrantie*, best described as a large rodent and commonly known as "grass cutter."

The Atlantic Ocean, Lake Volta, Lake Bosumtwi, and the many rivers provide a variety of sea and freshwater fish. Fresh fish can be baked or fried and put in soups or stews, or it can be grilled and served on the side with a staple such as *kenkey*. The most popular large fish include tilapia, sea bass, barracuda, and mudfish (or catfish) that can be caught in many rivers in Ghana. Tilapia was once an inexpensive fish and was considered "poor man's" food. Although it was enjoyed by most people, elite families were sure not to serve it when they entertained guests because of its low status. Recently, however, grilled tilapia and *banku* have grown in popularity and their cost and prestige have escalated. Smoked fish are a common sight in the markets or on the roadside. Usually smaller fish, smoking preserves them and allows them to be saved for later consumption or to be shipped to other regions. Along the coast, shrimp, snail, soft-shell crab, and lobster are also available.

Ghanaians also eat porridges frequently, especially as easy to digest and rehydrating foods for infants and as popular breakfast dishes for all ages. Ghanaian porridges are made from rice, millet, wheat flour, or corn. They are very filling and can satisfy a person for much of the day. The most popular types of porridge include "rice water," "Tom Brown," and *koko*. Evaporated milk and sugar are usually added to the porridges to give them a desirable flavor and a creamy texture.

Additional foods provide flavor and spice or add variety to the Ghanaian diet. The primary cooking oil comes from red palm nuts. The oil is high in cholesterol, but it contains high levels of vitamins A and E and adds a distinctive flavor to Ghanaian foods. Coconut oil is occasionally used as well. One of the most popular sauces used to add spice to food is *shito*. *Shito* is a hot pepper sauce that is made with fresh peppers and served with many foods but especially with fish and *kenkey*. Many societies rely on fruits such as coconuts, bananas, avocados, pineapples, oranges, papayas, and lemons to balance their diets. Ghana's most famous crop, of course, is cocoa. It is one of the country's major exports and is used to make chocolate, but few Ghanaians eat sweet foods on a regular basis and most of the cocoa is exported.

There are similarities between Ghanaian, Caribbean, and U.S. cooking. Cultural links, beginning with the trans-Atlantic slave trade and continuing in the present with Ghanaian emigration to other countries, have spread Ghanaian cuisine around the world. Many foods commonly found in the southern United States and the Caribbean, such as okra, greens, and black-eyed peas, are also popular with Ghanaians and many other West Africans. Groundnut soup has become one of the best known African foods and is popular with Africans and non-Africans alike. Ghanaians living abroad crave their traditional cuisine and, thus, scores of Ghanaian restaurants have been established in cities all over the United States.

BEVERAGES

Beverages are also important in Ghanaian customs. There are certain rules that apply to drinking in Ghana. In traditional society, alcohol was associated with power and, therefore, it was not considered proper for children, adolescents, or women to drink. There are rituals that must be followed when accepting a drink from someone. In all Ghanaian societies, visitors are first given a seat and then water or some other drink before they are asked the purpose of their visit. During festivals and religious ceremonies, libations of water, palm wine, or other alcoholic beverages are poured to pay respect to the gods.

Ghanaians drink large amounts of water to combat the hot temperatures. In general, no liquids are taken before a meal in order to leave more room in the stomach for food. It is common for Ghanaians to eat until their stomachs can take no more. Water is usually left until the food is finished, and is then gulped down quickly. It is becoming more common, however, for elites and restaurant-goers to have a beer or soft drink with their meals.

Fruits can be found in most rural areas and they are sold everywhere. Coconut milk is a popular drink. Mangos, pineapples, and oranges are sometimes made into juices. Non-alcoholic drinks also include ginger beer, a spicy, refreshing drink made from ginger root, and *askenkee* (iced *kenkey*), a milky drink made by mashing *kenkey* in water, adding sugar, and refrigerating. Soft drinks such as Fanta, Coca-Cola, Pepsi Cola, Mirinda, Sprite, Muscatella, and others are very popular and are available in all areas of the country.

Some Ghanaians give their children bitter medicine drinks made from local materials to promote general health, fight specific maladies, and induce sleep. There are also drinks that act as laxatives, cleansing the body by purging the infections from within. The medicinal drinks are produced from local leaves, roots, and tree barks.

Ghanaians consume alcoholic beverages for recreation and ritual purposes. Drinking is primarily a social activity and it is frowned on for Ghanaians to drink alone. The popularity of locally produced alcoholic beverages is regionally specific. *Akpeteshie* is a high-alcohol, homemade gin that is popular throughout Ghana. It was banned during the colonial era, but continued to thrive as a cheaper alternative to high priced imported liquor. Since independence, the production of *akpeteshie* has increased, both at the formal and the informal level. The consumption of alcohol is related to wealth and status. *Akpeteshie* is associated with lower- and working-class life, while more expensive imported liquors mark middle- and upper-class status.[1]

Pito is a fermented, low-alcohol drink made from Guinea corn (sorghum) that is common in the northern regions of Ghana. Because Guinea corn is the main crop of many northern societies, brewing *pito* is an important social activity in the courtyards of residential compounds. There are specially assigned areas in which to store the large pots and brew the *pito*. Drinking *pito* at open-air bars is a popular leisure time activity and a regular source of entertainment.

Palm wine is tapped from a palm tree using different methods. Depending on the type of tree, Ghanaians may fell the palm tree first and let the liquid ferment before tapping it or tap the tree at the top while it is still standing. The alcoholic content of palm wine varies according to the fermentation time. The best tasting palm wines are usually found in rural areas because they are taken directly from the tree and not diluted with anything else. In urban areas, palm wine is often mixed with water and sugar, diluting the strength and taste. Palm wine was once used on most ceremonial and ritual occasions, but spirits are sometimes now used instead because of the higher status that they carry.

Other popular alcoholic beverages are the locally produced Ghanaian beers available throughout the country. These include Star, Club, ABC, and Gulder, as well as Guinness stout, an Irish beer now brewed in Ghana that is believed to give strength. Bitters, a drink made from gin and herbs, is becoming popular with young men in the urban areas, who associate it with increased sexual potency.

Festival Food and Drink

Food and drink are essential for life. Ghanaians do not see death as the end of life and, therefore, those who have died must be given food and drink from time to time. The gods provide protection and happiness so they too must be propitiated. There are food dishes associated with specific festivals and ceremonies in Ghana. All the important life events, such as naming, puberty, marriage, and death, have food and drink associated with them. A drop of water is given to children when they are named, officially welcoming them to the family. Libations are poured during puberty rites, weddings, and funerals to pay respect to the ancestors and gods. Liquor and palm wine are important elements of bridewealth, the gifts that the family of the groom gives to the family of the bride. Local festivals also include a great deal of feasting, each festival having a particular dish or dishes associated with it.

During the Ga festival of *homowo*, a great feast is held on the most important day. The ritual meal of *homowo* is *kpekpei*, a corn flour dish served with palm soup. Women begin the preparation long before sunrise because everything must be finished by noon to allow for the other rituals. The *kpekpei* is made from steamed, unleavened corn dough that is pounded in a mortar. It is salted and mixed with palm oil and always served with palm soup during *homowo*. The *kpekpei* and soup are put into earthenware pots. Some is given to the owners of the house, who sprinkle it around the entrances to pay respect to the souls of departed ancestors. Some is given to the *mantsemei*, (chiefs) who, usually accompanied by lively drumming and dancing, walk around sprinkling it in the public areas under their jurisdiction.

All festivals in Ghana are based on the ritual use and consumption of food and drink to pay tribute to the gods and ancestors who provide for the people. Ceremonies that mark the end of the growing season pay tribute to gods and ancestors for helping produce an abundant harvest. One of the most popular is the yam festival, celebrated by Akan peoples. To thank the gods, yams are pounded and sprinkled all over the village or city, and in rivers, lakes, and shrines. Libations of palm wine or *akpeteshie* are poured for the gods, and animals are sacrificed. After all the proper rituals are finished, the festival-goers take part in eating and drinking to celebrate a successful season.

The ritual sacrifice of cows, sheep, and goats is commonly practiced to propitiate the gods during important ceremonies and festivals. The most popular festival is probably the *aboakyer*, or deer hunt festival, held annually at Winneba. During this festival, teams of *asafo* companies compete to see who can capture a live deer. The deer is then sacrificed to the gods and the entire community enjoys enormous amounts of food, drink, music, and dancing. Other traditional festivals of similar status include the *afahye* festival, celebrated by the people of Cape Coast, *bakatue* festival, held in Elmina, and the *kundum* festival, celebrated by the Ahanta and Nzema of the Western Region.

DRESS

Ghanaians attach considerable importance to dressing themselves according to their status and the nature of the occasion. Dress includes not only the clothes that people wear, but also the ornamentation and accessories that affect the way in which people project their image to others. What one wears is an indication of socioeconomic status, age, education, and marital status. Ghanaians of all classes exert time and effort into their personal appearance. They make sure their shoes are shined, their pants and shirts are ironed, and their hair is well-groomed.

Many features of traditional dress codes are still apparent throughout the country. Foreign clothing styles that satisfy traditional mores are incorporated and adapted, while others are adopted by youth, much to the dismay of older generations. For both men and women, wearing shorts is frowned upon. Boys and girls regularly wear shorts in public, but once people reach the age of puberty, the wearing of shorts undermines their adult status. Around the home, both men and women are free from these social restrictions. Such sanctions are relaxed in the urban areas, where young men and women frequent the beach and discos, and women wear short skirts and tight tops.

Men and women continue to wear traditional styles of dress in both the rural and urban areas. Women generally wear a set of two cloths as a wrapper or skirt, plus a blouse, jewelry, and a head-tie. The two-yard piece of cloth that is worn around the waist is called a *lapa* and is the most common everyday clothing style of women in the rural areas. Women might also wear a *lapa* or *lapas* wrapped around the entire upper and lower body. Another piece of cloth can be used to carry a child on the back. Head-ties are a common feature of Ghanaian female dress. They are yard-long pieces of cloth that are wrapped around the head, usually covering all of the hair. Head ties can be worn in a variety of styles which often have specific names. They are fastened by tightly securing one end of the fabric in the wrap or by tying both ends together. The fabric of the *lapa* and head-tie may match or may be of completely different patterns. More formal dress might include a skirt, a blouse, a purse, and various accessories.

The "*kaba* and slit" is becoming a popular style of dress for women to wear to work, formal dinners, and weddings. Many banks, restaurants, and other workplaces use it as their company uniform for women. Six yards of cloth are used to make the *kaba* (blouse), slit (skirt), and a cover cloth. This style comes in many different forms. The blouse may have a high or low neckline, it may have a stiff or puffy sleeve that extends outward from the shoulders or extends down the arms slightly, and it may be made from lacy material or locally produced prints. The skirt can be hip-hugging, it can be loose, or it can be fashioned in an A-line style.

Menswear ranges from *agbada* (long gowns, usually worn over loose shorts) to variations of an oversize smock, called *fugu,* worn with long pants made from imported or Ghanaian fabric. Ghanaian traditional dress reflects regional and ethnic identities, but the spread of national ideas and increased migration has blurred those lines. Men in northern regions often wear long tunics sewn from strips of rough cotton cloth. Smocks are made from a similar cotton cloth and can be worn by all social groups for all occasions. *Agbada* gowns are derived from the flowing gowns of the Muslim *ulama* (learned men) in North Africa, but the Ghanaian style is more colorful. *Agbada* are now worn by men of all regional and religious backgrounds and in all areas of the country. The cloth for traditional garments can be plain, feature designs and patterns of colors, or be elaborately embroidered. For festive or ceremonial occasions, men and women in the southern regions usually wear a large, eight-by-twelve-foot piece of cloth in a toga style. The cloth can come in many different patterns and designs, including hand-made *kente* and *adinkra,* or factory-made wax prints. In general, men have adapted the Western-style shirt and pants more readily than women have taken on Western fashions. This is likely due to the fact that men are more apt to migrate and be exposed to new ideas of dress. The politics of a multiethnic workplace also promote a greater variety of dress styles and more emphasis on Western clothing styles.

There are a number of ways to wear cloth. Children commonly cover their bodies with a piece of cloth and fasten the ends behind their neck. Young women also wear the cloth in this manner, especially when they are doing chores around the house. The *Mewo me biribi di* ("I am self sufficient") style is associated with kings, chiefs, and wealthy men. Another way to wear untailored cloth includes leaving the bottom to dangle on the ground, signifying that you have enough money to buy more cloth and a wife at home who will wash it. Those who cannot afford the proper cloth for a certain ceremony may wear *mokwaa ntoma fra* ("borrowed to wear"). The wearers do not want to damage or dirty the cloths that are borrowed from family or friends and, thus, they wear their cloth much higher off the ground, often at knee level, and hold it close at the sides. This is generally associated with people of lower status.

Among the Asante, boys and girls traditionally dressed differently from the time that they were born. Although the differences today more often relate to types of Western-style clothing, the gender variances remain. While there are few restrictions on the type of Western-style clothing that children can wear, the styles of traditional clothing that can be worn relate to age and status. Although it is a waning practice, young girls don waist beads before anything else. They gradually add additional items of clothing as they mature. When they reach five or six years of age, they wear a cloth to cover their genitals, and at the age of seven or eight they began to wear a larger cloth that reaches from their waist to their knees. Tradition did not require that they cover their knees until they became women. Today, a girl's first *kaba* and slit provides a day of great happiness and gives her status above those still wearing "childrens' " clothes. Around the age of eight, boys begin to wrap a single piece of cloth around them and tie it around the neck. The loop around the neck was important because it distinguished them by age and status from adults, who wore cloth in a toga style, with the end thrown over the left shoulder and arm.

There are three main types of traditional cloth in Ghana: factory-made, plain cloth that is usually fashioned into Western-style clothing; traditional cloth with batik-like patterns and symbols that are increasingly being manufactured in Ghanaian factories; and "country cloths," hand-woven from various materials into narrow strips that are sewn together to form larger pieces. The textile industry in Ghana has made advances during the last decade. It now manufactures quality cloth decorated with many different types of wax prints. Factories produce special types of cloth to commemorate important holidays or special events. During the most recent elections, political parties commissioned special cloths printed with their party logos or the image of their candidates. One of the best selling cloths was the "millennium" cloth that celebrated the beginning of the new millennium. Hand-woven cloths come in many different designs and can be fashioned into any

A woman at a festival wearing traditional cloth and metal and bead bracelets; her arms and face are adorned with body painting.

of the popular garment styles. Like pieces of art, hand-woven cloths such as *kente, adinkra,* and other "country cloths" are valued for craftsmanship and artistic style.

Ceremonial Dress

Ghanaians wear fancy clothes for many social occasions. Weddings and Sunday religious services call for elaborate dress, whether traditionally tailored Ghanaian cloth or Western clothes. Dress is also important in the celebration of funerals and naming ceremonies. All-night wake-keeping on Fridays and burials on Saturdays demand certain types of cloth, depending on the age and status of the deceased and the relationship of the audience to the deceased. The elite use a celebration, such as a naming ceremony, to display their wealth to their family and friends by wearing expensive cloths cut in the newest fashions. Naming ceremonies, weddings, and funerals are frequent and popular social occasions that offer everyone a chance to wear their

Men wearing traditional cloth and holding carved wooden staffs at a festival.

finest cloth and enjoy the company of friends and family. It would be difficult to pass through any part of a city or any village on a weekend without encountering one of these ceremonies.

Cloth has value beyond its economic worth. It has often been given by the groom's family to the bride's family as part of the bridewealth. In Ga culture, a full traditional wedding is called a "six cloth" marriage, relating to the quantity of cloth that must be given to meet the bridewealth requirements. Cloth can represent Ghanaian ethnic and national pride. When President Bill Clinton visited Ghana, his Ghanaian counterpart, Jerry Rawlings, presented a piece of traditional cloth to him as a symbol of the bonds between Ghana and the United States, similar to the bonds that are created between two families.

Different types of cloth are appropriate for certain ritual and ceremonial events. *Kente* is the most popular cloth for festive occasions, while *adinkra* cloth is usually worn at funerals (see Chapter 4). *Kente* cloth is brightly colored and was once worn exclusively by Akan royalty. Africans all over the continent now wear *kente* and it has become popular with African Americans as a symbol of their ties to the continent. *Kente* can identify a person's place of origin and sometimes their station in life. *Adinkra* cloth comes in a variety of colors and its stamped images relate to proverbial expressions in Akan culture. Some of the *adinkra* images, such as the *sankofa* bird, have become symbols of the links between Africans and African Americans.

Specific colors should be worn for specific occasions. The Akan use dark colors such as black and brown for funerals. The immediate family and close relatives wear dark red cloths because red is a sign of passion and is believed to contain protective powers. At other times, *kuntunkuni*, an older, obviously aged black cloth, is worn to express profound grief over the death of an important family member. White cloth is worn for joyous occasions such as naming ceremonies, marriages, or funerals for a person who has lived a long and happy life. The many colors of *kente* cloth represent various human traits and connote status (gold), vitality (yellow), renewal (green), and spiritual purity (blue). *Kente* is usually worn on ceremonial and festive occasions. Perhaps the most elaborate exhibition of colorful cloth in recent times was the 1995 silver jubilee celebration of the *asantehene*. One observer counted about 1,000 chiefs and queen mothers dressed in a colorful collage of traditional cloths and other regalia, with the most important participants donning *kente* cloth.[2]

One of the most impressive Ghanaian ceremonial garments is the *batakari*, or war shirt. The shirt is a product of the northern regions and is tied into military power. It is also seen, however, in Asante society, reflecting the influences of northern cultural practices and Islam in the royal court of Asante. The Asante adopted the shirt and added amulets made by Muslim *malams*, a small but influential group on the *asantehene*'s court during the rule of Osei Tutu and Opoku Ware. In the time of the Asante Empire, it was worn by Asante generals to give them courage and help ward off evil spirits on the battlefield. The *batakari* of northern Ghana, made from heavier hand-woven cotton and also covered with numerous amulets, serves a similar military and spiritual purpose. Today, *batakari* is a ceremonial dress and worn by men throughout Ghana on special occasions.

Ornamentation

Individual preferences in jewelry, accessories, hairstyles, and bodily ornamentation form an integral part of traditional and modern dress in Ghana. In general, ornamentation varies by gender, generation, status, and context. Genuine high status is gained through age, respect, and wisdom, but a high-status look can be created by what one wears. In general, money is rarely saved for a rainy day, for that day may never come. It is better to spend it now and enjoy the fruits of life. One of the ways to spend it is to buy fine clothes and shoes and wear them often. Status can also be gained by dis-

playing certain items, such as gold jewelry, expensive watches, and lux
purses. For women, expensive, imported cosmetics and perfumes
wealth and a worldly style.

The Asante, with their wealth in gold, have skilled craftspeople w
duce elaborate gold objects for royalty and for ceremonial use. Gold is w
in copious amounts by Asante royalty. One of the most impressive objects
is the ceremonial heavy gold badge worn around the neck by distinguished
members of the royal court who are close to the king. At the most important
ceremonies, the *asantehene* and influential paramount chiefs have worn so
much gold jewelry and armlets that assistants have had to walk beside them
to support the weight of their arms. The Asante believe that gold has spiritual
power and can provide protection to those who wear it. Other societies see
gold as a destructive force that hinders spiritual power and prefer to wear
silver jewelry instead. Regardless of the type of material, metal jewelry plays
an important role in traditional cultures. Diviners often advise clients to wear
metal bangles or other forms of metal ornamentation to give them spiritual
guidance and protect them from evil spirits.

In much the same way, beads can be indicators of wealth and status and
provide spiritual protection. The meaning and symbolism of beads vary between ethnic groups. In many groups, a string of small, fine beads are
wrapped around the waist of young girls from the time they are born as a
protective device and a sign of age and marital status. In Dangme society,
the wearing of *nyoli* and *tovi* beads identifies certain people as priestesses.
The number of beads indicates the rank of the priestess and identifies her
deity. Bead bracelets are also worn by chiefs to signify their position in society.

The human body can also be a form of art in itself, displaying sophisticated
body markings, hairstyles, or painted designs. Elaborate body painting and
specific hairstyles may be used in ceremonial contexts to identify a particular
position or display ethnic pride. Some body adornments last forever, while
others are only intended as temporary displays. They all help indicate the
social status or group identity of their wearers. During their traditional festival, the installation of a chief, and girls' puberty rites, Dangme priestesses
paint their bodies with chalk, vegetable mixtures, and charcoal. These designs
are determined by the instructions that the priestess receives from her personal deity. The act revitalizes the bond between the priestess and her deity.
Although they are less common today, small, permanent facial markings are
also used to identify a particular ethnic group or signify ascension to a specific
age level.

Coiffures and hats, like beads, can be associated with ceremonial meanings,
but hairstyles are also an important part of everyday dress. Wearing hair short,

These elaborately painted signs for hair salons depict styles of haircuts for men and women. In the background, street signs show the direction to various places, including a cellular phone company, a pharmacy, and a bar.

in dreadlocks, braided with extensions, or straightened says much about individual personality and values. Haircuts often have names that reflect the wearer's beliefs. In the 1950s, one of the popular styles for men was called "freedom now." Hairstyles, especially among women, can provide insights into a person's age, socioeconomic, and marital status. Just as school children wear uniforms that identify them as students, most are also required to keep their hair short because they are not yet considered adults. Hair can also play a role in mourning. Among the Akan, the immediate family of the deceased shave their heads and place the hair in a pot, which is then taken to the cemetery to appease the spirits.

Western Fashions

Dress and identity are intimately related. Dress is a nonverbal symbol, but it says much about a person. Something as simple as tying a red sash around one's head provides a powerful symbol of resistance, a symbol Ghanaian students and other groups frequently use when they are protesting against administrative or government policies that they believe are hindering their development. The wearing of Western dress has a long history in Ghana and also played an important role in the projection of individual and group identities during the colonial era.

Christian missionaries expected Ghanaian converts to put on European-style clothing, disparaging African dress and seeing it as "native" and "uncultured." Western dress was associated with high civilization. Some elite Ghanaians chose to don Western clothes to separate themselves from other Africans and give them entrance into European society. Africans and Europeans alike could be seen wearing clothes, such as heavy woolen suits, corsets, and plumed hats, unsuited to the tropical heat. There are even reports of some elite African clubs fining members who were seen wearing traditional clothes in public.

But there were also people who fought against the European ideas of dress. In 1931, Ephraim Amu (1898–1995), a Presbyterian minister, conducted a church service wearing Ghanaian clothes. He was reprimanded by the Synod Committee of the Gold Coast and given a choice between wearing "proper" religious clothes while preaching or not preaching at all. For Amu, it was not a difficult decision: "I felt the attire in which we preach is ridiculous. . . . In this hot country it is stifling to wear a black suit with vest and everything which I did wear for sometime. By the time one went through all that, one was fully wet with perspiration."[3] When he showed up the following Sunday wearing *kente* cloth, he was dismissed from the Presbyterian Training College.

Western-style dress became associated with colonial power. When the nationalist movement gathered steam in the 1950s, leaders began to wear traditional clothing as a symbol of their independence from the colonial elite and their desire for self-government. Kwame Nkrumah instructed others to wear traditional smocks and donned one himself at Ghana's independence celebrations in 1957. Throughout his rule, Nkrumah promoted the wearing of traditional clothes, frequently sporting smocks and *kente* cloth, as a symbol of Ghanaian cultural pride and as a tool to foster a national identity. Subsequent presidents and other notable figures have also worn Ghanaian traditional clothing regularly and in high profile situations. The former first lady, Nana Rawlings, wore the *kaba* and slit style of dress often and, by doing so, created new interest and stirred the development of new styles in women's clothing.

As information about the world beyond localized places becomes more available through international media forms such as movies, television, and the print media, there is an increased exchange between cultures. Ghanaians

One of the ubiquitous tailors, working at his sewing machine.

today wear a variety of clothing styles, sometimes Western dress, sometimes a combination of Western and traditional dress, or sometimes traditional clothing, especially for ceremonies. Tailors and seamstresses work out of shops that can be found in all cities and villages. Women may take Ghanaian cloth to a tailor to sew a dress style that they found in a fashion magazine or saw on television. Denim materials may be taken to a tailor to be made into a Ghanaian-style shirt or a skirt. Tailors may also use both Ghanaian cloth and imported cloth in the same garment.

The type of dress often depends on the environment and the generation of the person wearing it because dress makes a direct comment on personal identity. When going to a disco, for example, young people tend to dress in fancy Western clothes, symbolizing a high status and knowledge of Western fashion. On the street, clothing varies from traditional garments to a dignified Western-style suit. It is common to see men wearing a Ghanaian shirt with khaki pants, or women wearing a T-shirt with a waist-wrap.

Western clothes can be bought at a variety of places in Ghana. People can buy fabric in stores, at the market, or at roadside stands and bring it to tailors to get it made into any style of garment that they desire. They may also visit one of the many stores in the cities that sell new clothing, although this is cost prohibitive for some. The desire for Western clothing has promoted the development of a new and flourishing industry. The markets for second-hand clothing, *obroni wawu* ("clothes of dead white people"), are extremely popular and sell just about any style of clothing worn in the West. The T-shirts, pants, blouses, ties, and shoes are shipped in bulk to Ghana and are sold at prices far lower than those charged for most locally made goods. At least some of the changes in dress, then, seem to be encouraged by economic factors.

Traditional styles of dress and Western fashion are interrelated.[4] One may buy a piece of Ghanaian cloth and have it made into a Western-style garment. *Kente* cloth is made into ties and coats, mainly for the international market. Tailored suits made in Ghana or abroad signify knowledge of international styles in corporate and political milieus, but wearing them does not necessarily mean the complete acceptance of this style. It is a conscious decision to present oneself to a particular audience in a particular way. Many elite Ghanaians were educated abroad and have an understanding of Western culture. They know that, at times, it is best to don the Western suit in "power" meetings, while at other times it behooves one to wear traditional clothes. It is also important to remember that, just as Western styles and ideas are imported into Ghana, so too are Ghanaian styles of dress becoming increasingly popular in parts of the Western world. Just as Ghanaian food can be found throughout the United States and the Caribbean, Ghanaian fashions, such as *kente* cloth have been adopted and adapted by African Americans to celebrate their cultural heritage.

Lastly, Ghanaian fashion, like Western fashion, is constantly undergoing change. Unlike some traditional cloth that is closely associated with particular ceremonies and religious rites, fashion trends are dynamic and change according to the context. Wearing a cloth in a toga style to work might be comfortable and cool, but it would be difficult because one must constantly make adjustments to keep the loose ends in place. Fashion designers react to the needs and interests of society and create new styles of clothing that reflect those interests. Ghana has a number of skilled fashion designers who create new styles for the workplace, entertainment venues, and casual environments. Some designers own fashionable shops in Accra, while others host fashion shows on local television stations. Ghanaian designers utilize the wealth of local textile designs and patterns to create garments that reflect innovations in traditional styles. A number of fashion designers living in Ghana are gaining fame on the international scene by using Ghanaian fabrics and designs to create a wide variety of styles, including European suits and African shirts.

NOTES

1. For a discussion of alcohol and status, see Emmanuel Akyeampong, *Drink, Power, and Cultural Change: A Social History of Alcohol in Ghana, c. 1800 to Recent Times* (Portsmouth, NH: Heinemann, 1996).

2. Judith Perani and Norma H. Wolff, *Cloth, Dress and Art Patronage in Africa* (Oxford: Berg, 1999), 98.

3. Quoted in Kojo T. Vieta, *The Flagbearers of Ghana: Profiles of One Hundred Distinguished Ghanaians* (Accra: Ena Publications, 1999), 440.

4. For a discussion of ethnic dress and world fashion, see Joanne B. Eicher and Barbara Sumberg, "World Fashion, Ethnic, and National Dress," in Joanne B. Eicher (ed.), *Dress and Ethnicity* (Washington, DC: Berg, 1995).

6

Gender Roles, Marriage, and Family

Ebusua Ye Dom ("The Family Is a Crowd")

—Akan proverb

GHANAIAN families are truly a crowd. They can include extended families spanning three and four generations. Traditional family, marriage, and gender relations affect individual development and are instrumental in determining the overall social organization of society. They are dynamic institutions that reflect traditional patterns of lineage descent and concepts of family structure, as well as changes brought about by Islam, Western religion and culture, education, migration, and changing economic conditions.

LINEAGE AND SOCIAL PATTERNS

In general, a lineage is an extended kinship group living in compounds or towns that are near one another, although increased migration has changed the geographical component of the relationship. A lineage system provides the basic framework for organizing traditional society and managing complex relationships. Lineage systems determine the control and dissemination of property, ensure the maintenance of social laws, and play a vital role in ceremonial and religious rites. They also define the nature of communal identity and the process of political succession.

The framework and social organization of the family vary depending on the type of descent system practiced. There are two prominent types of descent systems in Ghana: matrilineal and patrilineal. The Akan practice matrilineal descent, while most other groups practice patrilineal descent. Matrilineal societies trace descent exclusively through females, while patrilineal societies do so through males. Regardless of the type of system, these relationships establish membership in a kinship group.

In the Akan matrilineal descent system, lineage membership is determined through the mother. Males and females are both members of the matriclan (*abusua*), but only female links are used to determine future generations. The *abusua* includes siblings, the children of female siblings, and maternal uncles and aunts. Each lineage has a unique status and identity within society, represented by property rights and specific symbols. The branches of the family tree derive from a female founder, with each branch led by an elder or chief. Individual branches possess minor family stools (carved symbols of family and status), but a lineage stool that can be traced to the female head ultimately links the extended family together.

Although women have a high status in Akan society because of their important position within the matrilineal descent system, men continue to hold most of the traditional leadership positions in the lineage of their mothers. Wives and children in matrilineal systems do not traditionally inherit status and wealth from their husband or father, but rather from their mother's brother. This is changing, however, as wealth becomes more individualized. It is now customary for men to make a will leaving self-acquired property to their sons. This became more common during the early twentieth century when cocoa farmers and businessmen amassed large amounts of money and property. Early deaths of male household heads left wives and children with little economic security or access to family resources, and often caused disputes between the immediate family and the rest of the lineage. Recent laws have attempted to streamline the system of inheritance. The 1985 Intestate Succession Law, for example, gives greater recognition to the rights and power of the nuclear family upon the death of a husband or father, while still recognizing the collective ownership of lineage property.

Outside the Akan areas, patrilineal descent is the most common form of lineage system. In patrilineal systems, individual and family social identities are attached to the extended family of the father. A traditional household consists of the paternal grandparents, parents, unmarried daughters, some or all of the sons, and their wives and children. Children belong to the patrilineage and most property is handed down directly from the father to his sons, while women may receive and use property relating to everyday domestic activities, such as cooking pots, plates, and other household goods, or land on which to grow crops.

Marriages between people of different ethnic groups with different lineage systems confuse the issue of descent and identity for the children. If the mother is from a matrilineal group and the father is from an ethnic group that practices patrilineal descent, the child can experience duolineal descent, obtaining full lineage rights from each of his or her parents. On the other hand, children in the reverse situation are at a disadvantage because they do not have rights of inheritance from either of their parents. Kinship links with people from outside of one's lineage are still recognized, but they do not have the same relationship and obligations as those tied directly into a particular descent system.

Various social benefits and obligations bind lineage members together. The extended family operates as a mutual aid society. Members have the right to receive help with financial matters, entitlement to lineage property, and the security of knowing that they will receive a proper funeral when they die. Obligations to the lineage keep members in good standing and permit them to draw on the membership benefits. Families are responsible for ensuring that their members receive the moral and ethical instruction that is necessary to make them comply with their obligations. Individual behaviors and actions reflect an individual's moral character, as well as that of the entire family.

RITES OF PASSAGE

One of the most important responsibilities of lineage membership is participation in rites of passage celebrating birth, puberty, marriage, and death. The ceremonies help determine family organization, domestic hierarchies, and future lineage relationships. They provide status and represent the growth of the lineage. Each event is marked by specific rituals that teach children how to be responsible adults, show married couples how to live together and respect one another, or send the deceased on their journey to the ancestral world with dignity and respect.

Birth

The birth of children is a joyous occasion for Ghanaian families. Children represent wealth and the future continuance of a lineage. It is believed that the spirits of the parents live on through their children. Pregnant women are considered beautiful and given special privileges by others. They are also, however, considered fragile and vulnerable to evil spirits. Barrenness and miscarriages are believed to be caused by these spirits, and thus women will sometimes seek guidance from a diviner in order to enhance their chances of conception or to protect the fetus from harm. Among the Akan, fertility symbols such as *akuaba* dolls may be carried around during pregnancy to ensure a healthy baby that resembles the idealized symbol of beauty depicted by the statue's exaggerated female features.

When children are born, they are kept indoors for seven days, the period when they are most vulnerable to physical and spiritual harm. Most Ghanaians believe that a child is a wanderer from the spiritual world and may "decide" to go back to that world at any point during the first week. After this period, the child undergoes an elaborate naming ceremony that celebrates the birth and officially acknowledges the child. These "outdooring" ceremonies are called *kpodziemo* by the Ga, *abadinto* or *dzinto* by the Akan, *sunna* by the Dagomba, and *vihehedego* by the Ewe. During these ceremonies, the child's name is called out by the father or an elder, and the guests repeat the name aloud, formally welcoming the child into the community.

Outdooring ceremonies are accompanied by different kinds of rituals, depending on the ethnic group. Among the Ga, drops of water and alcohol are put on the children's tongues so that they will know the difference between good and evil. Babies may also be given a small piece of food, such as *kenkey*, so they will appreciate the staple food of the Ga people. Other groups raise the child toward the sky three times as an introduction to heaven and earth. Libations are poured and sacrifices of goats or chickens are made to ask for good health and to protect the child against evil. After the naming is finished, friends and relatives bestow many gifts on the initiate and the family. This is followed by a grand celebration with feasting and dancing.

Most Ghanaian groups have special names associated with the day of the week on which children are born as well as a name for their age relationship with other children in the family. A male Akan child born on Friday, for example, is called Kofi, while one born on Saturday is Kwame. Females are Afua and Ama, respectively. The eldest child takes the name of Opiesie, while the second is Maanu. Ewe groups also have special names for children born at night or on a rainy day. In areas where Islamic influence is greater, the naming ceremony is led by a *mallam*, who suggests several names and allows the community to choose from among them. Christian families often give both traditional names and Christian names to their children.

Initiation

The next major stage in a person's life is the transition from childhood to adulthood. Initiation into adulthood symbolizes a rebirth and is accompanied by special ceremonies that teach the initiates about cultural, social, and religious values. The ceremonies may involve information about sex, health, folklore, beliefs, hunting, farming, and performance and fine arts.

For females, initiation takes place after they have had their first menstrual period. Whether it is the Ga *otufo*, the Krobo *dipo*, or the Akan *bragoro*, all traditional Ghanaian societies celebrate girls' transition to adulthood. The lessons begin with the skills and knowledge they will need to live a fulfilled adult life. The process involves learning the cultural traditions and social mores of society through folklore, games, and practical experiences. Domestic skills such as cooking, cleaning, and caring for children are also emphasized because the woman will need proficiency in these areas to attract a good husband.

There are a number of steps in Akan female puberty rites (*bragoro*). After her first menstruation, the girl is brought to the queen mother to determine whether she is physically and spiritually ready. The girl's mother then announces the initiation to the community and other females are invited to help. They first perform the enstoolment rite, where the initiate sits on a stool and rises three times, then sits on the stool again. The stool sits atop a cloth, sometimes *kente*. Next to the initiate is a brass basin filled with water to protect her from evil spirits. The women sing and dance and pour libations to thank the ancestors and gods for bringing the girl safely to this point. Family and friends bring presents and place them around her. The girl's body is then prepared for initiation. She is ritually bathed, her hair, fingernails, and toenails are cut, and she is dressed in a new cloth and adorned with beads and jewelry. The community welcomes the girl into adulthood by pouring libations, offering various food items for her to taste, and enjoying more music and dancing. In the final stage, the initiate walks around town, announcing her transition to adulthood and thanking the community members for their contributions to her successful rite of passage. Although most Ghanaians today do not go through the same initiation rites as their elders, less elaborate activities still lend significance to an important stage in life.

Male initiation into adulthood revolves around a similar concept of preparing initiates to become responsible adults and fulfill their obligations to society. Boys generally undergo initiation between the ages of ten and fourteen. In some societies, they are taken outside of town, where they undergo physical tests for endurance and participate in competitive games. Boys are also taught occupational skills during their initiation so that they will be better able to support themselves and a family during their adult life. The Gas, Ewes, and others are usually circumcised during this time because circumcision represents cleanliness and it is believed that enduring the pain will make the boys physically and mentally stronger. Carved figures and masks are used to ask the spirits of ancestors for blessings in the transition. Akan and Ga families may present initiates with a gun, a symbol of their readiness for battle and hunting, or a cutlass signifying their ability to begin farming on their own.

Marriage

Unlike marriage in many other parts of the world, marriage in Ghana is seen as a requisite stage in life, rather than an option, and remains the most important social institution. Marriage sanctions reproduction, still believed by many to be the most important function of the union between a man and a woman. Children are a sign of status and wealth. They represent a successful marriage, provide valuable domestic help around the house, and can contribute agricultural labor. Marriages between individuals from outside their kinship groups, are most common under customary law. Through marriage, new social contacts are made and kinship ties are extended. Marriages serve to establish alliances between families and between communities.

The importance of marrying and creating children made arranged marriages common at one time. Families had to be confident of the status and character of their child's mate, especially when it reflected on their own lineage. This is, however, most uncommon today. Arranged marriages focused more on family considerations than on personal ones. They linked two families together for political, social, or economic reasons. For the individual, love was often not an issue. In general, men were older than their wives in arranged marriages. An older man would likely have more status in the community, and thus the union would be considered more prestigious and advantageous for the wife's family. The age and status differences between women and their husbands, however, often reinforced women's position of subservience within conjugal gender relations.

Today, men and women are more likely to choose their own partners, but marriage continues to revolve around much more than the union of two people. It is still, primarily, a union between two families. Young people must inform their families of their intentions and ask for permission to begin the steps necessary to begin the process leading to the marriage rites. In some cases, educated urbanized couples must work hard to convince their families to agree to their wishes because the families may not be well known to each other.

There are three main types of legal marriage in Ghanaian society. The Marriage Ordinance, a remnant of the colonial era, permits only monogamous marriages, while both customary law and the Marriage of Mohammedans Ordinance allow for polygyny (one man having multiple wives). Marriage under the ordinance and customary marriages exist throughout

Ghana, but Islamic marriages are predominantly found in the northern regions and among Muslim communities living in large urban centers. A fourth type of marriage, consensual union, is a result of the changing personal and geographic relationships between men and women and between young people and their families. Although they are becoming more frequent today, they do not fit into the traditional concept of marriage.

Customary marriages, representing more than 80 percent of conjugal unions, are by far the most common. In 1985, the government enacted the Customary Marriage and Divorce (Registration) Law, which introduced a standard system of registration for customary law marriages. The marriage of Mohammedans Ordinance provides a similar system for Islamic marriages; once registered, they are regulated by Muslim laws. Most Muslim marriages, however, are never registered and are therefore regarded as customary law marriages. Even Ordinance marriages, those carried out in an official court or Christian church, generally take place only after many of the traditional customs have been completed.

Customary marriages revolve around long-standing traditions that begin the process of linking the two families. The groom and his parents or close relatives greet the woman's family to seek their consent. They pour libations, share a "notification" drink signifying their intentions, and discuss the gifts necessary to formalize the marriage pact. During the interlude between the first discussion and the formal presentation of the gifts, each family checks out the background, reputation, and medical records of the other, to ensure that the union is justifiable and will not bring disrepute.

Bridewealth, the gifts given by the groom's family to that of the bride, represents each family's approval of the other and its acceptance formalizes the marriage contract. It is not, in the crudest sense, payment for the sale of a family's female child into marriage. It is not simply compensation for the loss of a woman's labor around the house. Bridewealth symbolizes gratitude and appreciation for the family's cooperation in allowing their daughter to marry. It creates a symbolic and physical bond between the two families. The costs vary, depending on the society and the status of the families involved. Bridewealth may include bottles of liquor or wine, pots of palm wine, kola nuts, tobacco, and money. The groom's family may also expend a great deal of wealth in the presentation of cattle, goats, chickens, and a variety of other gifts. The costs associated with bridewealth force many young men to delay their marriage rites until they can collect the necessary resources. The costs also result in increasing numbers of consensual marriages, where the young people live as a married couple, but have yet to complete the marriage rites.

Inappropriate behavior by the husband or wife may result in divorce and the forfeiture or demand for return of the bridewealth. If a woman leaves the marital home without a valid reason and there is no hope of conciliation, her family is expected to return the gifts and officially dissolve the marriage. If a man mistreats his wife or otherwise disrespects the marriage, he may forfeit the bridewealth. A woman's inability to conceive and a man's impotence are considered grounds for dissolution of the marriage compact because the couple will not be able to produce offspring. A woman unable to bear children is looked on with suspicion. She is sometimes accused of being a witch or having committed immoral acts earlier in her life for which she is now being punished. The amount of bridewealth is often quite substantial and thus serves to enhance the level of commitment by all parties involved. In cases where there are problems, the families often act as counselors and attempt to mend the rift between the couple if possible, or assist in negotiating a settlement if it is not.

Divorce is generally not approved of in Ghanaian societies, but it is becoming more common, especially in urban areas and in marriages under the Ordinance. Couples in Ordinance marriages need only show that their relationship has deteriorated beyond reconciliation to justify divorce. In general, women have more financial freedom in urban areas. They often engage in trading activities or have a full-time occupation, and this makes separation from their husband's resources more feasible. Difficult economic times, especially in export cropping and mining, have put a strain on family budgets and made it difficult for husbands to support their families on their wages alone. Still, the official divorce rate remains lower in rural areas, though the figures do not include people whose marriages are no longer viable but who have not filed the official papers.

The justifications for divorce in traditional society are limited. A husband can claim divorce if his wife is barren, has deserted him, is practicing witchcraft, or has committed an adulterous act. It is more difficult for women to justify divorce, but a husband's impotence, neglect, cruelty, or desertion are valid justifications. Adultery on the part of the husband is not a justifiable ground for divorce. Such acts do not result in disgrace unless the husband's mistress is married to another man. In certain groups, divorce proceedings can only be raised by one of the spouses. Among the Ewe, for example, the wife must initiate divorce, while in northern groups, it is almost always the male who does so. Problems arise, however, if the wife seeks some financial or property settlement. In both matrilineal and patrilineal customary systems, a woman generally has no direct rights to her husband's property. Custody of children is determined by the type of descent system. In patrilineal societies, custody has been awarded to the father, while in matrilineal groups, the children have gone with the mother. These restrictions, however, are changing and children in both systems often live with their mother until at least their adolescence. The reasons for a woman to initiate divorce from her husband are often difficult to prove and thus, together with the likelihood of forfeiting the bridewealth, the lack of much hope for any financial reimbursement, and the potential loss of their children, makes formal divorces under customary marriage difficult.

Monogamy and polygamy both exist in Ghana. Monogamous marriage between one legally joined husband and wife is the most common form. Those joined under the Ordinance are required to remain monogamous while men married under customary law may take unlimited numbers of wives, and men married under Islamic law may take up to four. More than 70 percent of marriages in Ghana are monogamous, but not because of beliefs or customary sanctions. Many husbands currently engaged in monogamous relationships would marry additional wives if not for the economic resources they would need to do so. Exceptions are practicing Christians, especially Roman Catholics, who are restricted by their faith to a monogamous life. The educated elite are also more likely to enter into monogamous marriages.

Polygamy permits a spouse to marry at least one additional partner. In Ghana, the only form of polygamy is polygyny, in which the husband is allowed to marry several wives. It is unheard of for one wife to be married to more than one husband. Polygynous marriage has a long history. In most Ghanaian societies it is socially accepted and at one time was even preferred. Polygyny helped families establish more alliances with other villages through marriage. In societies where agriculture and domestic labor were essential to family prosperity, the more wives a man could marry, the greater chance he had of creating more children, and thus of enhanced social status and wealth.

Social customs also enhance the value of polygynous marriages. A pregnant wife will often go to her family home during the latter stages of pregnancy and remain there for up to six months following the birth of the child. At one time, wives were not allowed to cook for their husbands while they were menstruating, but this is rare today. Having more than one wife also means that a woman would always be around the house to tend to domestic duties and keep the husband from looking outside of the home for sexual companionship. Women, too, have benefited from polygamous marriages because society frowns on those who have reached an appropriate age but have not married. The average age of marriage for women is now approaching nineteen. If women have reached the age of thirty without marrying, however, people believe that there must be something physically or mentally "wrong" with them, or perhaps that they have committed indiscretions that have turned the spirits against them. Polygyny affords a greater percentage of women the chance to avoid such condemnation by entering into a legal marriage relationship.

Although polygyny still exists today, it is in decline due to religious, economic, and educational reasons. Even in polygynous marriages, it is now rare for a man to have more than two wives. Economic difficulties have reduced the resources available to complete the customary rites and maintain a sizable family. Declining agricultural production and rural-urban migration have also contributed by decreasing the importance of the labor function of polygyny. The highest rates of polygyny are found in northern Ghana among less educated women in areas where Islam is prominent. In the southern regions, where Christianity is more pervasive, religious teachings present polygyny as an abomination and preach against it adamantly. Geographical location and the increase in female education have also changed the demography of marriage. Women living in urban areas and those with at least secondary school education tend to marry later in life and enter into more conventional nuclear family structures. As the concepts of wealth and status become more associated with money rather than knowledge, age, and number of children, individuals are less likely to enter into polygynous marriages.

Another type of male-female union is *trokosi*, but this does not represent a typical marriage for many reasons. In *trokosi*, a young girl is given to the priest of a fetish shrine to ensure that no harm will come to others in the family. This occurs after some member of the family has committed an offense that the family believes will bring shame and potentially put the entire family at risk. Although the legal marriage age for females in Ghana is eighteen, females are sometimes betrothed to the shrines at a very young age and become the conjugal property of the fetish priest. They perform domestic and agricultural labor and often bear his children. Such early "marriage" and strict domestic obligations reduce the opportunities for these young women to seek an education and, for the most part, they are imprisoned in a life of unhappiness. Because it is seen by many as a form of slavery, the government passed legislation in 1998 banning this practice, but it is known to continue in spite of the legislation.

Death

The final rite of passage in the human world is death. Ghanaians do not mourn the dead as people do in many other countries. Death marks not the end of life, but rather a transition from the physical world to the spiritual world, to the world of the ancestors. Funeral ceremonies perform social functions, providing an opportunity for the people of a community to come together. It is not uncommon for Ghanaians to attend a funeral every weekend. It is traditional to show respect to the deceased by holding a proper funeral ceremony and providing everything they might need on their journey. For this reason, great amounts of money are expended on funeral celebrations, leaving many families with huge debts. The belief is that the deceased might have been poor in life, but they should not want for anything in death. Failing to pay the proper respect to the dead is considered a social disgrace for the descendants of the deceased. Even for those with meager economic resources, no expense should be spared. Due to the type of wood used for the coffin, the type of dress worn by the deceased and the mourners, and the music and drinks provided at the celebration, funerals often place families in a grave economic crisis.

The nature of the funeral ceremony depends on the age, status, and occupation of the deceased. The death of a child in its first few days of life merits little pomp because it is believed that the child's spirit never really belonged to the human world. The death of a chief, on the other hand, merits a large ceremony, with the entire community taking part. In the past, the burial and the funeral did not take place on the same day, but they are usually combined into a single event today. If the deceased is an important person, it is not uncommon for the body to be kept in a morgue for weeks, allowing time for family and relatives living abroad to arrange to attend. Funerals are held on weekends. The wake-keeping begins on Friday and often lasts the entire night. Saturday sees the burial and the performance of the funeral rites, which frequently continue on Sunday. Smaller gatherings follow on Monday, including thanking the mourners and "making accounts," or accepting donations from others. The funeral itself is accompanied by dirges and wailing by females; it is not considered proper for men to exhibit their emotions in public. Periodic rituals follow the funeral and help to complete the journey of the deceased. The first of the two most important rituals occurs forty days after death, when there is a "parting" ceremony to mark the spiritual departure of the deceased to the ancestral world, and the second occurs at the first anniversary of the death. The first anniversary ceremony also allows for the distribution of inheritance, and after this time, the widowed spouse, by customary law, can remarry.

Family Concept and Structure

The family is the most basic social unit in Ghanaian societies. Smaller than the lineage, it plays an active role in daily activities and provides for the maintenance of social security. The structure of the family differs widely from one ethnic group to another, but the inherent values are similar. Sometimes, the household structure resembles the traditional nuclear family of a husband, wife, and unmarried children. There are, however, almost always additions to this household structure, including elderly relatives, cousins, and brothers, sisters, nephews, and nieces of the husband and wife.

Extended families live close together, and occasionally three or four generations share a single residential compound. A typical compound consists of different sections for individuals, depending on gender and age, with a section reserved for the oldest male. Rooms are set aside for other adult family members, and some are reserved for extended family members living temporarily or permanently in the compound. In other cases, family members may occupy several neighboring houses in the same compound or town, with the wife or wives living separately from their husbands. Lineage patterns determine, in part, the nature of family and residence organization, but even within the same lineage system there are many variations.

Among patrilineal groups, such as those in the northern regions, the Ewe, and the Ga, residence patterns are varied. In the north, a household is often composed of two or more brothers, their wives, and their children. The eldest brother is considered the head of the household. Each husband is the head of his family and is responsible for its needs, but all of the adult males cooperate in the care and well-being of the entire household. Among the Ewe, a domestic group typically includes a husband and wife or wives, their children, and sometimes several dependent relatives. Over time, however, the household expands, taking in additional young and adult dependent relatives.

After marriage, Ga husbands and wives usually remain with their own lineages in separate residences. The husband lives in the men's compound of his father, while the wife stays in the women's compound of her mother. The mother raises the children until the age of thirteen, at which time boys move to their father's residence to learn an occupation and participate more in male activities. The male patrilineage compound usually consists of a family of brothers and their older sons, with married adult males having their own rooms. The women's compound consists of members of various patrilineages, including mothers, daughters, and their younger children. Women and children cook food and deliver it to the men's compound, and occasionally make nighttime visits to their husbands.

The traditional matrilineal Akan family structure is similar to that of the Ga in that the husband and wife live separately, but the matrilineal descent system also causes some differences. The female compound usually consists of a mother, her unmarried and married daughters, and their children, who form a cohesive matrilineal group. The husband, rather than staying in a men's compound, lives in his mother's house or that of a maternal uncle. This is called natolocal residence. A husband in this situation has obligations

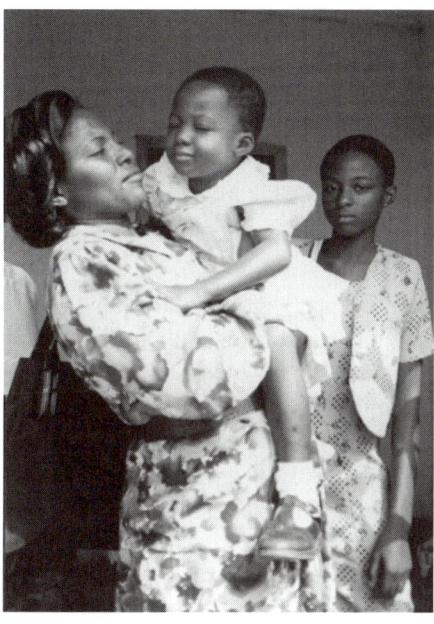

A mother and her daughters.

both to his own children and to those of his sister. Adolescent sons sometimes move to the houses of their fathers or to those of their maternal uncles, with the latter playing an important role in raising their sisters' sons. It is not uncommon to hear an Akan male refer to his maternal uncle as his father. Wives and daughters prepare meals and children deliver them to their fathers' houses. This arrangement is made easier because the houses of the husband and wife or wives are rarely far away from one another.

Although less common, two other residence styles are seen in the Akan. In one system, the husband, the wife, and their young children share a single house, much like a nuclear family. When the young males reach adolescence, they move in with their maternal uncle, while the daughters remain in their parents' house until the time of marriage. In another system, the family lives together, but the sons remain at their parents' house through adulthood, bringing their own wives and children into the house. This is advantageous for a family with agricultural labor demands. The availability of the sons' children adds to the family's resources. Daughters move out of the house when they are married and move in with their new husband.

Polygyny mandates special residential arrangements. The wives cannot all share a room with their husband. Rarely do all the wives even live in the same house because there is frequent tension among them over the attention of the husband and the amount of family resources that they and their children receive. Co-wives form a hierarchy, with the senior wife controlling the domestic scene and the most recent wife having the least say in decision making. In some cases, the senior wife will live with the husband, while the others stay with their own families. The wives more often live in a separate residence or residences, with sexual activities generally arranged at the husband's behest.

Urban families exhibit the same variety as their rural counterparts. Generally, in the oldest urban areas, patterns based on traditional models are more common. Areas of new growth, especially middle and upper class neighborhoods, tend to reflect the idealized model of the nuclear family, with the husband and wife sharing a home with their children. Even in these cases, however, other relatives frequently send their children to live with the urban dwellers because of higher quality educational facilities and better opportunities for increased wages in the city.

ROLES AND RESPONSIBILITIES

Within the family structure, hierarchical roles determine individual responsibilities in community and household organization. These roles are determined, in large part, by age, gender, and status. Traditional household relationships revolve around rules of family etiquette that demand certain patterns of interaction and determine behavior models. The movement of an individual from infancy to youth, to adulthood, and to old age influences the nature of these interactions, in terms of providing for and drawing on family resources according to one's abilities and needs.

Elderly people are the reservoirs of family tradition and knowledge in the cultural, social, and practical domains. Within a traditional household, elders provide advice and counseling rather than great amounts of physical labor. Elderly females tend to young children in a mother's absence and teach them morals, folklore, and skills. An Akan proverb emphasizes the dual-dependency relationship that exists between children and elders: "If your elders take care of you while cutting your teeth, you must take care of them while they are losing theirs." Elders are seen as the closest link to the ancestors, and they preside over ceremonial rites related to birth and death. They are to be accorded honor and respect by younger people because of their age and life experiences, and they are greeted, seated, and served first at social gatherings.

Children, in contrast, are at the bottom of the social ladder. They are valued, to be sure, but they are also taught to respect age and status and perform their duties without objecting. Children are expected to learn the

Young children enjoying themselves on a home-made rocking horse.

mores of the community so that they do not disgrace themselves and their family, their elders, and their ancestors. They learn by watching adults and by participating in games and other activities that reinforce social values and help them develop physically and mentally. They learn traditional roles and receive moral, ethical, and religious instruction from their family and the community as a whole.

There are different domestic expectations for girls and boys. If capable, children are required to assist their parents in the family modes of production. Girls, however, generally have more responsibilities around the house than boys. They begin to help their mothers when they are very young. Although there are no legal barriers preventing female children from receiving education, domestic responsibilities often force them to drop out before beginning secondary school. A twelve-year-old girl in a rural middle school, for example, rises early in the morning to sweep the house and outside areas, fetch water from the stream, boil water and cook breakfast, clean the breakfast dishes, and dress her infant brother, all before she goes to school. She has one older brother, one younger by three years, and one in infancy. When she returns from school, she prepares *fufu*; sometimes her brothers help her with the pounding. After she has cleaned the mortar and pestle, she has to take food to her father's house and collect the used dishes for washing. It is easy to see that she has little time to devote to her studies.[1]

Her brothers have far fewer chores to do and find more time to devote to their studies and engage in fun. Part of the justification for a young girl's tasks is that she must learn how to manage domestic activities and make her future husband happy. Some parents are reluctant to send their daughters to school at all because their labor is needed around the house. A few still believe that, because a woman's primary duty is child bearing and domestic work, acquiring an education will make her less desirable to all prospective suitors. The gap between males and females in educational achievement reflects the additional demands and cultural constraints on female children. At the primary level, the male to female ratio is virtually even, but subsequent grades show a widening gap, culminating in a ratio of less than one in four female students at the university level. At all levels of secondary and university education, female enrollment is increasing, but the discrepancies are still significant.

Parents also have roles to perform in the household. As mature adults, they are expected to provide the financial resources and basic needs for their children, as well as food and shelter for their elders. Within this structure, however, there are sharp differences based on gender.

Men still largely control traditional Ghanaian society. Men retain power in traditional households, in community life, and in most government positions. In all areas, important decisions are usually made by men, although women are increasingly playing an important role. Regardless of residence structure and location, husbands are expected to provide for the health and well-being of their wives and children. Ghana's Criminal Code lists the items that must be provided as food, clothing, shelter, healthcare, and anything else necessary to preserve life. There are, in theory, provisions for women to go to court if they feel their husbands are not meeting their obligations to the family, but in reality this rarely happens. Wives are expected to respect their husband's authority in the household, care for children, and carry out regular domestic duties. They are, increasingly, asked to provide a greater share of the financial needs of the family as well.

Women do, however, play important roles in domestic, economic, and political life. They perform many daily activities that keep both the household and the larger community running smoothly. They work inside the home rearing children, preparing food, and cleaning. From a young age, most Ghanaians acquire a social understanding of gendered activities in domestic work. They are taught that domestic chores are women's work. This holds true regardless of a woman's level of education or work schedule. Boys, at least until they reach a certain age, are expected to help their sisters, and in modern nuclear families where both spouses are working, husbands often perform some domestic duties.

The nature of traditional relations between husband and wife was once embedded in economic conditions. Rarely was romantic love part of the equation. Mutual respect between the two and economic security were often the highest things that women aspired to in their marriage. Increasingly, however, women are choosing husbands based on more personal factors, and are contributing toward the basic finances of the household, as well as food and school fees. The differential rate of education leaves many women without sufficient education to assume professional positions; thus many of them earn money through trading, office work, or other economic enterprises. Market traders, especially those in major urban centers, can become economically and socially independent and protect themselves against the possible inability of their husbands to provide sufficient support. It is becoming more common for husbands and wives to keep their financial resources separate, especially in the southern areas. Where the husband is delinquent in his duties or where a child has been born out of wedlock, women may contribute virtually all of the resources necessary to raise and educate the child or children. Such cases, estimated as around 30 percent of households, are becoming more common today, especially where two people form a relationship without performing the customary marriage rites or, perhaps, make only the initial offerings to the woman's family with the intention of completing the process later.

In societies where the husband and wife do not share a household, there is tension over the division of resources and women are being called on to provide a greater amount. In matrilineal communities, in particular, a husband is obligated to provide for his wife and children, as well as for the matrilineage, with extra resources usually going to the latter. Asante men are expected to provide money for food and pay for school fees, while women pay for other items their children need, such as clothing. Difficult economic conditions make it impossible in many communities for the husband both to support his family and make contributions to his matrilineage on his salary alone.

Educated Ghanaian women, despite the constraints on them, can achieve high status through their professions, working in prestigious positions as doctors, lawyers, and judges. Women dominate the secretarial and nursing professions, and they play a significant role in education, serving as teachers at every level from primary school to university. Increasingly, women are acting in supervisory roles and earning the same wages and benefits as men in similar capacities. Many men and even some women, however, find it difficult to work under a female supervisor.

In some societies women hold significant offices. The queen mother in Asante and Ga society, for example, wields influence over the affairs of the community. The queen mother is usually the sister of the chief and, as the mother of his heir, she is seen as the most important mother in Asante society. With advice from elders, she helps to nominate the candidate for the stool and gives advice to the chief, especially in matters related to women's affairs such as birth, initiation, and marriage. She is also seen as the guardian of the moral education of the younger generation. The Ga stool mother, who holds a similar position at the lineage level, has an important role in rituals dealing with lineage descent.

SOCIAL CHANGE

Traditional Ghanaian family structures, roles, and institutions are undergoing rapid transformation due to changing economic emphases, the increase in education and migration, and broadened global influences. New identities emerge and the roles of the extended family have had to change. Many people choose to focus solely on the deterioration of the traditional lineage system, yet it still functions, even under severe constraints, and continues to bring people together in kin-based relationships. This is true, although to different degrees, in both the rural and urban areas.

In the rural areas, traditional lineage obligations remain important, but they have also adapted to new economic conditions and rural-urban migration. The expansion of cash crop agriculture and wage labor, for example, altered the concept of wealth and emphasized the individual over the lineage. Cash crops made land a valuable commodity, especially in the cocoa growing regions of the Akan. Individual sale of land creates problems within the authority structure of the lineage. Opportunities for wage labor take people away from their home environment, making lineage obligations more difficult to fulfill and putting people in situations where they cannot rely on the usual benefits of lineage membership.

Rural-urban migration changes the composition and function of the family in both the rural and the urban areas. Many young men and women move to the cities for a variety of reasons, but the most prominent is the hope of economic gain. The lucky ones acquire jobs, gain skills, and earn wages far beyond those available to them in their home areas. Migration alters the nature of social organization. The obvious aspect is the physical loss of young men and women who would otherwise have been active participants in rural family and economic life. The cyclical balance in the household relationship between youth, adults, and elders is more difficult to maintain with infrequent interaction widening the divisions between generations.

Wage labor also helps young men subvert social restrictions on the acquisition of wealth and status. Economic independence diminishes the influence of family resources. In such cases, young men now provide their own bridewealth, thus reducing parental influence. Arranged marriages are far less common. In general, marriages have become less formalized with respect to customary traditions. Among the Ga, for example, a traditional marriage was called a "six cloth" marriage, representing the elaborate ceremony surrounding bridewealth. It is more common today for Ga couples to perform the *afayinodaa* ("offering a drink") marriage. This involves assuming a marital relationship after the groom presents a small amount of money or gifts, but it does not include as much family involvement. In cases where the full traditional marriage ceremonies are not performed, it is much easier for the wife to leave her husband. Though the descent system can determine who will have custody of the children in a broken marriage, the children tend to remain with their mothers when full customary rites are not performed.

Education, too, influences the nature of family interaction. It certainly has a positive impact on the growth and development of children, but it also leads to changing concepts of family values and generational dynamics. Like wage labor, education enhances the independence of young men and women, but it also broadens the gap between young and old. In the traditional system, elders had status because of their vast knowledge of traditional culture and society. Formal education, however, has undermined that role by transferring the control of knowledge to educated youth and this has altered the assessment of status.

Changing family patterns and interactions impact many aspects of social life. Urban nuclear families, for example, do not provide the same arrangements for the care of elderly relatives or young children with working parents. Day care, unheard of in the rural areas where female relatives, adolescent daughters, or elders are always around, becomes more important for urban nuclear families when both parents are working.

Urban family size has decreased due to changing economic conditions and expansion of education. Children are still important contributors to the domestic environment and may help in their mother's or father's work, but there is little need for large families when agricultural production is not the main economic activity. The high costs associated with formal education and the time children spend away from the house also make large families impractical. Educated women generally marry later, thus reducing the number of children they have during their fertile years. The overall effect on family size, however, is less profound, because educated couples have access to better healthcare facilities and, thus, their children have a lower infant mortality rate.

Western culture is a pervasive element of social life that effects individual attitudes about family in varying degrees. Particularly, in the more affluent urban areas, family life assumes features similar to that of the Western world. Husbands and wives live together in the house, share duties, and practice a more egalitarian decision making process. Children in these homes experience different stimuli through educational activities. They increasingly spend time away from home with schoolmates and other peers, and absorb a greater share of their values from adults who are not part of their extended family. School life extends beyond the normal school hours and encompasses social activities that further alter children's relationship with their parents and their siblings.

The increasing availability of television, video, and films emphasizing foreign, especially Western, expressions of familial love has influenced sexual relations in Ghana. Many people have lived abroad and returned with Western ideas about male-female interactions. Younger couples, for example, are more apt to "go out" to a movie or to dinner and generally spend greater amounts of their leisure time together. Ghanaian culture does not emphasize outward and public expression of love. It is still rare to see a couple kissing in the open or holding hands in a romantic way. The decline in arranged marriages and the impact of Western culture, however, have made such sights more common among young couples. These ideas and behaviors spread quickly from urban to rural areas, just as changing rural cultural patterns continue to influence the urban environment.

In the face of constant change, lineage and family structures remain important in Ghanaian life. The distance between migrants and their families reduces contact and communication between them, but rarely does it sever lineage bonds entirely. Even long-term urban residents rarely consider the city to be their home. Many migrants plan to return to the rural areas after having achieved their goals, or perhaps just to escape city life. Some young men leave a wife and children behind while they seek financial security in the urban environment. There is no immediate or complete separation of the two worlds. Although the types of interactions are altered, there is still a mutual dependency between them. Money replaces work in the fields or labor around the house. New urban migrants continue to meet some of their lineage obligations by sending cash to their homes for the care of their parents and the education of younger siblings. Some also build houses in the rural areas in preparation for retirement.

It is, therefore, important to see the continuity in extended family relations. Although the nature of the household has changed, migration has actually widened some lineage branches, bringing together in the city people who would not otherwise be dependent on each other. The social security function of the lineage continues to have relevance. Urban migrants reach out to their extended family for assistance with housing, food, a loan to start a business, or school fees. Their sponsors are meeting their lineage obligations by providing for the children of relatives. Well-off families are best able to provide support to extended family members, and their houses often act as meeting places for the new urban kinship members who are eager to hear news of their home. This creates a different type of benefit-obligation cycle, but it continues to support the overall function of a lineage by bringing people together and creating links to the next generation.

Rapid social change has changed familial patterns, reduced customary rites in the institution of marriage, and led to shifting power in gender interactions in the household and the community as a whole. Ghanaian family structures have adapted to new economic activities, changed demographics, increased formal education, and pervasive foreign cultural influences. The lineage continues to be a source of collective security for its members and, by adapting to the multiple stimuli of modern life, it offers a broader pattern of organization for society.

NOTE

1. Yaw Boadu-Ayeboafoh, "Is It a Curse to Be a Girl?" *Daily Graphic,* 25 May 2001.

7

Social Customs and Lifestyle

SOCIAL CUSTOMS in Ghana include ceremonies celebrating family life and rites of passage, festivals bringing people of the community together, religious holidays to strengthen common spiritual bonds, and national holidays focusing on important events of the independence era. Lifestyle has many aspects to it, including sports and leisure, cinema, and everyday events and happenings. Lifestyle patterns reflect the growing availability of outside cultural stimuli, changing economic conditions, and increased educational levels. This chapter elaborates on the formalized social customs that are required in interpersonal relations and discusses a few of the traditional festivals in Ghana. It also looks at the various types of activities that engage Ghanaians of all ages on a day-to-day basis, and how these activities differ in rural and urban areas.

SOCIAL RELATIONS

Every society has patterns of behavior that help to organize social relations and determine acceptable and unacceptable actions in particular situations. Apart from urban centers such as Accra, Cape Coast, Sekondi-Takoradi, and Kumase to a lesser extent, where a greater degree of outside influences have affected the actions of some people, there is a general formality to social interactions throughout the country. The fundamental basis of these interactions is determined by the factors of age and status.

In general, Ghanaians value interpersonal interactions. Similar to lineage and family, the needs of a group are valued over those of the individual. Greeting is an important custom. Whether buying something at a store, entering someone's house, or meeting someone on the street, greetings are always given first. In the rural areas, greetings are usually conferred in the dominant local languages, but "good morning," "good afternoon," and "good evening," are common in the cities, especially among the urban elite. When meeting an individual, it is proper to greet them, shake their hand, and inquire about their health and the health of their family. There are various ways to greet people. Sometimes, two males shake hands and punctuate it by touching their index and middle fingers together and pulling apart to make a snapping sound. This is a newer custom and is thus, not usually done if one is shaking the hand of an elderly man or woman. Some people in northern Ghana bow when they greet others, while others crouch down or prostrate themselves before elders or superiors, and especially before chiefs. When encountering a group of people, there are also expected procedures. Individuals are expected to greet all of the group members individually beginning with the person on the right, even if only intending to speak to one person quickly. Failure to acknowledge everyone in the gathering may be considered an insult.

Any handshakes or gestures should be done with the right hand because many Ghanaians consider the left hand to be dirty. It is an insult to be offered the left hand as a greeting or to be handed or receive something with it. Even gesturing with the left hand is inappropriate. This custom is changing with younger people, but it still demands a considerable following. If the right hand is engaged, people might offer their wrist or forearm for the other person to grasp lightly, or one may offer the left hand with the statement, "I do not give you my left hand," to show that no social insult is intended.

Social relations are very important in Ghanaian society. One commonly found aspect of this is visiting the homes of friends and family. Visiting in both urban and rural areas is most common on Sundays or at the end of traditional festivals. When visiting a friend's or family's house, visitors are welcomed and made to feel comfortable. It is customary to remove shoes, especially sandals and flip-flops, when entering, although this too is changing in many of the urban areas. People are first offered a seat and a drink, such as water, a soft drink, or a beer, to welcome them. After completing the proper greetings, visitors explain the reason for their visit. The people often share recent news and events in the community and elsewhere. Just as greetings demand a certain protocol, so does leaving. One does not simply leave their guests at the door and bid them farewell. It is customary for the host to walk with the visitors, either taking them to their car, helping them find a taxi, or giving them a ride home. In general, Ghanaians do not walk around while eating in public, except in areas around "chop bars" (see Chapter 5), or public events such as soccer games where food stands are abundant. Visitors who arrive while food is being served are invited to eat with the host.

Ghana is a very expressive and oral-based society. Whether in the smallest village or the largest city, news travels fast, due in part to people's desire to know what is going on in the village or across town. Private matters often become public very quickly in Ghana. Skilled public speakers are valued for their use of proverbs, especially at the courts of chiefs. People also appreciate a good storyteller and humorous tales. Ghanaians are knowledgeable and enjoy discussing issues of local politics, sports, philosophies, and culture. Heated discussions amongst people are not frowned upon and often entice others to join in with their own opinions. Ghanaians are also well-versed on international issues from reading newspapers and magazines, listening to radio broadcasts of Voice of America and BBC, and watching international television news shows such as CNN.

Public gender relations and patterns of dress are generally conservative by Western standards. Showing public affection between men and women, even between husbands and wives, is rare. It is common to see friends of the same gender holding hands while walking or talking, but members of the opposite sex rarely show affection in public. Grooming and overall neatness are also important because they are outward reflections of one's character. Women are discouraged from wearing tight or revealing clothing. In general, women's skirts, dresses, and pants cover their knees, and more often reach mid-calf length, especially in the more Muslim societies of northern Ghana. It is also rare to see men wearing shorts. These traditional mores on public display are changing quickly however. Urban youth, in particular, are exposed to more images of Western culture in films and written publications, as well as personal interactions. They frequently wear clothes that older generations see as too tight or too short, and express feelings for their partner more openly.

Children are taught to comply with certain rules regarding their elders. They greet them with terms of respect, help them with heavy loads, and offer them their chair. People of age and status are addressed as "mother," "father," "grandmother," or "grandfather." Every language has its own words for these terms of address. People close in age call each other "brother" and "sister," while those only slightly older, may be called "uncle" and "auntie," regardless of whether they are related or not. In contrast to Western society, it is not a sign of shyness or shiftiness for a child to look at the ground while talking to an elder; it is a requirement. Children who look elders in the eye are challenging their status and authority. Children who fail to observe these social values are considered untrained and uncultured.

FESTIVALS AND HOLIDAYS

Throughout the world, people hold festivals and celebrate holidays to commemorate important community, religious, and national events. Ghanaian festivals reflect the rich tradition and culture inherited through indigenous customs, Islamic and Christian practices, and colonial influences. Rites of passage, such as naming ceremonies, puberty, marriage, and death are accompanied by rituals, celebration, and pageantry. The rites of passage focus on membership in the lineage and the initiate's changing role within the community. These are discussed more in Chapter 6.

Traditional Festivals

Traditional festivals are centered on the religious, socio-economic, political, and cultural beliefs and values of a society. During the festival period, people return to their homes to celebrate their family ties and reinforce the customs and values of the community. There are common underlying features of traditional festivals in Ghana. These are closely tied into traditional belief systems and the emphasis on ancestors, spiritual protection, and purification. When people die they move to the ancestral world, but remain a guiding force in the land of the living. Traditional festivals recognize this and pay tribute to the ancestors and previous leaders, seeking their spiritual protection through libations of food and drink. The rituals associated with traditional festivals are also a means to purify the community. They act as a way to cleanse society and provide hope for a new year. Although festivals are associated with the beliefs and values of a society, they are also a time of celebration, a time filled with colorful displays, music and dance, and plenty of feasting.

Festivals continue to change as the social and cultural contexts that surround them are altered. Many incorporate modern forms of music and dance, not into the ritual itself, but as a form of entertainment during the festivities. Christians, who at one time were not allowed to participate directly in the rituals, have a more visible role now. It is not uncommon for many societies to hold a formal church service during a festival to bless the ongoing events. Population growth has forced changes to some practices. During the Ga festival of *homowo*, for example, people come from the inland areas to the original coastal towns to celebrate the extended family. In the past, people came on the same day and their relatives waited for them on the outskirts of towns to escort them home with a lively procession of music and dance. Accra, in particular, is now too big and too congested for this custom to continue. Another example of changes that have occurred in the celebration of traditional festivals is the introduction of new sports and other competitions into the events. The *aboakyer* festival in the coastal city of Winneba, for example, opens with various sporting activities, including a regatta, a cross country race, and soccer games.

Children and elders adorned in traditional dress and holding ritual objects for the annual Ga celebration of *homowo*.

Many festivals take place soon after the staple crop is harvested and are a form of thanksgiving to express gratitude for a successful agricultural season. Priests and chiefs play the most important roles by leading the rituals of purification and dedication. Priests are the intermediaries with gods, while chiefs are the link to ancestral leaders. Important traditional festivals include *aboakyer, homowo, odwira, glidzi*, the yam festival, and *damba*.

Aboakyer

The *aboakyer* festival is one of the oldest and most popular festivals in Ghana today. Also known as the "deer catching" festival, it centers on a competition between two *asafo* companies to find and catch a live deer first. The *asafo* companies were once military groups called together to defend the community. Although they still perform community service, they are now more ceremonial and act as social organizations for men. Membership in a particular group is tied to common symbols which are exhibited with pride.

All companies have their own unique colors and flags that differentiate them from one another. During *aboakyer*, the *asafo* companies dress in traditional battle-dress and, after undergoing a purification ceremony at the beach and receiving blessings from the chief, they set out to catch the deer. Once the deer is caught and the winning company presents it to the chief, it is sacrificed to the god, Penkye Otu.

Believed to be more than 300 years old, the festival is held annually in Winneba, usually the first weekend in May. *Aboakyer* commemorates the first settlement of the Effutu people in Winneba. It is accompanied by drumming, dancing, and spirited processions. When the deer is presented to the shrine of Penkye Otu, the chief priest receives information from the god about the outlook for the upcoming year and informs the community.

Homowo

The most important festival for the Ga is *homowo. Homowo* ("hooting at hunger") is a thanksgiving festival that celebrates the corn harvest. *Homowo* brings all Ga people from the outlying villages to the original coastal settlements. There is a belief that anyone failing to celebrate *homowo* will be punished by the ancestors. Oral tradition states that there was a period of famine when millet would not grow. After planting corn, however, the crops flourished and, thus, the main dish of *homowo* is *kpekpei*, a dish made from steamed corn. There are many elaborate rituals that surround the *homowo* celebration.

Preceding *homowo*, there is a one-month ban on drumming, dancing, and general loud behavior within all Ga traditional areas. At the end of the thirty days, priests perform special rites and mark the beginning of the festival. *Homowo* is related to the principle occupations of traditional Ga society, fishing and farming. As the time nears for the ban to be lifted, there are a series of events. Among them are the opening of the fishing season, bringing living and dead family members together through rituals of gift giving and purification, eating the *homowo* meal, performing the *homowo* dance, and observing the "day of remembrance."

Each of the original seven Ga coastal towns celebrates the festival on a different day. In Accra, the celebration starts on Thursday. The people that live outside the city who return to celebrate with their lineage are called *soobii* ("Thursday children"), while those in Teshie, to the east of Accra, return on Monday and are called *juubii* ("Monday's children"). Before they enter the town, priests walk around ritually clearing the streets for the returnees to make their way home. Before the ceremony, it is customary for daughters-in-law to bring their mothers-in-law firewood, and sons-in-law give gin to their fathers-in-law to represent social harmony.

On the eve before the celebration, people stay in their houses as ancestors are believed to be walking the streets. Elderly women spread *akpade* (red clay) on the doors of their houses to protect the inhabitants from evil spirits. Before eating the ceremonial meal, some of the *kpekpei* is sprinkled around the entire neighborhood and around all of the houses, and libations are offered to the ancestors. During the meal, the family eats together. Children, women, and senior men all eat from a single bowl, dismissing the usual age, gender, and status divisions. The "day of remembrance" follows the *homowo* celebration. On this day, women mourn family members who passed away and men greet relatives and friends, wishing them well in the coming year.

Odwira

The *odwira* festival of the Akans gives thanks for the harvest of new yams, mourns those who passed away during the previous year, and pays tribute to ancestors for their guidance. It is centered on the Akan calendar, which breaks down the year into forty-two-day cycles, called *adae*. The *adae* ceremony is held twice every cycle, with the *akwasidae* held on Sunday, and the *awukudae* taking place the following Wednesday. These ceremonies honor ancestors. The Asante ceremonies, for example, recall the greatness of the Asante state. Priests pour libations to cleanse the community of evil spirits and ask for ancestral guidance during the next month. The chiefs also lead a parade and display gold and other objects of the Asante state so that the public can share in their spiritual power. On the sacred day of *adae*, all markets are closed. With few exceptions, no hard labor is performed.

There are nine *adae* in a year and the last one, *odwira*, marks the biggest annual festival of the Asante. *Odwira* falls on the Wednesday *adae* ceremony, *awukudai*. Like the Ga *homowo*, there is a ban on noisemaking and dancing, but it lasts the length of one *adae*. This period is called *adaebutuw*, or "turning over" of the *adae*. The *odwira* festival lasts one week, with special rituals on each day. Tuesday marks the parade of new yams, which are banned from consumption until this point. Wednesday is a day of mourning and fasting to commemorate all those who have died during the past year. In contrast, Thursday is a day of feasting and the entire community pays tribute to their ancestors. During the night, however, people stay inside because it is a time for the ritual procession of the dead. Friday is the climax of the *odwira* festival. There is a great *durbar* (procession of chiefs) and lavish gifts are presented for the ancestral spirits to thank them for their protection and for promoting the previous year's good fortunes.

Ewe Festivals

There are many different festivals celebrated among Ewe societies. *Hogbetsotso* celebrates one Anlo Ewe group's exodus from central Togo, where they lived under an oppressive ruler. In the Wli area, the home to the highest waterfall in West Africa, there is a festival that pays tribute to that natural landmark. One of the largest Ewe festivals is the biennial *glidzi* festival of the Ewe in the Adaklu area. During the week-long festival, people who have moved away return to visit the ancestral shrine and participate in the drumming, dancing, and purification rites. On Friday of the festival week, men dress up in traditional war-dress and sacrifice a goat at the shrine of the village founders to ensure prosperity in the year ahead. Like many festivals, the festival ends with a *durbar* and plenty of drumming and dancing.

For those Ewe who live in farming areas one of the most important celebrations is the yam festival. Among the many varieties of food stuffs grown in the Volta Region, the Ewe celebrate the harvesting of yams because it requires the greatest amount of work to cultivate. Like the other festivals, the yam festival celebrates the harvest, remembers those who have died during the past year, and pays tribute to ancestors to provide protection in the future. Priests and chiefs play major roles and there is much ceremonial dancing, drumming, and feasting. It is also a celebration of community and a time to greet everyone and express good wishes for the upcoming year. In the town of Peki, the yam festival concludes with the purification of the house by one of the household males. Taking a piece of burning wood from a fire, the purifier waves it in every corner of the house and, when finished, runs to the outskirts of town to banish the wood and the evil spirits that it harbors into the bush.

Damba

Some traditional festivals combine indigenous beliefs and values with those of other religions, such as Islam. Most people in the northern regions of Ghana celebrate the annual *damba* festival. It was originally an Islamic festival, but is now celebrated by Muslims and non-Muslims alike. Held in August, *damba* is actually two festivals. The first one marks the birth of the Prophet Mohammed and is called the *somba damba*. It is ushered in by the appearance of the *damba* moon, the new moon in the third month of the Islamic calendar. During the first night there is much drumming and dancing to welcome the start of the festival. The nine days before *somba damba* are filled with drumming and dancing, as well as Islamic prayers by Muslims to renew their faith. On the tenth day after the appearance of the moon, the *somba damba* festival begins.

The second festival celebrates the naming of the Prophet and is called *naa damba*. Upon the completion of the first festival, people begin to prepare for the second and the entertainment wanes. Also known as the "chief's festival," it begins seventeen days after the appearance of the *damba* moon. The *naa damba* festival, like the first, combines traditional rituals, such as paying tribute to ancestors, with Islamic prayers. During the ceremonial slaughter of a cow, a chief reads verses from the Qur'an while dancers move around the animal. The women use the meat to cook the festival meal. After eating, everyone dresses in their best clothes and moves toward the dancing area. It is a day of great pageantry. When the chief arrives, the drummers begin to play and people begin to dance. The merrymaking continues on and off until the following day, when everyone breaks away to conclude the *damba* period by greeting their friends and neighbors and wishing them well. The long celebration is an enjoyable period for people in the northern regions.

National Holidays

There are numerous national holidays celebrated by all Ghanaians. National holidays are joyous times and feature a variety of cultural and entertainment activities. In all areas, performances of traditional and modern styles of music and dance are common. During many festivals, sporting competitions or friendly matches between community groups take place. In the coastal areas, people flock to the beach to picnic and enjoy the company of friends.

Secular holidays include New Year's Day, which is marked by various social events, religious services, and music and dance of all types. Independence Day is on 6 March. It celebrates the day when the British flag came down and the new Ghanaian flag arose at midnight in 1957. During the evening of 5 March, the celebration begins in Accra with speeches and music in Kwame Nkrumah Memorial park. People remain until the official moment of independence and return to Black Star Square the following day for a parade of military personnel, school children, and various public and private groups. During the Independence Day celebrations, people don traditional dress and wave Ghanaian flags all over the country. A speech by the president punctuates the festivities. Labor Day is celebrated on 1 May, the day that honors workers worldwide. The first of July marks the day that Ghana became a republic in 1960. The people who work in Ghana's main economic activity, agriculture, are honored on 6 December, known as Farmer's Day. Boxing Day, which falls on the day after Christmas, is a colonial remnant of the British and is a time to celebrate with friends and family.

Ghanaians, regardless of their religious faith, also enjoy national holidays during important Christian and Islamic celebrations. Christian holidays include Good Friday, Easter Sunday and Easter Monday, commemorating the death and resurrection of Jesus Christ. Christians hold long church services the night before Christmas and continue again on Christmas day. Gift giving is not common, but it is a day to remember family and friends.

The Muslim holidays of Ramadan, *Eid-el-Fitr* and *Eid-el-Adha*, and *Eid-el-Kabir* are also celebrated in Ghana. Ramadan, usually held in March or April, is a purification period for Muslims. It requires thirty days of dedicated fasting and abstinence from sex during the daylight hours. During this period, people wake before sunrise to eat a large meal and eagerly look forward to sunset with anticipation for water and another feast. *Eid-el-Fitr* marks the end of Ramadan and is looked to with great eagerness. The events around *Eid-el-Adha* commemorate Abraham's sacrifice of his son. The period symbolizes the Muslim ideal of sacrifice and spiritual dedication, and celebrates family and friends. The *Eid-el-Kabir* marks the culmination of the *hajj*, the sacred pilgrimage that all Muslims, if they are able, take to the Islamic holy land during their lifetime. During this time, Muslims make animal sacrifices to thank Allah for providing for them.

Ghanaian youth, especially those of the middle and upper class, have begun to adopt some of the Western holidays as well. Valentine's Day, for example, is popular with love-struck youth in urban centers and, although less so, throughout the country. From February first, young men begin patronizing shops to buy cards and expensive gifts for their loved ones. The gifts express affections for the other person, but they also act as a status symbol and are an attempt to impress that person and others who see the item. The media plays an important role in promoting Western-derived holidays. Newspapers, radio, and television stations promote Valentine's Day raffles. They offer free movies and cozy dinner buffets, and sponsor events such as blind dates, as well as other valentine activities. Other holidays, such as Mother's Day and Secretary's Day are also gaining some followers today.

PANAFEST

The largest international festival in Ghana is the Pan-African Historical Theatre Festival (PANAFEST). Beginning in December 1992, the biennial PANAFEST gathering attracts people from all over the world. The festival promotes the links between Africans and African Americans and focuses on the development of the African continent and its peoples. The main mediums of entertainment emphasize the common heritage of all African peoples, and include drama, dance, music, and other forms of creative arts. The bulk of the festival events are held in Accra and Cape Coast.

LEISURE AND ENTERTAINMENT

The bulk of everyday life depends, as anywhere in the world, on the type of economic livelihood that is most prominent in a particular society. Leisure and entertainment styles are, in part, determined by the nature of social institutions and the available cultural stimuli. Very much like people do in Western communities, urban Ghanaians play sports, listen to music, watch television, go to movies and bars, and attend dances. Rural leisure time, however, is different because of a more homogenous culture and limited entertainment options.

Sports and Games

Sports, whether playing them or watching them, are an important aspect of Ghanaian leisure activity. Popular sports include soccer, boxing, field hockey, table tennis, cricket, netball, volleyball, and basketball. Soccer, however, is the king of sports and has a huge following in Ghana. From the time they are young, boys begin to play soccer with any round object available to them, from small plastic balls to orange peels. They play anywhere. Children set up soccer fields in any open spaces and use rocks to mark the goals. "Gutter to gutter" is a short game of soccer that is played on city streets. Soccer was first introduced early in the colonial era, but it did not become widespread until after the Second World War with the increase of urban populations. Currently, the national league consists of teams from most of the different regions. Some regions, especially the Greater Accra, Ashanti, and Central Regions have many teams. Clubs attract thousands of fans to their stadiums, the largest of which is National Stadium in Accra. People support their team with outward displays of team colors and energetic vocal cheers. The clubs with the most followers are Asante Kotoko, based in Kumase, and Hearts of Oak, based in Accra. A meeting between these two clubs generates enormous excitement both within and outside of the stadium. People live and breathe soccer. It is a common topic of discussion in daily activities and stimulates lively discussions.

Ghana has enjoyed some success at the international level. The Under-17 team, in particular, has won the World Cup twice in recent years, but the older players have yet to match them. Every young boy dreams of playing for the Black Stars, Ghana's national team. People vigorously support the national team, but they also do not hesitate to criticize the players and coaches for defensive lapses, selfishness, and misplayed balls. When it comes to soccer, everyone is an expert! There are many Ghanaians playing soccer in European leagues. In fact, the first black professional soccer player in the British league,

Boys playing "gutter-to-gutter," a type of soccer that is played on city streets.

Arthur Wharton, was a Ghanaian. Ghana's most famous soccer player of all time is undoubtedly Abedi Pele, who was voted the best player in Africa three times.

The second most popular sport in Ghana is boxing. Boxing also began during the colonial era when some missionaries saw it as a good activity to keep young men off the streets. The Ga of central Accra are known for their boxing prowess. Ghanaian boxers have enjoyed success at the international level, winning numerous medals in the Commonwealth and Olympic games. Ghana's greatest fighters include Ike Quartey, Emmanuel Clottey, and Azumah Nelson. Nelson, also known as "The Terrible Warrior," was a three-time world boxing champion in the featherweight and super-featherweight divisions before retiring in 1998.

Track and field events are also common in Ghana. Almost every school at every level holds competitions in the various events. Athletes compete in zonal, regional, and national contests. Ghanaians particularly excel in the sprints and short relay-races, with sprinters winning international competitions and faring well at the Olympics.

The government sponsors an annual National Sports Festival to find new talents and promote the development of Ghanaian sportsmen and women. Athletes representing each of the administrative regions come together to

A painting promoting one of the local boxing gyms in Accra and one of Ghana's top fighters, Ike Quartey.

compete for honors in soccer, netball, handball, basketball, volleyball, table tennis, tae-kwon-do, boxing, speed walking, badminton and field hockey. The sports festival is also a time to have fun and enjoy good-natured competition. Many groups, such as the military, the police, fire services, and university sports associations, sponsor teams to compete in the games.

Ghanaians in rural and urban areas enjoy playing board games. One of the oldest games is *oware*. *Oware* is similar to backgammon, but it is played with marbles (or stones) on a board that has two rows with six holes on each side. The goal of the game is to move the game pieces around the board and capture those of the opposition. Draughts, sometimes called "African checkers," is also popular. Two men sitting under a shade tree with the wooden board resting between them is a common sight in all areas of Ghana. The games are played with a certain style, with participants slamming the small wooden pieces against the board to emphasize a good move. Bystanders watch the game with interest, waiting for their turn to play.

Young men playing draughts (African checkers) at the end of the day.

Cinema

Going to the cinema was once a popular social activity for urban Ghanaians. Every major city had at least one cinema and Accra had as many as
twenty at one time. Action films and American westerns attracted the biggest
and most vociferous crowds. Indian and kung fu movies were also popular
with youth. The Ghanaian cinema experience is very different than that of
most Western societies. Ghanaians voice their pleasures and displeasures, they
debate every move of the protagonist and antagonist, and laugh openly and
often. Going to a cinema is an exercise in social relations. People get up and
move around frequently, talking to friends in the audience. The rural areas
were not left out of the cinematic loop. Without a proper cinema to attend,
vans outfitted with a projector and speakers plied all areas of the country
showing films in open courtyards and town squares. The announcement of
a mobile cinema van was likely to bring out everyone in the community.

Film first became popular in Ghana during the 1920s, when private businessmen established the first cinemas in Accra, Takoradi, and Kumase. In
1939, the British established the Colonial Film Unit, and during the Second

World War, the colonial administration used the mobile cinema vans to show propaganda films throughout the country. Following the war, they made documentaries and "educational" films that emphasized Western culture and knowledge, and demeaned African traditional values. The basic premise was that the Western way of life represented "civilization," while Ghanaian values and beliefs were "uncultured" and "savage."

Other types of films were also made before independence. *The Boy Kumasenu* (1952) was Ghana's first full-length feature film. It portrayed the experiences of a boy who moved from a rural village to Accra, a common occurrence in the post-war period. After independence, the Ghanaian government attempted to use film as a means of education and as a way to foster national unity. Mobile cinema vans proved to be effective carriers of films promoting civil education and health issues. Although a number of films were produced, Western movies continually gained a stronger foothold in the cinemas.

Unfortunately, the Ghanaian film industry has produced only a few films in recent times. The two most famous feature films are Kwaw Ansah's *Love Brewed in an African Pot* (1981) and King Ampaw's *Kukurantumi: The Road to Accra* (1983). Both films link the present and the past, modern urban culture with rural traditional life. *Love Brewed in an African Pot* explores class differences in contemporary society and draws parallels to beliefs in traditional witchcraft. The film shows that neither of them are acknowledged as a physical reality, but both have a strong impact on everyday life. *Kukurantumi*, as the subtitle suggests, is about a lorry driver in a rural village who loses his job, moves to Accra, and sees his traditional lifestyle slowly chipped away. The films were popular because, unlike the many Western movies, they portrayed images and themes that were familiar to Ghanaians. Both films received international attention and received many awards. Since *Kukurantumi*, however, there have been few new productions of celluloid films in Ghana.

Economic problems made it difficult to maintain steady film production. Shrinking revenues and the fall of the cedi during the early 1980s created problems for the film industry. Prices of staple items increased much faster than salaries, and people had less money to spend on luxuries and entertainment. The improvements in the television infrastructure provided viewers with a cheap and easy alternative to the cinema. Although the number of televisions per person is low, extended family gather around one to watch their favorite shows. Today, Accra has only one remaining cinema that shows celluloid films, and even that is infrequent.

Since the early 1980s, however, a video film industry has developed and expanded rapidly. The advent of video in the Western world did not escape

Ghanaian entertainment circles. Videos became widely available everywhere in the country and small, video theaters were established. Video technology also changed film production. As people started businesses to record various social and religious events, they also began to use the cameras in other ways. Novice filmmakers began to experiment with video cameras and produce raw but popular films that gave attention to Ghanaian issues and attracted a mass audience. Soon, experienced filmmakers also realized the financial benefits of video production, and today new video films are introduced regularly.

Both Ghanaian and Western videos are widely available in stores and roadside stands throughout urban centers. Advertisements can be found everywhere. From large banners hanging over streets and exciting trailers on television, to small chalkboards in front of small video theaters. New video films generate excitement within a community. When a new video is released, a large truck might be decorated with bright signs and banners emphasizing scenes from the movies, and a band is hired to play. The truck and band parade through the major streets of cities, much like the announcement of traveling concert parties of old. Some of the actors ham it up for the crowd, while others mingle on the streets selling copies of the video.

Cinemas have been replaced by video theaters, which are more accessible and usually much cheaper. Anyone can establish a video theater with somewhat minimal expenses. The obvious needs include a television and a VCR. One also needs a venue. Video theaters consist of a room, either attached to a house or a separate building. They are commonly constructed from local materials, but sometimes are more elaborate and built to accommodate an upscale audience. The number of seats varies according to the expected audience. Unlike cinemas, video theaters can be established anywhere in Ghana. Many people flock to these theaters to watch Western, Nigerian, and Ghanaian films. Following the films, people often discuss them with their friends and family.

The popularity of video films arises from their themes, which express commonalities with their viewers. They often explore some aspect of traditional witchcraft and the impact of spiritual forces. While the physical imagery of the films is usually based in urban domestic life, the unseen spiritual reality is always present. Video films address class and gender issues, and depict problems and features of modern urban life, including crime, corruption, love, and poverty.

Everyday Life and Leisure

Everyday life varies dramatically between the rural and urban areas, but there are also similarities. Societal values and patterns of behavior are undergoing a constant process of change due to economic factors and increases in education. The types of leisure and entertainment most common to a society are largely determined by the available cultural stimuli.

The differences between rural and urban life are profound, but people living in both areas also exaggerate them. Many tend to express the dichotomy in idyllic terms that favor traditional life. The fast pace of city life is contrasted with the relaxed atmosphere of rural society, the noise of the city is set against the serenity of the countryside, and the cold, cruel social relations of the urban environment are the antithesis of the warm, friendly family life found in the village. These differences reflect the reality as well as the ideal of traditional life. Rural life has not remained unchanged. It has a long history of economic, social, and cultural exchange that continues to modify everyday patterns of existence.

Most Ghanaians live in the rural areas in villages ranging in size from a few families to thousands of residents. Rural societies are agriculturally based and, thus, farming activities take up a large part of the day. Some people also practice animal husbandry, with younger children tending to smaller animals such as goats and sheep. Women spend their time doing domestic chores such as cleaning, cooking, collecting firewood, and fetching water, as well as helping with farming duties. Men who farm are busiest during the planting and harvesting seasons. Although there have been attempts to introduce mechanization, most farming is still done by hand and with plow animals. Small farms either do not need to use tractors or cannot afford the expense of purchasing equipment, even when it is shared between a collective of farmers. Other traditional occupations include blacksmiths, tailors, and carvers. Children are expected to help their parents and learn the skills necessary to continue the family tradition. They are groomed to take over household and family responsibilities when they reach adulthood. During the dry season, after the harvest, everyone has more free time, which is spent doing repairs to equipment and homes, visiting friends, and enjoying leisure activities. Most of the major festivals are held during this time.

Changing economic systems and the expansion of Western education, however, are affecting rural patterns of life. Rural farmers are increasingly growing export crops to pay for school fees or buy manufactured goods. The development of wage labor offers jobs for young men and women, affecting the traditional economic and social system. Rather than relying on family and lineage structures for support, sons and daughters are able to earn money on their own. The labor economy increases individualism and diminishes the impact of traditional lineage relations. Some young men and women who migrate to the cities in search of employment never move back to their homes, altering the traditional patterns of inheritance and distribution of wealth.

The increase in Western education has introduced new factors into rural life. Schools can be found in even the remotest villages today. Both boys and girls often attend, at least through the primary level. During these years, the school environment consumes the majority of the student's time. Schoolmates, rather than siblings, become their best friends. Teachers, rather than parents and elders, assume the most important role in the socialization process. Educated children often do not want to stay in the village and work on the family farm. Rural men and women want to explore the increased opportunities offered in urban areas and often migrate to one of Ghana's cities at some point during their lives. Some leave only for a few years and return to the family farm or business, while others find their niche in the city and establish their lives there. Those from small villages who want to continue their education past the primary level, find that they must move to an urban center to attend the nearest school.

Leisure time in the rural area differs from that of the city because of the more limited number of options. After the workday, people may gather together for storytelling, to share news about other community members, or to discuss local, national, and international issues. People gather around a television or radio to listen to the news or one of the many other radio programs available to them. They may attend a video theater and see the latest Ghanaian film. *Pito* (see Chapter 5) and palm wine bars are popular places to meet friends, listen and dance to music, and unwind from the day.

In the urban areas, there are a greater variety of economic, social, and cultural choices. The economic system of the city is more diversified and people work in a variety of professions that determine a large part of everyday life. Unlike in rural areas, wage labor forms the majority of the occupations. Cities include many of the same professions that are found in the rural areas, but there are also a greater number of other jobs. One needs money to live in the city, as transport, food, and basic amenities require at least minimal incomes. People take jobs to meet those expenses. Small traders selling manufactured goods, food, or art on the streets, in the markets, or in shops form a majority of the urban workforce. Most government, industrial, and other business-type jobs are in urban areas as well.

Quality educational facilities are more widely available in the cities. Western education has created and promoted new professional occupations, such as doctors, lawyers, and accountants. But it has also encouraged the growth of a middle class that is engaged in business, technological, and industrial ventures. People gain prestige not by age and social status as with elders and chiefs, but by their level of education and their standard of living. Their wealth is derived from individual means. The wide varieties of opportunities in the cities offer people aspiring to monetary wealth a better chance of success and the communal aspect of lineage is, thus, diminished. As large numbers of people continue to migrate from the rural to the urban areas social problems associated with city life, such as crime and prostitution, continue to grow as well.

City lifestyles cover a wide spectrum. A few people are wealthy and live in large houses with all of the modern conveniences. They have cars and sometimes even drivers, a sign of status and prestige. They go to work in offices, hospitals, or businesses. At home, they might have a hired staff who take care of domestic duties. At other times, extended family members staying with them are expected to do some housework. Some people live in middle-class homes or apartment complexes and enjoy a comfortable life by all standards. Most people, however, live in ad hoc neighborhoods of small, often one-room houses. They rely on mass transit to get to and from their workplaces and, in general, have far less social mobility than people of other classes.

Urban leisure and entertainment reflect the diversity of people and availability of cultural resources. Class differences, in part, determine the type of activities in which people participate. Urban wage labor creates money for basic amenities, but it also affects the organization of leisure and entertainment by creating differences in disposable income. The lower classes might attend a video theater, have a drink at one of the ubiquitous "spots" (small outdoor bars), or spend time relaxing, listening to music, and dancing with friends. The middle and upper classes have more disposable income. They are apt to seek entertainment at upscale hotels, bars, discos, restaurants, and theaters. They also spend more time with their nuclear family, dining together, watching television, and traveling. Some urban elite enjoy time in their home village. They establish large farms and grow export crops such as pineapples, mangoes, and cassava. They often construct nice houses in the village, both to get away from city life and as a means of displaying their status. Regardless of economic class, coastal populations enjoy attending concert parties and going to the beach, especially on Sunday. Beach outings are a time to spend with friends, play soccer, and swim. In larger cities, such as Accra, Cape Coast, and Kumase, big music festivals are often held on Sunday afternoons and holidays.

In general, leisure and entertainment time, like social relations, are valued. Whether in the rural or urban areas, people enjoy spending time with others, sharing stories, playing games, and having new experiences. As class differences become more pronounced and Western cultural influences more available, sharper contrasts arise in Ghanaian lifestyles.

8

Music and Dance

Music and dancing is the best medicine to make man feel healthy and to get rid of frustrations.

—Rebecca Atanga[1]

MUSIC AND DANCE can be found in almost every aspect of Ghanaian cultural life. They are often inseparable forms of artistic and emotional expression. Music and dance styles fall into four main categories: traditional, neo-traditional or neo-folk, popular, and Christian. The last three, in particular, are forms that have become pervasive only since the Second World War. They all, however, contain many different genres that continue to evolve with changes in the historical and cultural environment.

Society is in a process of constant change; so too are music and dance forms. External influences, such as Islam and Christianity, and internal influences, such as local and regional trade, affects the development of Ghanaian music by conveying cultural traits from one society to another. Islam had a more profound impact on musical cultures of northern Ghana, while Christianity affected those of the central and southern regions to a greater degree. In general, societies did not convert en masse and accept all the tenets and customs of a foreign religion, but they did borrow cultural items and adapt them for their own use. Musically, such influences are found in the types of instruments that a group employs. The trans-Saharan trade, for example, brought Sahelian instruments common in areas of Mali to the northern peoples of Ghana. The *seprewa*, which resembles the *kora* used by the *griot* musicians of Mali, probably came from the north and was adapted

A musician and dancer outside the Akuma
Village Cultural Center.

to local conditions. Christianity and colonialism, on the other hand, brought brass instruments to the coast and spurred developments in brass band music in the southern regions. Christianity also introduced Western-style church hymns which have evolved to form a distinct Ghanaian type of choral music.

Music and dance styles may change through local trade and intermarriage, resulting in traits shared by various musical cultures. The *asafo* music of warrior organizations, for example, is found in the Akan, Guan, Ga, Adangbe, and Ewe areas of Ghana, while the Dagomba have a music and dance type called *kanbonwaa*, a combination of local and Akan styles. Another type, *jongo*, can be found in many societies of northern Ghana.[2] Instruments such as the *atumpan* (talking drum) and the *fontomfrom*, considered Akan instruments, can now be found in Ga, Ewe, Dagomba, and Wala ensembles. When artistic styles are transferred from one society to another, the language, playing techniques, and dance forms often change as well. The Hausa *donno* (hourglass or pressure drum) originally came into northern Ghana from Nigeria. It can now be found throughout southern

A man with his large collection of albums and videotapes.

Ghanaian music cultures, each group adapting its sounds into their own music and dance styles.

Modern transport and communication networks also encouraged the dissemination of music and dance styles. Better roads and faster vehicles make contact between cultures much easier. Artists can perform in their styles and also learn from the music and dance resources of their hosts. Radio technology and the expansion of radio broadcasts, especially the liberalization of the airwaves in the early 1980s, have allowed local Ghanaian styles and foreign music to spread more quickly and to a wider audience than before. Television, too, provides a visual and auditory medium through which to access a variety of music and dance styles.

Music and dance are popular forms of ceremony and recreation in Ghana. Men and women of all ages meet formally and informally to listen and dance to a variety of rhythms. Musicians create sounds to send a message, inspire their listeners to action, or to provide a backdrop for entertainment and leisure. Whether in the presence of a chief and dignitaries or in a nightclub with friends, dancers listen to the rhythmic patterns of music and reveal their

A performer clad in costume, wearing an
"Atta-Mills for President" T-shirt.

skills through their posture, gestures, and steps. All varieties of music and
dance in Ghana invite people to join in, to play an active part in social
occasions.

TRADITIONAL MUSIC AND DANCE

It is important to understand the instruments used and types of traditional
music, but it is also crucial to see their function and recognize the dynamic
relationship between the music and the musical environment that is closely
tied to the larger social and cultural contexts. Traditional performances of
Ghanaian music draw no line between audience and performers. They often
take place in an open area, with the musicians surrounded by the audience
rather than placed before the audience on a stage. There is little physical or
psychological distance between them. The audience not only listens to the
music but partakes in it through dance and ceremony.

Functions

Many types of traditional music and dance are functional and their performance is limited to a particular context. Music and dance have social roles and functions through which Ghanaian societies express their culture. Different types are performed for funerals, weddings, harvest festivals, or work activities. The meaning of the music in these contexts is closely related to the ideas and feelings associated with the occasion.

The names and instruments used for traditional music are sometimes taken from the nature of the social occasion. The Akan, for example, have a category of songs, *asrayere* (visiting the wives), which were performed by women while the men were away at war. These songs functioned to unite the women and show their support for their warrior men. The Akan also have songs called *bradwom* (*dwom*: song) for the puberty rite (*bragoro*). In general, music reveals the customs and ideals of a society. Drums should only be played by Akan men because of the potential impurities of women during menstruation. During female puberty rites, however, women are allowed to play *donno* drums because men are not important elements of the ceremony. The drumming and singing celebrate the passage of girlhood to womanhood and help to teach the initiates some of the duties they will need to perform as adults.

There are songs for all activities and various social and age groups. Recreational music is the most common type. Music and dance accompany sports events, children's games, beer-drinking, family time, and storytelling. Music and dance are often accompanied by singing to express sorrow or joy, or to give a rhythm to work patterns, such as the pounding of *fufu*, a staple food prepared from cassava, yam, or plantain. Children incorporate singing into games and storytelling, and use music to impart lessons. Children play games like *aboo asimensa* and *nteewa. Aboo asimensa* ("a stone has hit my hand") begins with the children sitting in a circle. While singing, they take a stone from their right hand and place it on the ground in front of the person to their right. The object is to pick up each stone and pass it on before the next is placed before them. A player who misses a stone is eliminated. The back-and-forth movements are accompanied by a swaying of the body toward the direction in which the stones are moving and a song to provide a rhythm for those movements. *Nteewa* is a clapping game, usually performed by young girls in a circle. They move in the circle and, while singing, clap in an alternating (up and down) rhythm with the people on either side of them. The object of this game is to remain in rhythm, to sing and clap on specific beats, and continue to move the body and legs at a different pace.

Music is used to impart a message. A group of Asante children might sing a song to a habitual bed-wetter in an attempt to correct the practice. Parents also use music to communicate a message to their children. A Ghanaian cradle song reflects important values of society:

> If you are hungry, cook yourself a meal.
>> Why do you cry?
> You are the child of a yam farmer.
>> Why do you cry?
> You are the child of a cocoyam farmer.
>> Why do you cry?[3]

This song not only shows children that they need to take action to satisfy their needs, but it also reveals the potential wealth of the land and shows pride in the agricultural profession.

There are songs and dances for women, songs and dances for men, and songs for warrior groups and chiefs. The music of the *asafo* companies, for example, once included all able-bodied Fante men who came together during community crises. These companies have evolved into social organizations and music plays a vital role in their proceedings. Their military history is evident in the lyrics of the songs. *Asafo* companies used drums to announce the arrival of the enemy and call the men of the community together. The drums can call the name of a specific company and relate the nature of the meeting. Drums and singing were used to celebrate a victory:

> He has killed the Southerners.
> He has killed the Northerners.
> It is *Asafo Apagya.*
> The Umbrella tree.
> The Umbrella tree has branches above and below.
> The crafty Umbrella tree.
> King, Hail the helper![4]

Today, *asafo* companies are most active during community festivals and in performance of community service. In a procession, drums may announce the arrival of a certain company whose music and dancing attract many followers in the community. *Asafo* drummers also call the company together to perform service such as extinguishing a fire or improving a road.

Dancing can also relate a story and portray historical images important to an ethnic group. The *agbekor* dance of the Anlo Ewe, for example, employs movements and costumes that present the experience of the Anlo Ewe during battles fought while migrating through hostile lands to their current location. Some Anlo Ewe dances relate to a later historical era, presenting comical images of German and French colonial soldiers marching upright with a staff in one hand. These dances tell a story, but they might also elicit laughter from the audience.

Instruments

Many types of instruments are used in Ghanaian musical performances. There are various types of drums and other percussion instruments, such as bells, iron gongs, rattles, and percussion sticks. Some of the most common drums include the following:

Atumpan—pairs of "talking" drums associated with Akan royalty and used for transmitting messages. They are inclined at a 45 degree angle and played with two sticks shaped like the number "7";

Donno—an hourglass-shaped drum whose pitch is varied by squeezing tension strings on the side. The changes in pitch are recognized as a language and can be used to communicate;

Gome—a large, square-framed drum on which the player sits and plays with both hands and feet. The sound is changed by altering the skin tension with the feet and the instrument serves as a bass drum. It is believed that it was brought from Jamaica via Fernando Po and is the essential instrument in many neo-traditional drumming and dance styles;

Fontomfrom—pairs of huge drums about five feet tall that are used with the *atumpan* talking drums to praise Akan and Guan royalty. At one time, their status was elevated and no one was allowed to own one without the approval of the chief; and

Kpanlogo—a conga-shaped drum that is played with the hands, it is probably Ghana's most well-known drum, and is used in festivals, funerals, and naming ceremonies. It is important in many styles of music, especially the Ga neo-folk style, *kpanlogo*.

There are also many different types of melody instruments. These include, for example, flutes, fiddles, xylophones, and harps:

Atenteben—a bamboo flute with seven holes, it originated with the Akan and is used as a solo instrument or in ensembles;

Gonje—a single-string fiddle from the Dagbon area in northern Ghana, mounted on a calabash gourd covered with animal skin and played with a bow. It is played in praise of a chief;

Prempremsiwa—like a large *mbira* of southern Africa, it is a rectangular box with three metal prongs fixed over a sound hole on the front. The player sits on top of the box and plucks the prongs with both hands;

Gyil—a xylophone from the Upper West region of Ghana, tuned pentatonically and consisting of wooden blocks mounted over resonating calabash gourds with holes bored at the sides. It is now played in all regions of the country;

Seprewa—a traditional harp lute of the Akan, tuned heptatonically. It has eight to ten strings arranged vertically in two rows. The strings reach from a wooden neck to a wooden box that serves as the resonator.

Ghanaian instruments are not simply mass produced as many instruments are in the Western world. The significance and meaning of each instrument goes far beyond its exterior. An Akan talking drum, for example, must be carefully tended so that it can speak a drum language. The master drummer must follow the proper ritual involved in making a new drum or preparing one for a performance. The spirits of the drum components, the wood of the body and the pegs, the bark for lacing strings, and the animal skin, must all be respected:

> Wood of the drum, Tweneboa Akwa.
> Wood of the drum, Tweneboa Kodua.
> Wood of the drum, Kodua Tweneduro.
> Cedar Wood, if you have been away,
> I am calling you; they say come.
> I am learning, let me succeed.[5]

This is one verse, relating to the wood of the drum, of a "Drum Exorcism." It is performed as a tribute to Tweneboa Kodua, the spiritual ancestor of drummers who lives in the Tweneboa wood.

The making of a Kasena calabash drum also demands more than cutting and covering the calabash. A Kasena craftsman, for example, must perform certain rituals to ensure that the spirit of the drum is satisfied, allowing it to speak correctly. Pebbles from the yard of a woman known as a gossiper are placed inside the drum so that it will be talkative. The skin of a frog's neck is added so that the drum will stay responsive. At one time, a lion skin was put inside the drum to ensure that it would roar. Today, other things, such as pieces of metal, are inserted, creating a rattle effect to accompany the drum sound. The Akan, too, make additions to some percussion instruments to make them rattle and produce more sound. They may attach a metal ring to

A musician repairing a worn xylophone and preparing to cover a drum.

a drum head or add items to xylophones or chordophones to enhance the effect. Dancers often wear bracelets to produce a sound that, as they move in their dancing, keeps tune with the rest of the music.

Musicians

Traditional musicians and dancers learn their skills from a very young age. Musicians learn their skills informally through social interactions and frequent exposure to music. Participating in childrens' games and listening to stories that employ singing and dancing introduce children to different types of music and dance and encourage the development of their own music and dance resources.

At one time, sons born to a father who was a master drummer of an Akan state were trained to assume that position at the death of the elder. Master drummers were well-versed in the drum language of the *atumpan* and had a vast knowledge of history and tradition. Intensive training began with techniques of drumming and memorization of rhythms. Students were expected to devote their energy to training and some were forbidden to play any games during their free time. Fluency and clarity of expression of the drum language can only be obtained through years of practice and awareness of the form and meaning of the musical and verbal texts. As one expert notes, the sound and the language are intricately linked: "if a drummer learns to reproduce sequences of rhythmic groups accurately . . . he can become fluent at playing the drums but he cannot translate the sounds into words."[6] Once a drummer became skilled, he enjoyed great prestige within society. While engaged in the act of drumming, a person is considered a "sacred person and is immune from assaults and annoyances."[7] There were also certain taboos associated with drummers. Others had to carry the drums for the musician, because it was believed that if they carried their own instruments on their head it would make them insane. The power and prestige of the drummer, however, has diminished in recent times. The declining resources of chiefs and the increased availability of higher education make jobs in financially rewarding areas more appealing.

Today, Ghanaian musicians often take a different path to musical development. Rebecca Atanga's story is a common story of Ghanaian musicians; a story of migration out of a village, into a city, and subsequently out of Ghana to the West. Atanga began to play music during her childhood in the village of Yua, in northern Ghana, very close to the Burkina Faso border. Her father was an amateur musician who played the *kologo*, a two-stringed guitar, to entertain guests in the family compound. When she was young, she was part of a group of children that played at the homes of elderly people who had died. They sang, danced, and drummed in the evenings until the day of the burial. She then performed in her school's dance group, where she learned different dances and rhythms through cultural exchanges with other schools from as far away as Guinea.

As her musical aspirations grew, Atanga moved to Bolgatanga, a larger city and the capital of the Upper East Region, and worked as a musician and dancer at a bar and café owned by her brother. It was there that she began to hear different types of African popular music and began to develop a repertoire that would later serve as the basis of her musical career. Wishing to expand her musical skills, she attended the University of Ghana, Legon and studied music. After marrying a touring musician from the Netherlands and moving to Amsterdam, she enrolled at Amsterdam Music School. Like many Ghanaian musicians, Atanga's career took off when she left Ghana and honed her skills away from her home. In 1998, she released her first CD, *Bayete*.[8]

Types of Music and Dance

Asante *adowa* is perhaps the most widely known traditional music and dance form in Ghana and has become popular with other ethnic groups. *Adowa* was originally a ceremonial dance that relied on graceful and dignified walking movements. The dance is usually preceded by a chorus of voices and two gongs, with two drums joining in. Once the introduction has attracted the attention of the audience, the *atumpan* drums begin to play. As in many other Ghanaian dances, different instruments direct different aspects of the dance. Parts of the body adjust to specific drum rhythms, while gong patterns control body movements like spins and bows.

In the Kasena area of Northern Ghana there is a music and dance type called *jongo,* which is performed during times of celebration, such as harvest festivals, weddings, or the last stages of funeral celebrations. Jongo employs a variety of percussion instruments, including large calabash drums (*kori*), larger cylindrical drums (*gullu*), hourglass-shaped drums (*gungwe*), and small calabash bowls played with sticks. Flutes (*wui*) provide the melody. When the music starts, the audience participates by dancing. The best dancers are rewarded with money stuck to their foreheads; the money is then given to the musicians in payment for playing at the ceremony.

Court music and dance are performed for royalty and the people who attend royal gatherings. A royal ensemble of musicians attached to the *asantehene* and the Asante paramount chiefs perform *kete* music and dance. Traditionally, these musicians were tied to royal houses and performed at functions associated with the king and the paramount chiefs. Although the musicians are no longer supported fully by the Asante royalty, they still perform when asked to do so. *Kete* music is predominantly drum music, but it also includes *odurugya* flutes. There is a bass drum that provides the "timeline," or essential rhythm, that all other instruments follow. There is a master drummer who leads the ensemble and plays complex patterns, and another drummer whose rhythms fit with those of the master drum.

Many drum rhythms speak a language that conveys a message. A master drummer must have a vast knowledge of the different rhythms that can be used in different situations. If a *kete* ensemble, for example, is playing a song and the paramount chief leaves his chair and starts walking, the master drummer should segue into a piece appropriate to the moment. One specialist suggests that the *kete* piece, "Apente," could be used because it expresses the message "the chief walks; he is not in a hurry," and advises the chief to walk carefully.[9]

Kete dancing also demands great skills. Solo dancers, for example, are judged by the way they move their bodies, picking up specific rhythms from particular drums. The feet may be moving in duple beats, the body may be leaning to the side in a faster rhythm, and the arms moving at yet another pace, but all must be presented in a relaxed and dignified manner suitable for a court dance.

NEO-TRADITIONAL OR NEO-FOLK MUSIC

Traditional music and dance continue to change as new forms of creativity and outside influences are introduced. When a type of traditional music incorporates elements of popular music, it becomes neo-traditional or neo-folk. Neo-folk music types do not replace traditional styles of music, but represent new additions to the Ghanaian musical repertoire. Neo-folk musical styles combine elements of traditional music, previous recreational styles, and popular styles like highlife. The new styles maintain basic elements, such as the emotional, spiritual, and cultural values, but incorporate recreational and popular rhythms and steps that reflect the environment of their creators.

Kpanlogo

Kpanlogo, a drumming and dance style created and disseminated by urban youth, originated in Accra during the early 1960s. It represents an attachment to the past as well as a progressive attitude toward the future, and it is a symbol of Ghanaian urban neighborhood youth. A young Ga carpenter, Otoo Lincoln, named the dance after a story his grandfather told him when he was a child. His friends, Okulay Foes and Ayitey Sugar, developed a drumbeat to accompany it. *Kpanlogo* grew out of earlier traditional styles, such as *oge* and *gome*, and was influenced by contemporary highlife and even rock 'n' roll dancing. It spread rapidly among the youth of other ethnic groups. *Kpanlogo* has become entrenched today; most young people would tell you that it is an old Ga music and dance style that has existed for a very long time. It is an example of the indistinct boundaries between "traditional" and "popular" music. One does not evolve into the other. They continuously influence each other in a dynamic, two-way relationship. According to one authority "the claim that anything in Africa that sounds cultural must be ancient and anonymous is an oversimplification that separates the actual, individual creators from their works."[10]

Kpanlogo usually uses three drums, with the supporting drummers playing a responsive beat and the lead drummer playing solos against that rhythm. *Kpanlogo* groups also use other instruments including a *gome* drum, a beaded gourd shaker, rattles, double bells, and wood blocks. The central instrument is the *kpanlogo* drum. A master *kpanlogo* drummer must be inventive and, using a call and response pattern with the other main drummer, have the ability to constantly improvise, moving to a variety of different rhythms according to the context and the changes in a dancer's movement.

Kpanlogo is popular with young people, largely because of the physical nature of the dancing. It is sometimes called by its nickname, *lolo*, reflecting the characteristic movements of the body, especially the hips and shoulders, which occur in the basic dance steps. It incorporates pelvic thrusts and twists influenced by Elvis Presley and Chubby Checker. One observer notes that the movements are "slightly irreverent." When young men are dancing "it is exceedingly macho," and the young women dancers make it "very, very sexy."[11] Although there was a great deal of resistance from the Ga elders when it was first introduced, *kpanlogo* is now performed at Ga funerals and wakes and can be heard in many parts of Ghana during recreational time.

Ga Cultural Groups

Another development in Ghanaian music began in the early 1970s, with what one musician calls a "folk revival."[12] These bands blended traditional music with highlife and created "cultural" highlife music. The first band to develop this style was Wulomei (traditional priests in Ga society). Influenced by earlier neo-traditional styles, Wulomei added the electric guitar to a traditional ensemble. The founders, Saka Acquaye and Nii Ashitey, sought to indigenize highlife music and create a style that would draw the attention of youth away from foreign music. The group's success led to the formation of many more bands like them, and this type of music remains popular with many groups in Ghana today.

Ga cultural groups play various types of music, from Ga traditional songs and older neo-folk styles like *kolomashie, oge,* and *kpanlogo,* as well as popular highlife music. Like *kpanlogo* groups, they use the *gome* drum to provide the bass line. They also feature Ga percussion instruments such as congas, calabashes, and gongs. The electric guitar, a chorus of female vocalists, and bamboo flutes perform the melody. During performances, Wulomei dresses in traditional cloth, merging traditional music imagery with the instruments and sounds of other influences.

Simpa

Another type of Ghanaian neo-folk music is a recreational drum and dance style of the Dagbon area called *simpa.* Created in the 1930s, *simpa* blends traditional Dagomba and Hausa music, neo-folk music such as *gome,* and popular highlife. Its name is derived from the traditional name for the town of Winneba, one of the Fante ports where highlife originated. *Simpa* performances generally take place outdoors in the evening. Young men play the instruments, which include conga drums, square-frame drums, a gong-gong, rattle, and sometimes a Hausa pressure drum and a trumpet. Young females form the chorus and sing a variety of songs from traditional, highlife, and other contemporary popular music forms.[13] *Simpa* music continues to change, incorporating Western pop styles and adopting new messages relevant to current trends in Dagomba society.

Just as the Ga elders resisted *kpanlogo*, Dagbon elders originally resisted *simpa* music because they considered it a youth music that encouraged delinquency and promiscuity. Nevertheless, it grew quickly and numerous *simpa* bands formed. Its influence also grew with time. In 1969, there was a succession conflict between two royal houses and *simpa* was banned because the songs were deemed to be inflammatory. *Simpa* is now accepted as a traditional Dagomba music style and, though still a recreational music played by young people, it is sometimes played at naming ceremonies, weddings, and funerals.

Ghanaian neo-folk music comes in many different forms. It is at the forefront of maintaining traditional music, not by locking it into a time capsule and forcing it to remain unchanged, but by finding a place for it within modern social contexts. Such music, regardless of its point of origin, appeals to all Ghanaians by cutting across ethnic and generation lines.

POPULAR MUSIC AND DANCE

The roots of contemporary popular music go back to the early age of contact with the West and the spread of the Atlantic trade and missionary activity. Popular music developed during the colonial era and continues to change through a dynamic relationship with global cultural forces. Many new styles have developed with the introduction of Western instruments and musical influences. After independence, material changes affected the development of popular music: electric guitars replaced box guitars, electric organs replaced pianos, and amplifiers allowed popular music to reintroduce African drums into a small band without drowning out the other instruments. New styles, too, are brought into the local musical culture and incorporated into already existing musical forms.

Ghana's most significant and longstanding popular music is highlife. It dates from the early 1920s and continues to thrive and generate new music and dance styles throughout Ghana. Popular music and dance are defined by the nature of their performance setting. Though there is a continuous and

c̩   between traditional and popular music in Ghana, the
di̩   is that popular music does not serve any function
wit̩   although it is often used as entertainment following
offic̩   ̩nds and movements of highlife, reggae, and hiplife,
howev̩   ̩sive; they can be heard in homes, open-air bars, nightclubs,
stadium snows, and festivals.

Highlife

Highlife is a blend of traditional and imported music, and is certainly the
most internationally well-known music style of Ghana. Highlife began in the
1920s, when musicians began to incorporate imported influences, such as
the foxtrot and calypso, into Ghanaian rhythms like, *osibisaba* (Fante) and a
guitar style from Liberia *dagomba*. During the early period, large orchestras,
like the Jazz Kings, Cape Coast Sugar Babies, and Accra Orchestra, played
at high-class clubs in towns along Ghana's coast. Playing for the colonial
elite, they continued to rely on Western dance styles such as the foxtrot,
quickstep, and waltz but began to Africanize them. Dress codes and high
entrance fees at many clubs limited the clientele to the elite, and the name
"highlife" was coined to reflect this lifestyle. A brother of E.T. Mensah
(1919–96), one of the most popular highlife musicians of the time, related
his memories of such a scene:

> The people outside [the clubs] called it highlife as they did not reach
> the class of the couples going inside, who not only had to pay a relatively
> high entrance fee of about 7s 6d, but also had to wear full evening
> dress, including top-hats if they could afford it.[14]

By the 1940s, highlife developed two main branches, dance band highlife
and guitar band highlife. The latter, most popular among the Akan people,
relied on a smaller, usually acoustic band and is more common in the rural
areas. The guitar was easily integrated into the music because of musicians'
familiarity with other Ghanaian stringed instruments. The playing style of
the *seprewa* was combined with the similar guitar method of *dagomba*, introduced by Kru seamen from Liberia, which became the classic two-fingered
technique of the highlife guitar. Guitar band highlife included singing, acoustic guitars, drums, claves, and occasionally the *prempremsiwa*. Guitar band
highlife grew in popularity when E.K. Nyame (1921–77) and his Akan Trio
gave concert party performances. Nyame sang mainly in Twi and made more
than 400 records. When he died in 1977, he was given a state funeral, which

tens of thousands of fans attended. Koo Nimo is probably the most influential player of acoustic guitar highlife today and continues to advance the form.

By the 1950s, guitar band highlife was most closely associated with concert party performances. Guitar bands played with concert party troupes or sometimes served as both actors and musicians. Concert parties used slapstick comedy to portray common problems of everyday life. Increasingly performed in the vernacular, the music and dramatic performances addressed issues of migration, youth, poverty, politics, love, marriage, and death.

Dance band highlife developed in the urban areas during and after the Second World War when smaller, professional bands began to emerge. The most popular highlife musician of this type was E.T. Mensah, known as the "King of Highlife." His group, the Tempos, led the change from the big band, Western-focused styles of the earlier years to smaller ensembles more adaptable to the new musical influences brought in during the Second World War. E.T. Mensah recognized that he and the Tempos had Africanized highlife music and changed the rhythmic emphasis: "We evolved a music type thereafter relying on basic African rhythms, a criss-cross African cultural sound so to speak. No one really can lay claim to its creation. It had always been there entrenched in West African culture. What I did was give highlife world acceptance."

During the war, Mensah played with a Scottish sergeant in a multiracial band, Leopard and His Black and White Spots. With Mensah on saxophone (he later began playing the trumpet), the band performed mostly for British and American soldiers, playing jazz and swing and other popular dance music. After the troops departed, the band began to play for Ghanaians and the nature of the music changed. Incorporating influences from calypso and Afro-Cuban percussion, the Tempos developed a new highlife style that became popular throughout West Africa. The Tempos made their first of many recordings with Decca in 1952 and, after splitting and reforming with new members, registered as the first professional dance band in Ghana the following year. When Mensah played with Louis Armstrong and his All Stars during their first visit to Ghana in 1956, his popularity exploded and this new form of highlife attracted new followers. At the time of independence in 1957, Mensah composed a song that celebrated the event, "Ghana Freedom Highlife." The words of one verse go as follows:

> Ghana, we now have our freedom
> Ghana, land of freedom
> Toils of the brave and the sweat of their labor
> Toils of the brave which have brought results.[15]

E.T. Mensah and the Tempos inspired many new highlife bands throughout Ghana, and after many journeys throughout West Africa and Europe, Mensah certainly deserves his name, the "King of Highlife."

Another musician who could certainly lay some claim to the title was King Bruce (1922–97). His contributions to Ghanaian music culture are enormous. He remained important in the music scene from the 1950s to the 1980s and supported more than 150 musicians with his management of the "BB" groups, named after their bands which always started with the letter "B." These included the Barbecues, the Barons, the Bonafides, the Barristers, the Boulders, Big Soyaaya, and, the most famous of these, the Black Beats. King Bruce's legacy was recalled in 1999 when the Queen of England visited Ghana and his song, "The Queen's Visit," written soon after independence, was played on radio and television[16]:

> This is the day five million Ghanaians will go gay.
> Queen Elizabeth and Prince Phillip will be here that special
>   day.
> We'll drink and dance the whole day and put on Kente fine,
> On that Thursday, 12th November 1959.
>
> Seven long years we waited since coronation.
> To Canada and then Nigeria she brought jubilation.
> Now here are drummers stamping on the mighty fontomfrom.
> The Queen has come at last to Ghana from United Kingdom.[17]

Highlife captured its listeners because of its Africanized rhythms and lyrical content. The lyrics often served as social commentary. A song by E.K. Nyame's band, for example, "Nsuo beto a, mframa dikan" ("Before It Starts Raining, the Wind Will Blow"), was interpreted as a warning to President Kwame Nkrumah about his impending downfall:

> Before it starts raining
> The wind will blow.
> I warned you but you did not listen
> Before trouble starts,
> There will be a flag (to warn you).
> I warned you but you did not listen.[18]

Dance band and guitar band highlife flourished during the 1950s and early 1960s before declining in popularity. The central reason for their decline was the rise of Western popular music and Ghanaian acculturation of the popular music scene. The younger generation began to see highlife music as too "colo" (colonial), and associated it with the attitudes of the colonial period. They turned to new forms developing in Africa—Congo music, Afrobeat, and Afro-rock—and the West—rock 'n' roll, soul, and rhythm and blues. The dissemination of African music via recordings and radio spurred the interest of a younger generation. Congo music, in particular, became very popular. Originating in Central Africa, it combined local rhythms and Latin American music. It offered a new rhythm for dancing and introduced intriguing steps like the "cha-cha-cha."

By the end of the 1960s, Fela's Afro-beat had arrived and delivered a further blow to highlife music. Afro-beat, often sung in Pidgin English, merged African and Western languages and rhythms and was very danceable. Unlike some purely Western forms, this style of music liberated Ghanaian musicians from earlier "copyright" music and allowed for greater creativity. The final indicator of the changing musical climate occurred when Accra hosted the "Soul to Soul" concert in 1971. It was the biggest Western-oriented pop festival held in Ghana and attracted such performers as Les McCann, Wilson Pickett, Roberta Flack, the Staple Singers, Ike and Tina Turner, and Santana to Black Star Square where they performed before an audience of more than 100,000 people.

The late 1960s and early 1970s were a dynamic period in the history of Ghanaian music. Spending only a few weeks in Accra, one could experience a wide array of musical styles. From the music of syncretic churches to the traditional music and dance of festivals and the variety of music at hotels and nightclubs on weekends, there was always something to please music seekers. Highlife and rock 'n' roll bands like the African Brothers and the Avengers played at places like the Star Hotel and the Metropole; the National Music and Dance Troupe frequented the Ambassador Hotel; and visiting groups such as Fela made several appearances.

During the 1970s, however, the previously vibrant Ghanaian recording industry declined because of the shortage of vinyl for albums and the economic crisis that affected the entire country. Local music also suffered as youth began to listen more to American imports such as soul and disco. The popularity of highlife music began to wane, but it continued to influence the development of Ghanaian music. Although there are a few musicians today who continue to play the classic styles of the 1950s and 1960s, most artists integrated highlife and other popular influences of their era and developed new genres.

The most popular Ghanaian band of this period, Osibisa, did not even live in Ghana at the time. Formed in 1969 by a Ghanaian studying in London, the Afro-rock band became internationally famous and toured extensively, spreading their criss-cross rhythms, a mix of highlife, rock 'n' roll, and Afro-beat. The lead musicians learned their skills playing in a number of highlife and dance bands in Ghana before making the trip to London. The original band also consisted of musicians from Nigeria, Grenada, Antigua, and Trinidad. Osibisa's many tours of Ghana provided a source of inspiration for youth, and influenced bands such as Boombaya, Sawaaba Sounds, and Hedzolleh to play Afro-rock music. Osibisa also started a trend, which continues today, of Ghanaian musicians developing their skills and building their fame outside of their country.

Many highlife artists make the journey from Ghana to Europe or the United States to further their careers. This dislocation or exile often causes a change in their music. Just as Osibisa incorporated Caribbean influences from the musical culture of London and West Indian band-mates, Ghanaian highlife musicians in Germany integrated new stimuli into their repertoire and produced a new genre of highlife. Beginning in the late 1970s, George Darko and Lee Duodu incorporated synthesizers and electronic percussion into their music. Living in Hamburg, Germany, their style of music was nicknamed "burgher highlife," and quickly attracted many artists. Daddy Lumba was also an early name in the burgher highlife scene. He blended highlife, hip-hop, and reggae and continues to attract a strong youth following in Ghana. Though classic highlife music does not command the following it once did, its offspring continue to capture attention in Ghanaian popular music culture.

Reggae

It is not possible to discuss popular music in Ghana without looking briefly at the presence of Jamaican reggae. In the early 1980s, with the explosion of reggae superstar Bob Marley onto the international music scene, the danceable rhythms and relevant lyrics of reggae music made a strong impression on Ghanaian youth. It is not surprising that reggae caught on quickly. Previous Caribbean musical forms influenced the development of highlife music and its offspring. The lyrics of reggae music are closely tied to the liberation of all Africans from a history of oppression. Reggae music exalts the virtues of African culture and, for urban youth, provides a means of resistance against the "down-presser" man. It also offers a more "rootsy" musical alternative to the electronic music of the last few decades.

Reggae music carried with it the images of Rastafarian culture. Dreadlocked and dread-talking youth, wearing the red, gold, green, and black of the Rastafarians, can be found in Ghanaian cities, especially in the coastal areas. Society's impression of them, however, is not altogether favorable. The "Rastas' " often lower-class background and association with smoking marijuana has led many to see them as rogues and attribute the growth in illegal drug use, especially cannabis, to them. While the numbers of Rastafarians remains small, there is a sizable audience for reggae music. Attempting to change their image and contribute to the development of Ghanaian culture, the Rastafarians now hold an annual Emancipation Fair and Grand Reggae Festival to showcase talent in arts and craft, music, dance, poetry, and fashion in Accra.

Many people were happy to listen and dance to reggae music, but Ghanaian musicians also began to integrate reggae sounds into their own repertoire. Amakye Dede and Kojo Antwi, for example, have built formidable reputations in Ghana with their reggae-influenced highlife. African reggae, in general, has developed to the point where it is now a distinct musical idiom, very different from the Jamaican archetype. Another Ghanaian artist, Rocky Dawuni, sticks closer to traditional reggae music and, after coming onto the music stage in the early 1990s, has begun to make a name for himself in Ghana and abroad.

Hiplife

At the turn of the century, the most popular music in much of Ghana is hiplife. When rap and hip-hop music first developed in the United States, it attracted little attention in Ghana, but it slowly made inroads in the urban areas. Reggae still reigned as the most popular music of the youth. Today, American hip-hop and Jamaican reggae can be heard on Ghanaian radio stations and in clubs, but their most important influence is the cultural background that they have provided for new forms. Hiplife is a musical style that fuses hip-hop and rap with highlife rhythms. It is usually sung in a Ghanaian language and has become very popular. Ghanaian musicians absorbed the characteristics of hip-hop and adapted them to their own musical heritage to create a whole new musical culture. Although Gyedu Blay Ambolley was performing a form of rap in the early 1970s, hiplife emerged as a dominant force in Ghanaian youth culture in the early 1990s. Reggie Rockstone propelled hiplife into the mainstream by incorporating vernacular languages such as Twi. Rockstone's 1997 debut album, *Makaa, Maka!* ("I Said It, and That's That!"), brought the sound and language of hip-hop music to the Ghanaian masses in a localized form.

Rockstone was born in the United Kingdom, where he immersed himself into the 1980s hip-hop and rap scene. In 1994, he returned to Accra where he found a new generation of youth listening to American hip-hop and rap music. It was then that he decided to create this type of music, but sing it in Twi. His first hit, "Tsoo Boi," coined the term "hiplife." His newest album, *Me Na Me Kae*, employs both English and Twi lyrics for songs that sample a variety of musical styles. "Eye Mo De Anaa" ("Is It Sweet to Y'all?"), for example, draws from Fela Kuti's "Shakara" (1977), while "Keep Your Eyes on The Road" uses a well known highlife song from the 1970s.

Hiplife lyrics discuss common topics such as love and monetary matters, but some of them also touch on social issues like getting a visa, traveling, or unexpected pregnancy. Though undoubtedly a musical genre that appeals to the younger generation, the use of older samples and universal themes gives hiplife at least a potential appeal to a wider audience.

It quickly became evident that hiplife could be a commercially viable music form in Ghana and new artists and groups began to emerge. Part of its commercial viability came from the liberalization of the airwaves. In the mid-1990s, the government allowed the establishment of private FM stations. The new radio stations commercialized entertainment and provided a medium through which to distribute music to the masses. Many of them catered their programming schedule toward popular music and youth culture. Locally produced types of music such as highlife and gospel were common, as were imported forms such as rhythm and blues, reggae, and Western pop music. When hiplife burst onto the scene, however, it quickly took center stage and now receives the bulk of airtime on many radio stations.

At present there are a number of hiplife artists, singing in many different languages, including Twi, Ga, English, and Pidgin. The number of new artists continues to expand. Groups like V.I.P, Chicago, and Ex-Doe have been on the scene for a few years, while the latest hits by Tic Tac, Obrafo, Lord Kenya, Buk Bak, and Keteke command much airtime on local radio and attract huge audiences for live shows.

Still, there is a great deal of concern about the development of hiplife music. Hiplife remains a somewhat isolated Ghanaian musical form at this time, due in part to the language barrier and its "borrowed" beats. The music relies on samplings from other songs, many of them originally in Western forms. It, therefore, raises questions of "authenticity" and doubts as to whether it will ever assume a position next to the music of the Francophone countries on the World Beat charts. Many members of the musicians' union see hiplife music developing without a strong Ghanaian identity and believe that its reliance on foreign influences, lack of instrumentalists, and focus on individualism will make it a passing phase. Joe Mensah, past president of the Musician's Union of Ghana, recognizes that most rap forms of music imitate

African rhythm, therefore, imitation of foreign beats by Ghanaian musicians becomes a case of the "imitated copying the imitator."[19] Others, however, believe that for Ghanaian popular music to make an impact in the global market, it must continue to integrate different influences. Nana King, a musician and record producer, believes that Ghanaian youth culture today cannot be removed from American influence. He thinks, however, that hiplife has the potential to make an impact on its own: "The Ghanaian youth is so much used to the 'Yankee stuff,' but I believe in doing it the African way so if I can work to get a blend of the two, that will be perfect."[20] Whatever the future holds for Ghanaian popular music, King is probably correct in assuming that it will always blend foreign influences with local characteristics to create new and dynamic forms.

CHRISTIAN MUSIC

When Christianity began to take hold in the nineteenth century, Ghanaians sought new ways to Africanize church services by translating Christian hymns into vernacular languages and developing new styles of music that better expressed their worldviews.

Gospel Highlife

Perhaps the most common form of highlife in Ghana today is gospel music. Since the early 1970s, Charismatic, Apostolic, and Ethiopian Christian faiths have grown in great numbers, especially in the urban areas. Economic woes and government curfews in the early 1980s curtailed the musical development of many cities and led to the collapse of many bands. They also brought a surge in religious activity. By choosing to enhance the status of churches through tax breaks, and doing little to support musicians outside that structure, the government encouraged artists to move from nightclubs into churches and changed the nature of religious practice.

Unlike many of the European churches, African separatist churches employ music, dancing, and clapping to enhance the religious experience. In the late 1970s, they began to use guitars and promote gospel-highlife-pop fusions. The influx of musicians into churches in the early 1980s hastened the development of gospel highlife. The lyrics of gospel highlife are about biblical characters and are usually sung in vernacular languages. Bringing the largely male-dominated profession of musicianship into the church, gospel highlife also created a niche for female musicians and singers to practice their craft without invoking societal disapproval. The Genesis Gospel Singers, the

Daughters of Glorious Jesus, and the Tagoe Sisters are a few of the most popular female gospel highlife groups today.

Choral Music

Choral music, too, is found in the new musical expression of the Christian community particularly the African compositions for the Catholic Mass, experimental Protestant church music, and the music of spiritual churches or contemporary religious movements. It is also found in the music of the literate subculture, in the concert hall, formal parties, and parades. Choral music forms include imitative examples and recreated models, dubbed "neo-traditional art music," while others are a synthesis of Western and African models.

Many traditional Christian hymns were Africanized due to the efforts of one man, Ephraim Amu (1898–1995). After studying Western music in London, Amu began to compose church music in an African idiom. He was a preacher in the Presbyterian Church, but when he starting wearing kente cloth in the pulpit, the elders were shocked and he was forced to leave. He realized the need to Africanize church services to make them more meaningful to the mass of the population. One way of doing this was to translate and compose Christian hymns in vernacular languages. During the 1940s, when his first African hymn was performed in church, he expected to be thrown out but instead experienced quite a different reaction: "A heavenly silence descended on the congregation. I knew that I was right in thinking that African songs will appeal spiritually to illiterate members of the congregation."[21] The church authorities, however, did not see things the same way and he was removed from his teaching post at the Presbyterian Teacher Training College. The church authorities eventually realized the importance of vernacular hymns for illiterate churchgoers and the synod invited him to write more. Today, especially in the rural areas, it is not uncommon for church services to be performed entirely in the vernacular language.

Ephraim Amu also deserves the highest place among Ghanaian composers in the choral or "art music" realm. He wrote more than 200 choral compositions, of which 60 percent were in Twi, even though he was an Ewe. He used a classic palm-wine song first recorded by Kwame Asare, "Yaa Amponsah," to compose "Nnonan Ne Fa," a recreational song for students. Since it was perceived by many to be an unsuitable song for children, Amu was criticized, but it quickly became a popular song in Ghanaian schools during sporting activities. Another of Amu's compositions provided an alternative to "God Save the Queen" and "Land of Our Birth," songs popular at Empire

Day celebrations during the colonial era. Amu's song, "Yen Ara Asase Ni," expressed patriotism at a time when the colonial influence was still strong:

> This land is ours
> To us it is a priceless heritage
> Our forefathers shed their blood
> To win it for us
> It is now our turn
> To add to what they bestowed to us
> Arrogance, crookedness, and selfishness
> Have become so ingrained in our character
> Our love for our country has greatly diminished.
>
> (Chorus)
> If this nation will prosper
> If it will fall
> It is a truism
> The character of the people
> Will determine its fate.

The song became a symbol of Ghanaian pride and was sung during important events in the struggle for independence, including the 1948 shooting at the Christiansborg crossroads.

Due largely to the efforts of Amu, choral music is an extremely popular genre of music and is now pervasive in churches, theaters, and parade grounds and within particular social groups throughout Ghana. Through Amu's influence, an annual International African Choral Festival has been held at the National Theatre since 1998. The event is designed to bring together international and local choral groups to create a forum for musicians to share ideas and generate new directions in the development of choral music.

INSTITUTIONAL SUPPORT OF MUSIC AND DANCE

A number of institutions support the maintenance and development of Ghanaian music and dance forms. One of these is the International School of Music and Dance at the University of Ghana, Legon. Established in 1962, it is the preeminent institution encouraging creativity in Ghanaian music and dance forms. It teaches the theory and practice of music and dance techniques, including both Western and African forms. Attached to the Institute of African Studies, the Ghana Dance Ensemble consists of dancers, drummers, musicians, and technicians from all ethnic groups in Ghana. They learn music and dance from all regions of the country and, while maintaining the original movements, present them in a contemporary performance setting. The Ghana Dance Ensemble has performed as far away as Mexico City, and has taken extended tours of the United States and many European cities.

Ghanaian and foreign governments also support the development of Ghanaian arts. The National Commission on Culture, under the national government, provides funding for a variety of local and national festivals to promote music and dance as a means of enhancing national unity. The National Festival of Arts and Culture, for example, is held regularly in various parts of Ghana. It is a showcase of Ghanaian talent and includes traditional drumming and dancing, durbars, highlights of historical events, and cultural shrines. The festival also sponsors concerts of new Ghanaian musical styles. Foreign institutions also encourage the development of Ghanaian arts and create links with their countries. The German Goethe Institute, the French Alliance Française, and the American Embassy offer regular events showcasing music and dance groups from Ghana, Africa, and the West.

The private sector, too, assists the development of new artistic talent. Events like the Pop Chains, designed to showcase the talent of young artists, are becoming more common. Young musicians perform gospel, highlife, reggae, and hiplife songs. Mega-concerts showcase popular musicians and attract many fans to the National Theatre, the International Trade Fair Center, and the National Stadium in Accra, as well as to other venues throughout the country.

More than any other aspect of culture, the development and popularity of music and dance are encouraged by its prevalence in social customs and everyday life. Ghanaian music and dance continue to thrive through a circular process of adaptation and change. Traditional music and dance borrow from popular music and dance to create new styles. Popular styles build on traditional and neo-traditional forms and absorb outside influences, just as Christian music blends religious messages and secular genres.

NOTES

All songs were translated by the authors; notes indicate original source material.

1. Quoted in Elvis Ndubuisi Iruh, "The Songstress from Yua," *West Africa*, 4191, 18–31 May 1998, 503.

2. J.H.K. Nketia, *The Music of Africa* (New York: W.W. Norton, 1974), 7.

3. Ibid., 36.

4. J.H.K. Nketia, *Drumming in Akan Communities* (London: Thomas Nelson & Sons, 1963), 108.

5. J.H.K. Nketia, "The Role of the Drummer in Akan Society," *African Music Society Journal*, 1, 1 (1954), 37.

6. J.H.K. Nketia, "The Poetry of Akan Drums," *Black Orpheus*, 2, 2 (1968), 32.

7. Nketia, "The Role of the Drummer in Akan Society," 41.

8. Iruh, "The Songstress from Yua," 502–3.

9. Nketia, *The Music of Africa*, 129–30.

10. John Collins, *Highlife Time* (Accra: Anansesem Publications, 1996), 109.

11. John Miller Chernoff, "Africa Come Back: The Popular Music of West Africa," in Geoffrey Haydon and Dennis Marks (eds.), *Repercussions: A Celebration of African-American Music* (London: Century Publishing, 1985), 164.

12. John Collins, *Highlife Time*, 141. See also Chernoff, "Africa Come Back," 166.

13. See Collins, *Highlife Time*, 105–8.

14. Quoted in John Collins, *King of Highlife: ET Mensah* (Accra: Anansesem Publications, 1996), 2.

15. E.T. Mensah & the Tempos, *Day by Day* (Retroafric, 1994).

16. The queen was unable to come in 1959 and finally made her much anticipated trip to Ghana in 1961.

17. The first and last verses are above. Hear the full song on King Bruce and the Black Beats, *Golden Highlife Classics*, Retroafric, RETRO 13CD.

18. S. van der Geest and N.K. Asante-Darko, "The Political Meaning of Highlife Songs in Ghana," *African Studies Review*, 25, 1 (1982), 27–35.

19. "Highlife Must Have Ghanaian Identity," *Highlife Newsletter* (March 2001).

20. "Nana King's World," *UNEEK*, July/August 2000.

21. Amon Okoe, "Ahead of His Time," *Sunday Mirror*, 4 August 1963.

RECOMMENDED CDs

A.B. Crentsil and the Sweet Talks. *Hollywood Highlife Party*. P.A.M., 1997.

E.T. Mensah & the Tempos. *All for You*. Retroafric, 1990.

King Onyina. *King Onyina's Guitar Highlife*. P.A.M., 2000.

Koo Nimo. *Osabarima*. Adasa, 2000.

Mustapha Tettey Addy. *Master Drummer from Ghana*. Lyrichord, 1995.

Osibisa. *Happy Children*. One Way Records, 2000.

Various Artists. *Rhythms of Life, Songs of Wisdom: Akan Music From Ghana, West Africa*. Smithsonian Folkways, 1996.

Glossary

Aboakyer   A popular festival held annually in Winneba. Also known as the "deer hunt" festival

Abom   Garden egg (eggplant) stew

Abosom   Akan pantheon of lesser gods; also an Asante shrine closely associated with rulers

Abusua   The matrilineage in Akan society

Abusua ye dom   *Kente* cloth design meaning "the force of the extended family"

Adae   A day during the Akan calendar cycle to honor ancestors

Adaebutuw   A period of a forty-day ban on noisemaking and dancing before *odwira*

Adamu   the Ewe word for art

Adenkyem-dwa   Stool design depicting a crocodile with a fish in its mouth that represents power

Adinkra   Ceremonial cloth with stamped designs often worn at funerals

Adowa   Traditional Asante music and dance form

Aduafrol   A stew made from black-eyed peas, fried onions, tomatoes, and dried fish

Adwinasa   *Kente* design meaning "all motifs are used up"

Afa   An elaborate system of Ewe divination

Agbada   Long, flowing gown worn by men, especially Muslims

Agbekor   A drumming and dance style of the Anlo Ewe

Aggrey   High-quality beads worn by elders and chiefs

Akpade   Red clay that is spread on house doors during *homowo*

Akpeteshie　High alcohol, locally-produced gin

Akrantie　A small antelope commonly known as "grass cutter"

Akuaba　Akan fertility dolls

Akwasidae　The Sunday *adae* ceremony

Ananse　A personified spider and common character in Akan folk stories

Anansesem　The Akan word for all folktales dealing with animals

Asafo　Traditional Akan military associations

Asantehene　The Asante king

Asensie　Akan:"the place of pots," where terra-cotta portraitures of the deceased are buried

Askenkee　A derivative of "iced *kenkey*," a milky, non-alcoholic drink made from corn

Asrayere　Akan songs that were performed by women while the men were away at war

Atenteben　A bamboo flute with seven holes

Atumpan　"Talking" drums associated with Asante royalty

Awukudai　The Wednesday *adae* ceremony

Banku　A starchy food made from fermented corn

Batakari　War shirt covered with Muslim amulets and used to ward off evil spirits

Bokowo　Priests trained in the Ewe *afa* divination

Bradwom　Akan songs for female puberty rites

Bragoro　Akan female puberty rites

Bota　High-quality beads worn by elders and chiefs

Cedi　The national currency of Ghana

Damba　The new moon in the third month of the Islamic calendar marking the start of the *damba* festival

Dipo　Krobo puberty rites

Donno　An hourglass-shaped drum with a varying pitch

Dzinto　Akan outdoor ceremony when children are presented to the community

Eboore　Gonja Supreme God

Fontomfrom　Tall drums used with the *atumpan* drums to praise Asante chiefs

Fufu　A starchy food made with pounded yam, plantains, or cassava

Fugu　An oversize smock usually worn with long pants

Fumsoa　An Akan ritual used to detect those involved in suspicious deaths

Gome　A large, square-framed drum played with both hands and feet

Gonje A single-string fiddle from northern Ghana

Gye Nyame Popular *adinkra* symbol meaning "except God"

Gyil A pentatonically tuned xylophone consisting of wooden blocks mounted over calabash gourds

Halo A form of Ewe performance poetry that no longer enjoys much popularity

Hogbetsotso An Anlo Ewe festival celebrating the group's exodus from northern Togo

Homowo The annual Ga festival to commemorate the dead

Jollof rice A tomato and rice dish made in a single pot

Kaba A type of blouse usually worn with a skirt

Kanbonwaa A music and dance style of the Dagomba

Kenkey A starchy food made from cornmeal

Kente Expensive ceremonial cloth made by the Akan and the Ewe

Kla The life force of an individual in Ga society

Kofi broke man A dish of roasted plantains and groundnuts

Kologo A two-stringed guitar

Kontomire A stew made from spinach and *egusi* seeds

Kpanlogo A popular drum used in festivals, funerals, and naming ceremonies; also a neo-folk style of drumming and dancing

Kpekpei Steamed, unleavened corn dough that is served with palm soup

Kpodziemo Ga outdoor ceremony when children are presented to the community

Kuduo A metal urn used by the Akan

Kuntunkuni An older, obviously aged black cloth worn at the funeral of an important family member

Lapa A two-yard piece of cloth wrapped around the body

Mantse Ga chief

Mawu Ewe Supreme God

Mogya The blood of an Akan mother that binds her children to the matrilineage

Naa damba The second *damba* festival celebrating the naming of the Prophet Mohammed

Nteewa A popular children's game

Ntoro An Akan father's contribution to the personality and morality of a young child

Nwuni Mamprusi Supreme God

Nyoli Beads associated with priestesses

Nyonmo Ga Supreme God

Obaakofo mmu man   *Kente* cloth design meaning "one person does not rule a nation"

Obroni wawu   Second-hand clothing markets

Odwira   Annual Akan festival to celebrate the harvest and pay tribute to the ancestors

Ohene   An Akan chief

Okra (kra)   The spiritual part of humans, similar to a soul, in Akan society

Okyeame   A spokesperson or orator in Akan society; also the name of a literary magazine

Omo tuo   Rice balls commonly served with palm or groundnut soup

Onyame   Akan Supreme God

Osibisaba   A traditional rhythm that was precursor to highlife music

Pito   A fermented, low-alcohol drink made from Guinea corn

Posuban   Elaborate shrines associated with Fante *asafo* companies

Prempremsiwa   A large rectangular box instrument with three metal prongs

Ramadan   Muslim month of fasting

Sankofa   Popular *adinkra* symbol meaning "go back and fetch it"

Seprewa   A traditional harp lute of the Akan

Shito   A hot pepper sauce served as an accompaniment to many foods

Sika futuro   *Kente* cloth design meaning "gold dust"

Simpa   A neo-folk drum and dance style of the Dagbon

Somba damba   First *damba* festival marking the birth of the Prophet Mohammed

Sunna   Dagomba outdooring ceremony when children are presented to the community

Sunsum   Akan spirit that makes up individual character and personality

Susuma   The Ga unconscious mind that maintains the physical and psychological continuity of an individual between life and death

Tovi   Beads associated with priestesses

Tariqa   Muslim brotherhood

Toku kra toma   *Kente* cloth design meaning "Toku's soul cloth"

Trokosi   The giving of a young girl to the priest of a fetish shrine

Trowo   Ewe pantheon of lesser gods

Tuo zaafi   A starchy ball made from corn flour and served with a "slippery" okra stew

Vihehedego Ewe outdoor ceremony when children are presented to the community

Waakye Rice and beans mixed together with a bit of fried meat

Wodzi Ga pantheon of lesser gods

Wulomei Ga fetish priests; also the name of a band

Bibliographic Essay

Many of the books and essays used in the writing of this book have been published in Ghana and have seen only limited distribution. As they are difficult to find outside of the country, we have included only the most important of these as well as those that we have consulted as sources.

GENERAL

There are numerous general works about Ghanaian and African cultures and customs. These include: Philip G. Altbach and Salah M. Hassan (eds.), *The Muse of Modernity: Essays on Culture as Development in Africa* (Trenton, NJ: Africa World Press, 1996); Mary Jo Arnoldi, Christraud M. Geary & Kris L. Hardin (eds.), *African Material Culture* (Bloomington: Indiana University Press, 1996); Molefi Kete Asante and Kariamu Welsh Asante (eds.), *African Cultures: The Rhythms of Unity* (Westport, CT: Greenwood, 1985); Eric O. Ayisi, *An Introduction to the Study of African Culture* (London: Heinemann, 1972); William R. Bascom and J. Herskovits (eds.), *Continuity and Change in African Cultures* (Chicago: University of Chicago Press, 1959); Louis P. Bowler, *Gold Coast Palaver: Life on the Gold Coast* (London: J. Long, 1911); Roy Richard Grinker and Christopher B. Steiner (eds.), *Perspectives on Africa: A Reader in Culture, History, and Representation* (Cambridge, MA: Blackwell, 1997); John Kuada and Yao Chachah, *Ghana: Understanding the People and Their Culture* (Accra: Woeli Publishing, 1999); Jacob K. Olupona (ed.), *African Spirituality: Forms, Meanings, and Expressions* (New York: Crossroad, 2000); David Owusu-Ansah, *Historical Dictionary of Ghana* (Metuchen, NJ: Scarecrow Press, 1995); John Mensah Sarbah, *Fanti Customary Laws: A Brief Introduction to the Principles of the Native Laws and Customs of the Fanti and Akan Districts of the Gold Coast* (London: Cass, 1968); B.K. Swartz and Raymond E. Dumett (eds.), *West African Culture Dynamics:*

Archaeological and Historical Perspectives (New York: Mouton, 1980); Hope B. Werness, *The Continuum Encyclopedia of Native Art: Worldview, Symbolism, and Culture in Africa, Oceania, and Native North America* (New York: Continuum, 2000); and Kwesi Wiredu, *Philosophy and an African Culture* (Cambridge: Cambridge University Press, 1980). Brief biographies on important personalities in Ghanaian history can be found in Kojo T. Vieta, *The Flagbearers of Ghana: Profiles of One Hundred Distinguished Ghanaians* (Accra: Ena Publications, 1999).

INTRODUCTION

Individual groups and local histories are discussed in numerous works. For the Anlo-Ewe, see Sandra E. Greene, *Gender, Ethnicity, and Social Change on the Upper Slave Coast: A History of the Anlo-Ewe* (Portsmouth, NH: Heinemann, 1996). On the early history of the Krobo, see Louis E. Wilson, *The Krobo People of Ghana to 1892: A Political and Social History* (Athens: Ohio University Press, 1991). Although more limited than other regions, there are a number of works on the northern areas. These include: J.A. Braimah, H.H. Tomlinson, and Osafroadu Amankwatia, *History and Traditions of the Gonja* (Calgary: University of Calgary Press, 1997); A.W. Cardinall, *The Natives of the Northern Territories of the Gold Coast: Their Customs, Religion, and Folklore* (New York: Negro Universities Press, 1969); Esther N. Goody, *Contexts of Kinship: An Essay in the Family Sociology of the Gonja of Northern Ghana* (Cambridge: Cambridge University Press, 1973); and Eugene L. Mendonsa, *The Politics of Divination: A Processual View of Reactions to Illness and Deviance Among the Sisala of Northern Ghana* (Berkeley: University of California Press, 1982). No Ghanaian group has received more scholarly attention than the Akan, and particularly the Asante. A few of these works include: Joseph K. Adjaye, *Diplomacy and Diplomats in Nineteenth Century Asante* (Lanham, MD: University Press of America, 1984); Sara S. Berry, *Chiefs Know Their Boundaries: Essays on Property, Power, and the Past in Asante, 1896–1996* (Portsmouth, NH: Heinemann, 2001); Robert B. Edgerton, *The Fall of the Asante Empire: The Hundred-Year War for Africa's Gold Coast* (New York: The Free Press, 1995); Daryll Forde and P.M. Kaberry (eds.), *West African Kingdoms in the Nineteenth Century* (London: Oxford University Press, 1967); John K. Fynn, *Asante and Its Neighbours, 1700–1807* (London: Longman, 1971); T.E. Kyei, *Our Days Dwindle: Memories of My Childhood Days in Asante* (Portsmouth, NH: Heinemann, 2001); T.C. McCaskie, *State and Society in Pre-Colonial Asante* (Cambridge: Cambridge University Press, 1995); T.C. McCaskie, *Asante Identities: History and Modernity in an African Village, 1850–1950* (Bloomington: Indiana University Press, 2000); Minion K.C. Morrison, *Ethnicity and Political Integration: The Case of Ashanti, Ghana* (Syracuse, NY: Maxwell School of Citizenship and Public Affairs, 1982); Enid Schildkrout (ed.), *The Golden Stool: Studies of the Asante Center and Periphery*, Anthropological Papers of the American Museum of Natural History, 65:1 (New York: American Museum of Natural History, 1987); Ivor G. Wilks, *Asante in the Nineteenth Century: The Structure and Evolution of a Political Order* (London: Cambridge University Press, 1975); and Ivor

G. Wilks, *Forests of Gold: Essays on the Akan and the Kingdom of Asante* (Athens: Ohio University Press, 1993). For a discussion of Ga history and culture, see M.E. Kropp Dakubu, *Korle Meets the Sea: A Socio-Linguistic History of Accra* (New York: Oxford University Press, 1997); M.J. Field, *Religion and Medicine of the Ga People* (London: Oxford University Press, 1937; M.J. Field, *Social Organization of the Ga People* (London: Crown Agents for the Colonies 1940); Marion Kilson, *African Urban Kinsmen: The Ga of Central Accra* (New York: St. Martin's Press, 1974); and John Parker, *Making the Town: Ga State and Society in Early Colonial Accra* (Portsmouth, NH: Heineman, 2000). Two works portray various aspects of the historical development in the Cape Coast area: J. Hinderdink and J. Sterkenburg, *Anatomy of an African Town: A Socio-economic Study of Cape Coast, Ghana* (Utrecht: State University of Utrecht, 1975); and Christopher R. DeCorse, *An Archaeology of Elmina: Africans and Europeans on the Gold Coast, 1400–1900* (Washington, DC: Smithsonian Institution Press, 2001). The best book on rural-urban migration is John C. Caldwell, *African Rural-Urban Migration: The Movement to Ghana's Towns* (New York: Columbia University Press, 1969). For a specific discussion of Muslim immigration and identity, see Enid Schildkrout, *People of the Zongo: The Transformation of Ethnic Identities in Ghana* (Cambridge: Cambridge University Press, 1978). Various aspects of language have received scholarly attention. These include: M.E. Kropp Dakubu (ed.), *The Languages of Ghana* (London: Kegan Paul for the International African Institute, 1988); M.E. Kropp Dakubu, *Korle Meets the Sea: A Sociolinguistic History of Accra* (New York: Oxford University Press, 1997). Magnus Huber, *Ghanaian Pidgin English in Its West African Context: A Sociohistorical and Structural Analysis* (Amsterdam: J. Benjamins, 1999); Colin Painter, *Gonja: A Phonological and Grammatical Study* (Bloomington: Indiana University Press, 1970); and Diedrich Westermann, *A Study of the Ewe Language*, trans. A.L. Bickford-Smith (London: Oxford University Press, 1954). For a more general work on the role of ethnicity in identity and political formation, see Carola Lentz and Paul Nugent (eds.), *Ethnicity in Ghana: The Limits of Invention* (Hampshire: Macmillan, 2000).

Ghana's importance in the history of Africa is evidenced by the range and number of books that have been published. On the general history, see Basil Davidson, *Ghana: An African Portrait* (Millerton, NY: Aperture, 1976); J.D. Fage, *Ghana: A Historical Interpretation* (Madison: University of Wisconsin Press, 1966); David Owusu-Ansah and Daniel M. McFarland, *Historical Dictionary of Ghana*, 2nd ed. (Metuchen, NJ: Scarecrow Press, 1995); and W.E.F. Ward, *A History of Ghana* (London: George Allen and Unwin, 1969, first published in 1948). For more detailed works on precolonial history, see W. Walton Claridge, *A History of the Gold Coast and Ashanti, from the Earliest Times to the Commencement of the Twentieth Century*, 2nd ed. (New York: Barnes & Noble, 1964); K.Y. Daaku, *Trade and Politics on the Gold Coast, 1600–1720: A Study of the African Reaction to European Trade* (London: Clarendon, 1970); Ray A. Kea, *Settlements, Trade, and Polities in the Seventeenth-Century Gold Coast* (Baltimore: Johns Hopkins University Press, 1982); Thomas McCaskie, *State and Society in Precolonial Asante* (Cambridge: Cambridge University Press, 1995); Eva L.R Meyerowitz, *The Early History of the Akan States of Ghana* (London: Red Candle Press, 1974); and John Vogt, *Portuguese Rule on the Gold Coast, 1469–1682* (Athens: University of Georgia Press, 1979). The colonial era in Ghana has received much attention. The most prominent books include: Francis Agbodeka, *African Politics and British Policy in the Gold Coast, 1868–1900* (Evanston, IL: Northwestern University Press, 1971); A. Adu Boahen, *Ghana: Evolution and Change in the Nineteenth and Twentieth Centuries* (London: Longman. 1975); Raymond E. Dumett, *El Dorado in West Africa: The Gold-Mining Frontier, African Labor, and Colonial Capitalism in the Gold Coast, 1875–1900* (Athens: Ohio University Press, 1998); Roger S. Gocking, *Facing Two Ways: Ghana's Coastal Communities Under Colonial Rule* (Lanham, MD: University Press of America, 1999); and David Kimble, *A Political History of Ghana: The Rise of Gold Coast Nationalism, 1850–1928* (Oxford: Clarendon Press, 1963). On Ghanaian society and politics during the period of transition to independence, see Jean Marie Allman, *The Quills of the Porcupine: Asante Nationalism in an Emergent Ghana* (Madison: University of Wisconsin Press, 1993); David E. Apter, *Gold Coast in Transition*, later published as *Ghana in Transition* (New York: Atheneum, 1963); Dennis Austin, *Politics in Ghana, 1946–1960* (London: Oxford University Press, 1964); and Thomas Hodgkin, *Nationalism in Colonial Africa* (London: Muller, 1956). The rise and fall of Kwame Nkrumah has been documented in a number of works. See, for example: Basil Davidson, *Black Star: A View of the Life and Times of Kwame Nkrumah* (Boulder, CO: Westview Press, 1989); Bob Fitch and Mary Oppenheimer, *Ghana: End of an Illusion* (New York: Monthly Review Press, 1968); Trevor Jones, *Ghana's First Republic 1960–1966: The Pursuit of the Political Kingdom* (London: Methuen, 1976); and T. Peter Omari, *Kwame Nkrumah: The Anatomy of an African Dictatorship* (New York: Africana Publishing Co., 1970); Kwame Nkrumah was also a prolific writer and authored many works, including: *The Autobiography of Kwame Nkrumah* (Edinburgh: T. Nelson, 1957); *I Speak of Freedom: A Statement of African Ideology* (New York: Praeger, 1961); *Africa Must Unite* (New York: Praeger, 1963); *Consciencism: Philosophy and Ideology of Decolonization and Development with Particular Reference to the African Revolution* (London: Heinemann, 1964); and *Neo-colonialism: The Last Stage of Imperialism* (London: Nelson, 1965). Africanists have continued to take great interest in the history, politics, and economy of Ghana since 1966, producing works that include: T.E. Anin, *Essays on the Political Economy of Ghana* (Accra: Selwyn, 1991); Dennis Austin and Robin Luckham (eds.), *Politicians and Soldiers in Ghana, 1966–1972* (London: Frank Cass, 1976); E. Gyimah-Boadi (ed.), *Ghana Under PNDC Rule, 1982–1989* (Dakar: Codesria, 1993); A. Adu, Boahen, *The Ghanaian Sphinx: Reflections on the Contemporary History of Ghana, 1972–1987* (Westport, CT: Greenwood Press, 1989); Emmanuel Hansen, *Ghana Under Rawlings* (Oxford: Malthouse, 1991); Jeffrey Herbst, *The Politics of Reform in Ghana, 1982–1991* (Berkeley: University of California Press, 1993); M.M. Huq, *The Economy of Ghana: The First 25 Years Since Independence* (New York: St. Martin's Press, 1989); Paul Nugent, *Big Men, Small Boys and Politics in Ghana: Power, Ideology and the Burden of History, 1982–1994* (London: Pinter, 1995); Mike Oquaye, *Politics in Ghana, 1972–1979* (Accra: Tornado, 1980); Maxwell Owusu, *Uses and Abuses of*

Political Power: A Case Study of Continuity and Change in the Politics of Ghana (Chicago: University of Chicago Press, 1970); Deborah Pellow and Naomi Chazan, *Ghana: Coping with Uncertainty* (Boulder, CO: Westview Press, 1986); Robert Pickney, *Ghana under Military Rule: 1966–1969* (London: Methuen, 1972); Donald Ray, *Ghana: Politics, Economics and Society* (Boulder, CO: Lynne Rienner, 1986); Douglas Rimmer, *Staying Poor: Ghana's Political Economy, 1950–1990* (Oxford: Pergamon Press, 1992); and Kevin Shillington, *Ghana and the Rawlings Factor* (New York: St. Martin's Press, 1992).

RELIGION AND WORLDVIEW

For general books on indigenous African religion and worldview, see Noel King, *African Cosmos: An Introduction to Religion in Africa* (Belmont, CA: Wadsworth Publishing Co., 1986); John Mbiti, *Introduction to African Religion* (London: Heinemann Educational Books, 1979); John Mbiti, *African Religions and Philosophy* (Garden City, NY: Anchor Books, 1970); and S. Ottenberg (ed.), *African Religious Groups and Beliefs* (Meernt, India: Archana Publications for Folklore Institute, 1982). On Ghanaian indigenous religious beliefs and practices, see Kofi Appiah-Kubi, *Man Cures, God Heals: Religion and Medical Practice among the Akans of Ghana* (Totowa, NJ: Allanheld, 1981); J.M. Assimeng (ed.), *Traditional Life, Culture, and Literature in Ghana* (New York: Conch Magazine Ltd., 1976); Kwame Bediako, *Theology and Identity* (Oxford: Regnum Books, 1992); J.B. Danquah, *The Akan Doctrine of God: A Fragment of Gold Coast Ethics and Religion* (London: White Friars Press, 1968); Margaret J. Field, *Religion and Medicine of the Ga People* (London: Oxford University Press, 1937); Thomas McCaskie, "Komfo Anokye of Asante: Meaning, History and Philosophy in an African Society," *Journal of African History* 27:2 (1986), 315–39; Ebenezer Obiri Addo, *Kwame Nkrumah: A Case Study of Religion and Politics in Ghana* (Lanham, MD: University Press of America, 1997); Stephen Owoahene-Acheampong, *Inculturation and African Religion: Indigenous and Western Approaches to Medical Practice* (New York: Peter Lang, 1998); J.S. Pobee (ed.), *Religion in a Pluralistic Society* (Leiden: E.J. Brill, 1976); R.S. Rattray, *Religion and Art in Ashanti* (Oxford: Oxford Clarendon Press, 1923); and Harry Sawyerr, *God, Ancestor or Creator? Aspects of Traditional Belief in Ghana, Nigeria & Sierra Leone* (Harlow: Longmans, 1970). Works dealing with the spiritual worlds of the ancestors and witchcraft include: Elizabeth Colson, "The Father as Witch," *Africa*, 70:3 (2000), 333–58; Peter Geschiere, *The Modernity of Witchcraft: Politics and the Occult in Postcolonial Africa* (Charlottesville: University Press of Virginia, 1997); D.J.E. Maier, *Priests and Power: The Case of the Dente Shrine in Nineteenth-Century Ghana* (Bloomington: Indiana University Press, 1983); T.C. McCaskie, "Anti-Witchcraft Cult in Asante: An Essay in the Social History of an African People," *History of Africa*, 8 (1981), 125–54; Jane Parish, "The Dynamics of Witchcraft and Indigenous Shrines Among the Akan," *Africa*, 69:3 (1999), 427–47; and Judy Rosenthal, *Possession, Ecstasy, and Law in Ewe Voodoo* (Charlottesville: University Press of Virginia, 1998). On the importance of music and performance in Ghanaian religious practice, see Marion

Kilson, *KpeleLala: Ga Religious Songs and Symbols* (Cambridge: Harvard University Press, 1971); and Lawrence E. Sullivan (ed.), *Enchanting Powers: Music in the World's Religions* (Cambridge, MA: Harvard University Press for the Harvard University Center for the Study of World Religions, 1997).

Many authors have looked at the impact of Christianity on Ghanaian religious beliefs. Some of their works are: Nano O. Dankwa III, *Christianity and African Traditional Beliefs* (Jamaica, NY: Power of the Word Publishing Company, 1990); H.W. Debrunner, *A History of Christianity in Ghana* (Accra: Waterville, 1967); Kwesi A. Dickson (ed.), *Akan Religion and the Christian Faith: A Comparative Study of the Impact of Two Religions* (Accra: Universities Press, 1965); C.P. Groves, *The Planting of Christianity in Africa*, 4 vols. (London: Lutterworth Press, 1954); O.U. Kalu, *The History of Christianity in West Africa* (London: Longman, 1980); Birgit Meyer, *Translating the Devil: Religion and Modernity Among the Ewe in Ghana* (Edinburgh: Edinburgh University Press, 1999); Pashington Obeng, *Asante Catholicism: Religious and Cultural Reproduction among the Akan of Ghana* (New York: E.J. Brill, 1996); and J.S. Pobee (ed.), *Religion in a Pluralistic Society* (Leiden: E.J. Brill, 1976). The surge in Pentecostal churches and their influence on other forms of culture in Ghana has received attention from various scholars. See, for example: Rosalind Hackett, "Charismatic/Pentecostal Appropriation of Media Technologies in Nigeria and Ghana," *Journal of Religion in Africa*, 27:3 (1998), 258–77; Birgit Meyer, "Make a Complete Break with the Past: Memory and Post-Colonial Modernity in Ghanaian Pentecostalist Discourse," *Journal of Religion in Africa*, 27:3 (1998), 316–49; Birgit Meyer, "Commodities and Power of Prayer: Pentecostalist Attitudes Toward Consumption in Contemporary Ghana," *Development and Change*, 29 (1998), 751–76; and Robert W. Wyllie, "Pioneers of Ghanaian Pentecostalism: Peter Anim and James McKeown," *Journal of Religion in Africa*, 6:2 (1974), 109–2. The Seventh-Day Adventists are discussed in Kofi Owusu-Mensa, *Saturday God and Adventism in Ghana* (Frankfurt: P. Lang, 1993).

Writings on Islam in Ghana are many and include: Peter B. Clarke, *West Africa and Islam: A Study of Religious Development from the 8th to the 20th Century* (London: Edward Arnold, 1982); David Owusu-Ansah, *The Islamic Talismanic Tradition in Nineteenth-Century Asante* (Lewiston, NY: Edwin Mellen Press, 1991); Lamin Sanneh, *The Crown and the Turban: Muslims and West African Pluralism* (Boulder, CO: Westview, 1997); Enid Schildkrout, *Islam and Politics in Kumasi: An Analysis of Disputes over the Kumasi Central Mosque* (New York: American Museum of Natural History, 1974); J. Spencer Trimingham, *A History of Islam in West Africa* (Oxford: Oxford University Press, 1970); Ivor Wilks, *Wa and the Wala: Islam and Polity in Northwestern Ghana* (Cambridge: Cambridge University Press, 1989); and Ivor Wilks, Nehemia Levtzion, and Bruce M. Haight, *Chronicles from Gonja: A Tradition of West African Muslim Historiography* (Cambridge: Cambridge University Press, 1986).

LITERATURE AND MEDIA

For general works on African and Ghanaian literatures, see B.W. Andrzejewski, S. Pilaszewicz, and W. Tyloch (eds.), *Literatures in African Languages* (London: Cambridge University Press, 1985); Kofi Anyidoho, Abena P.A. Busia, Anne V. Adams (eds.), *Beyond Survival: African Literature & the Search for New Life* (Trenton, NJ: Africa World Press, 1999); Ruth Finnegan, *Oral Literature in Africa* (Oxford: Oxford University Press, 1970); J. de Grandsaigne (ed.), *African Short Stories in English: An Anthology* (New York: St. Martin's Press, 1985); Stephanie Newell (ed.), *Writing African Women* (London: Zed Books, 1997); Isidore Okpewho, *African Oral Literature* (Bloomington: Indiana University Press, 1992); Oyekan Owomoyela, *African Literatures: An Introduction* (Waltham, MA: Crossroads Press, 1979); and *A History of Twentieth-Century African Literatures* (Lincoln: University of Nebraska Press, 1993); and Richard Priebe (ed.), *Ghanaian Literatures* (Westport, CT: Greewood Press, 1988).

There are many books on the various forms of oral literature. Analyses and examples of folktales can be found, for example, in: Peter Adotey Addo, *Ghana Folk Tales: Ananse Stories from Africa* (New York: Exposition Press, 1968); Peggy Appiah, *Ananse the Spider: Tales from an Ashanti Village* (New York: Pantheon Books, 1966); Paul Radin (ed.) *African Folk Tales* (New York: Schocken Books, 1983); R.S. Rattray, *Akan-Ashanti Folktales* (London: Oxford University Press, 1930); and Jessica Souhami, *The Leopard's Drum: An Asante Tale from West Africa* (Boston: Little, Brown, 1995). A few works that discuss oral poetry and proverbs include: Daniel K. Avorgbedor, "It's a Great Song! *Halo* Performance as Literary Production," *Research in African Literatures*, 32:2 (2001), 17–43; Kofi Awoonor, *Guardians of the Sacred Word* (New York: Nok, 1974); Enock Azu, *Adangbe Historical and Proverbial Songs* (Accra: Gold Coast Government Printing Office, 1929); Ulli Beier and Gerald Moore (eds.), *Modern Poetry from Africa* (Harmondsworth: Penguin, 1966); Stella and Frank Chipasula (eds.), *The Heinemann Book of African Women's Poetry* (London: Heinemann, 1995); James Boyd Christensen, "The Role of Proverbs in Fante Culture," in E.P. Skinner (ed.), *Peoples and Cultures of Africa* (Garden City, NY: Doubleday, 1973), 509–24; S.S. Dseagu. "Proverbs and Folktales of Ghana," in J.M. Assimeng (ed.), *Traditional Life, Culture and Literature in Ghana* (New York: Conch Magazine Ltd, 1976); N.K. Dzobo, *African Proverbs: Guide to Conduct, Vol. 1* (Cape Coast, Ghana: University of Cape Coast, 1973); J.H.K. Nketia, *Funeral Dirges of the Akan People* (New York: Negro Universities Press, 1969); Mercy Amba Oduyoye, "The Asante Woman: Socialization Through Proverbs, Part I, *African Notes*, 8:1 (1979), 5–11; R.S. Rattray, *Ashanti Proverbs* (Oxford: Clarendon Press, 1916); Kwesi Yankah, *The Proverb in the Context of Akan Rhetoric: A Theory of Proverb Praxis* (Bern: Peter Lang, 1989); and Kwesi Yankah, *Speaking for the Chief: Okyeame and the Politics of Akan Royal Oratory* (Bloomington: Indiana University Press, 1995). For the interaction of oral literature and music, see J.K. Nketia, *Drumming in Akan Communities* (London: Thomas Nelson and Sons, 1963).

Many Ghanaians have published poems, novels, and short stories. It is impossible to list them all here, but the most important of them include the many novels by Ayi Kwei Armah: *The Beautyful One Are Not Yet Born* (Boston: Houghton Mifflin, 1968); *Why Are We So Blest?* (Garden City, NY: Doubleday, 1972); *Two Thousand Seasons* (Nairobi: East African Publishing House, 1973); *The Healers: An Historical Novel* (London: Heinemann, 1978); and *Osiris Rising: A Novel of Africa Past, Present and Future* (Popenguine, West Africa: Per Ankh, 1995). Novels and plays by other Ghanaian writers include: Kofi Awoonor, *This Earth My Brother* (London: Heinemann, 1972); K.A. Bediako (pseud. Asare Konadu), *Don't Leave Me Mercy!!* (Accra: Anowuo Educational Publishers, 1966); J. Benibengor Blay, *Conconut Boy* (Accra: West African Publishing, 1970); Cameron Duodu, *The Gab Boys* (London: Andre Deutsch, 1967); and Kobina Sekyi, *The Blinkards* (London: Heinemann, 1974). Ghana's best known poets are Ama Ata Aidoo and Kofi Anyidoho. Aidoo's works include: *No Sweetness Here* (Garden City, NY: Anchor Books, 1972); *Changes: A Love Story* (London: Women's Press, 1991); and *An Angry Letter in January and Other Poems* (Coventry, UK: Dangaroo Press, 1992). Those by Kofi Anyidoho are: *Elegy for the Revolution* (New York: Greenfield Review Press, 1978); *A Harvest of Our Dreams* (London: Heinemann, 1984); and *Earthchild, with Brain Surgery* (Accra: Woeli, 1985). Ama Ata Aidoo and Ayi Kwei Armah have also been the subjects of many works of literary analysis. On Ama Ata Aidoo, see Vincent O. Odamtten, *The Art of Ama Ata Aidoo: Polylectics and Reading Against Neocolonialism* (Gainesville: University Press of Florida, 1994); and Ada Uzoamaka Azodo and Gay Wilentz (eds.), *Emerging Perspectives on Ama Ata Aidoo* (Trenton, NJ: Africa World Press, 1999). For books about Armah, see Robert Fraser, *The Novels of Ayi Kwei Armah: A Study in Polemical Fiction* (London: Heinemann, 1980); Tommie L. Jackson, *The Existential Fiction of Ayi Kwei Armah, Albert Camus, and Jean-Paul Sartre* (Lanham, MD: University Press of America, 1996); Ode Ogede, *Ayi Kwei Armah, Radical Iconoclast: Pitting Imaginary Worlds Against the Actual* (Athens: Ohio University Press, 2000); K. Damodar Rao, *The Novels of Ayi Kwei Armah* (New Delhi: Prestige Books, 1993); Derek Wright, *Ayi Kwei Armah's Africa: The Sources of His Fiction* (London: Hans Zell Publishers, 1989); and Derek Wright (ed.), *Critical Perspective on Ayi Kwei Armah* (Washington, DC: Three Continents Press, 1992). For discussions of Ghanaian popular literature, see Ime Ikiddeh, "The Character of Popular Fiction in Ghana," in Christopher Heywood (ed.), *Perspectives on African Literature* (London: Heinemann, 1971), 106–16; Richard K. Priebe, "Popular Writing in Ghana: A Sociological and a Rhetoric," *Research in African Literatures*, 9:3 (1978), 395–432; Richard Priebe (ed.), *Ghanaian Literatures* (Westport, CT: Greewood Press, 1988); and Stephanie Newell, *Ghanaian Popular Fiction: "Thrilling Discoveries in Conjugal Life" & Other Tales* (Oxford: J. Currey, 2000).

The history and impact of drama can be found in: Kofi Agovi, "The Origin of Literary Theater in Colonial Ghana, 1920–1957," *Research Review*, Institute of African Studies, Legon, 6:1 (1990), 1–23; Ben Halm, *Theatre and Ideology* (Cranbury, NJ: Associated University Presses, 1995); Scott Kennedy, *In Search of African Theatre* (New York: Scribner, 1973); David Kerr, *African Popular Theatre: From Pre-Colonial times to the Present Day* (London: James Currey, 1995); and Sophia Lokko, "Theatre

Space: A Historical Overview of the Theatre Movement in Ghana," *Modern Drama*, 23:3 (1980), 309–29. For some of Efua Sutherland's plays, see *The Road Makers* (Accra: Ghana Information Services, 1961); *Playtime in Africa* (New York: Athenaeum, 1962); *Edufa* (London: Longman, 1967); *The Marriage of Anansewa* (London: Longman, 1975); Some of her plays have also been published in Fredric M. Litto (ed.), *Plays From Black Africa* (New York: Hill and Wang, 1968). The Concert party genre has received considerable scholarly attention in various works. These include: Kwabena Bame, *Come to Laugh: African Traditional Theatre in Ghana* (New York: Lillian Barber, 1985); Karin Barber, John Collins, and Alain Ricard, *West African Popular Theatre* (Bloomington: Indiana University Press, 1997); Catherine M. Cole, *Ghana's Concert Party Theatre* (Bloomington: Indiana University Press, 2001); and Efua Sutherland, *The Original Bob: The Story of Bob Johnson, Ghana's Ace Comedian* (Accra: Anowuo Educational Publications, 1970). The development of Ghanaian media is discussed in Clement E. Asante, *The Press in Ghana: Problems and Prospects* (Lanham, MD: University Press of America, 1996); Louise M. Bourgault, *Mass Media in Sub-Saharan Africa* (Bloomington: Indiana University Press, 1995); William A. Hachten, *Muffled Drums: The News Media in Africa* (Ames: Iowa State University Press, 1971); K.A.B. Jones-Quartey, *History, Politics and the Early Press in Ghana* (Accra: Assembly Press, 1975); Ernest Asamoah, *50 Years of Broadcasting in Ghana* (Accra: Arakan Printing, 1985); and UNESCO, *An African Experiment in Radio Forums for Rural Development, Ghana,1964/1965* (Paris: UNESCO, 1968).

ART AND ARCHITECTURE/HOUSING

For a discussion of the various form and functions of Ghanaian art, see Emmanuel V. Asihene, *Introduction to the Traditional Art of Western Africa* (London: Constable, 1972); Emmanuel V. Asihene, *Understanding the Traditional Art of Ghana* (London: Associated University Presses, 1978); Daniel P. Biebuyck, *Symbolism of the Lega Stool: An Ethnoscientific Approach to Akan Arts and Aesthetics* (Philadelphia: Institute for the Study of Human Issues, 1977); Timothy F. Garrard, *Akan Weights and the Gold Trade* (London: Longman, 1980); Lawrence Grobel, "Ghana's Vincent Kofi," *African Arts*, 3:4 (1970), 8–11, 68–70; Vincent Kofi, *Sculpture in Ghana* (Accra: Ghana Information Services, 1964); Olu Oguibe, "Anatsui: Beyond Death and Nothingness," *African Arts*, 31: 1 (1998), 48–55; George Nelson Preston, "People Making Portraits Making People: Living Icons of the Akan," *African Arts*, 23:3 (1990), 70–77; R.S. Rattray, *Religion and Art in Ashanti* (Oxford: Oxford Clarendon Press, 1927); Monica Blackmun Visona et al., *A History of Art in Africa* (New York: Harry N. Abrams, Inc., 2001); and Frank Willet, *African Art* (New York: Thames and Hudson, 1993). Scholars who have published studies on textile art include: Peter Adler and Nicholas Barnard, *African Majesty: Textile Art of the Ashanti and Ewe* (London: Thames and Hudson, 1992); Diane V. Horn, *African Printed Textile Designs* (Washington, DC: Stemmer House Publ., 1996); and Doran H. Ross et al., *Wrapped in Pride: Ghanaian Kente and African American Identity* (University of California Museum of Cultural History Textile Series, No. 2, 1998). For an excellent discussion and numerous photos of customized coffins, see Thierry Secretan, *Going Into Darkness: Fantastic Coffins from Africa* (London: Thames and Hudson, 1995; and Carol Beckworth, "Fantasy Coffins of Ghana," *National Geographic* (September 1994), 120–32.

Various aspects of traditional architecture have been studied in detail. See, for example: Nnamidi Elleh, *African Architecture: Evolution and Transformation* (New York: McGraw-Hill, 1997); Labelle Prussin, *Architecture in Northern Ghana: A Study of Forms and Function* (Berkeley: University of California Press 1969); Labell Prussin, *African Nomadic Architecture: Space, Place, and Gender* (Washington DC: Smithsonian Institution Press, 1997). Urban architecture has been discussed in: Claude Daniel Ardouin, *Museums and Archaeology in West Africa* (Washington DC: Smithsonian Institution Press, 1997); Janet Hess, "Imagining Architecture: The Structure of Nationalism in Accra, Ghana," *Africa Today*, 47:2 (2000), 35–58; and Janet Hess, "Exhibiting Ghana: Display, Documentary, and 'National Art' in the Nkrumah Era," *African Studies Review*, 4:1 (2001), 59–77. Some aspects of housing conditions, materials, and design can be found in various works. These include: J. Hinderink, *Anatomy of an African Town: A Socio-economic Study of Cape Coast* (Utrecht: State University of Utrecht, 1975); Tariku Farrar, *Building Technology and Settlement Planning in a West African Civilization: Precolonial Akan Cities and Towns* (Lewiston, NY: E. Mellen Press, 1996); K. Konadu-Agyemang, *The Political Economy of Housing and Urban Development in Accra* (Westport, CT: Praeger, 2001); D. Korboe and A.G. Ripple, "Family-Houses in Ghanaian Cities," *Urban Studies*, 29:7 (1992), 1159–72; and Irit Sinai, "Housing Types and Housing Uses in Kumasi, Ghana," in Hemalata C. Dandekar (ed.), *City Space + Globalization* (Ann Arbor, MI: College of Architecture and Urban Planning, 1998).

CUISINE AND TRADITIONAL DRESS

There are hundreds of books about cooking in African in general and in Ghana in particular. Some of these include: Alice Dede, *Ghanaian Favourite Dishes* (Accra: Anowuo Educational Publications, 1969); Harva Hachten, *Best of Regional African Cooking* (New York: Hippocrene Books, 1997); Dorinda Hafner, *A Taste of Africa* (Berkeley: Ten Speed Press, 1993); Jessica B. Harris, *The Africa Cookbook: Tastes of a Continent* (New York: Simon & Schuster, 1998); Tami Hultman (ed.), *The Africa News Cookbook: African Cooking for Western Kitchens* (New York: Penguin, 1986); Tebereh Inquai, *A Taste of Africa: An African Cookbook* (Lawrenceville, NJ: Africa World Press, 1998); Bertha Montgomery and Constance Nabwire, *Cooking the African Way* (New York: Lerner Publishing, 1998); Constance Nabwire et al., *Cooking the West African Way* (New York: Lerner Publications, 2001); Mary Ominde, *African Cookery Book* (Nairobi: Heinemann,1975); Laurens Van der Post, *African Cooking* (New York: Time-Life Books, 1971); and David Otoo and Tamminay Otto, *Authentic African Cuisine from Ghana* (Accra: Sankofa, 1997). For references to African cooking in the Americas, see Eric V. Copage, *Kwanzaa: An African-American Celebration of Culture and Cooking* (New York: Morrow, 1991); Ellen Gibson Wilson,

A West African Cook Book (New York: M. Evans, 1971); Jessica B. Harris, *Sky Juice and Flying Fish: Traditional Caribbean Cooking* (New York: Simon & Schuster, 1991); Jessica B. Harris, *Tasting Brazil: Regional Recipes and Reminiscences* (New York: Macmillan, 1992); Jessica B. Harris, *Iron Pots and Wooden Spoons: Africa's Gift to New World Cooking* (London: Fireside, 1999); Heidi Haughy Cusick, *Soul and Spice: African Cooking in the Americas* (San Francisco: Chronicle Books, 1995); and Diane M. Spivey, *The Peppers, Cracklings, and Knots of Wool Cookbook: The Global Migration of African Cuisine* (Albany: State University of New York Press, 2000). The history and cultural uses of a variety of Ghanaian drinks are discussed in Emmanuel K. Akyeampong, *Drink, Power, and Cultural Change: A Social History of Alcohol in Ghana, c. 1800 to Recent Times* (Portsmouth, NH: Heinemann, 1996). For a general study, see Lynn Pan, *Alcohol in Colonial Africa* (Helsinki: Finnish Foundation for Alcohol Studies, and Uppsala: The Scandinavian Institute of African Studies, 1975).

Discussions of various aspects of African and Ghanaian dress can be found in: Susan B. Aradeon, *Traditional African Dress and Textiles* (Washington, DC: Catalogue of the Exhibition of West African Dress and Textiles, at the Museum of African Art, 1975); Frances Kennett, with Caroline MacDonald-Haig, *Ethnic Dress* (New York: Facts on File, 1995); Kate P. Kent, *Introducing West African Cloth* (Denver, CO: Denver Museum of Natural History, 1971); Venice Lamb, *West African Weaving* (London: Duckworth, 1975); Judith Perani and Norma H. Wolff, *Cloth, Dress, and Art Patronage in Africa* (Oxford: Berg, 1999); John Picton and John Mack, *African Textiles* (New York: Harper & Row, 1989); E. Nii Quarcoopome, "Self-decoration and Religious Power in Dangme Culture," *African Arts*, 24:3 (1991), 56–65; M.E. Roach-Higgins et al. (eds.), *Dress and Identity* (New York: Fairchild, 1995); and Roy Sieber and Frank Herreman (eds.), *Hair in African Art and Culture* (New York: Museum for African Art, 2000).

GENDER ROLES, MARRIAGE, AND FAMILY

The topics of marriage, family life, and gender roles have been discussed frequently. For books about marriage, for example, see: John C. Caldwell, *Population Growth and Family Change in Africa: The New Urban Elite in Ghana* (Canberra: Australian National University Press, 1968); Mary Douglas and Phyllis M. Kaberry (eds.), *Man in Africa* (New York: Anchor Books, 1971); James L. Gibbs Jr. (ed.), *Peoples of Africa* (New York: Holt, Rinehart and Winston, 1965); Takiwaa Manuh, "Changes in Marriage and Funeral Exchanges among the Asante," in Jane Guyer (ed.), *Money Matters: Instability, Values and Social Payments in the Modern History of West African Communities* (Portsmouth, NH: Heinemann, 1971), 188–201; Christine Oppong, *Middle Class African Marriage* (London: Allen & Unwin, 1981); Christine Oppong (ed.), *Female and Male in West Africa* (London: George Allen and Unwin, 1983); and A.R. Radcliffe-Brown and Daryll Forde (eds.), *African Systems of Kinship and Marriage* (New York: Oxford University Press, 1965). On gender roles and relations, see: Jean Allman and Victoria Tashjian, *"I Will Not Eat Stone":*

A Women's History of Colonial Asante (Portsmouth, NH: Heinemann, 2000); J. Bukh, *The Village Woman in Ghana* (Uppsala: SIAS, 1977); L. Brydon, "Women in the Family: Cultural Change in Avatime, Ghana, 1900–80," *Development and Change*, 18 (1987) 251–69; Gracia Clark, *Onions Are My Husband: Survival & Accumulation by West African Market Women* (Chicago: University of Chicago Press, 1994); Akosua Gyamfuaa-Fofie, "Women's Role in Ghana's Social Development," in Stephanie Newell (ed.), *Writing African Women* (London: Zed Books, 1997); Nancy J. Hafkin and Edna Bay (eds.), *Women in Africa* (Stanford, CA: Stanford University Press, 1976); K. Little, *African Women in Towns* (Cambridge: Cambridge University Press, 1973); T. Manuh, "Women, the State and Society under the PNDC," in E. Gyimah-Boadi (ed.), *Ghana: Under PNDC Rule* (Senegal: CODESRIA Book Series, 1993); Christine Oppong (ed.), *Female and Male in West Africa* (London: George Allen and Unwin, 1983); C. Oppong (ed.), *Sex Roles, Population and Development in West Africa: Policy Related Studies on Work and Demographic Issues* (London: Heinemann, 1987); C. Oppong and Katharine Abu, *Seven Roles of Women: Impact of Education, Migration and Employment on Ghanaian Mothers* (Geneva: International Labour Office, 1987). Deborah Pellow, *Women in Accra: Options for Autonomy* (Algonac, MI: Reference Publications, 1977); Claire C. Robertson, *Sharing the Same Bowl: A Socioeconomic History of Women and Class in Accra, Ghana* (Bloomington: University of Indiana Press, 1984); and Claire Robertson and Martin Klein, *Women and Slavery in Africa* (Madison: University of Wisconsin Press, 1983).

SOCIAL CUSTOMS AND LIFESTYLE

There are many pamphlets on particular aspects of social customs and social mores that are published in Ghana, but there are only a few books and articles available. These include: Nana Araba Apt, *Coping with Old Afe in a Changing Africa* (Brookfield, VT: Ashgate Publishing, 1996); Nancy Braganti and Elizabeth Devine, *Travelers' Guide to African Customs and Manners* (New York: St. Martin's Griffin, 1995); and Sjaak van der Geest, "Money and Respect: The Changing Value of Old Age in Rural Ghana," *Africa*, 67:4 (1997), 534–59. For a discussion of particular leisure time activities, see Emmanuel Akyeampong, *Drink, Power, and Cultural Change: A Social History of Alcohol in Ghana c. 1800 to Recent Times* (Portsmouth, NH: Heinemann, 1996). On the history and development of African and Ghanaian cinema, see Olivier Barlet, *African Cinemas: Decolonizing the Gaze* (London: Zed Books, 2000); Manthia Diawara, *African Cinema: Politics & Culture* (Indianapolis: Indiana University Press, 1992); Frank N. Ukadike, *Black African Cinema* (Berkeley: University of California Press, 1994). For information on developments in popular cinema, see Birgit Meyer, "Popular Ghanaian Cinema and 'African Heritage,'" *Africa Today*, 46:2 (1999), 93–114. An interesting photographic publication is Stephen Marc, *The Black Trans-Atlantic Experience: Street Life and Culture in England, Ghana, Jamaica, and the United States* (Urbana: University of Illinois Press, 1992). On Ghanaian festivals, see E.V. Asihene, *Apoo Festival* (Tema, Ghana: Ghana Publ. Corp., 1980); A.A. Opoku, *Festivals of Ghana* (Accra: Ghana Publishing Corp., 1970); and Freda Wolfson, *Pageant of Ghana* (London: Oxford University Press, 1958).

Music and Dance

The study of Ghanaian music and dance has been the focus of many scholars. For a discussion of music in traditional societies, see: John Miller Chernoff, *African Rhythm and African Sensibility: Aesthetics and Social Action in African Musical Idioms* (Chicago: Chicago University Press, 1979); J.H.K. Nketia, *Drumming in Akan Communities* (London: Thomas Nelson and Sons, 1963); J.H.K. Nketia, *African Music in Ghana* (Evanston, IL: Northwestern University Press, 1963); J.H.K. Nketia, *The Music of Africa* (New York: W.W. Norton, 1974); Alan P. Merriam, *African Music in Perspective* (New York: Garland, 1982); and P. Klaus Wachsman, *Music and History in Africa* (Evanston, IL: Northwestern University Press, 1971). General studies of African popular music include: Wolfgang Bender, *Sweet Mother: Modern African Music* (Chicago: University of Chicago Press, 1991); Billy Bergman, *Goodtime Kings: Emerging African Pop* (New York: Quill, 1985); John Collins, *Africa Pop Roots* (London: Foulsham, 1985); Ronnie Graham, *Stern's Guide to Contemporary African Music* (London: Off the Record Press, 1965); John Storm Roberts, *Black Music of Two Worlds* (New York: William Morrow & Co., 1972); Chris Stapleton and Chris May, *African All-Stars: The Pop Music of a Continent* (London: Paladin, 1989); and Gary Stewart, *Breakout: Profiles in African Rhythm* (Chicago: University of Chicago Press, 1992). For studies on the various forms of popular music in Ghana, see: John Miller Chernoff, "The Popular Music of West Africa," in Geoffrey Haydon and Dennis Marks (eds.), *Repercussions: A Celebration of African-American Music* (London: Century Publishing, 1985); John Collins, *West African Pop Roots* (Philadelphia: Temple University Press, 1992); John Collins, *Highlife Time* (Accra: Anansasem Publications, 1996); John Collins, *King of Highlife: ET Mensah* (Accra: Anansesem Publications, 1996); and David Coplan, "Come to My Town, Cape Coast! The Social History of Ghanaian Highlife," in Bruno Nettl (ed.), *Eight Urban Musical Cultures* (Urbana: Indiana University Press, 1978), 96–114; The history and culture of dance is portrayed in: Ashenafi Kebede, *Roots of Black Music: The Vocal, Instrumental, and Dance Heritage of Africa and Black America* (Englewood Cliffs, NJ: Prentice Hall, 1982); Odette Blum, *Dance in Ghana* (New York: Dance Perspectives Foundation, 1973); Mawere Opoku, "The Dance in Africa" and "The Dance in Ghana," in Selma Jeanne Cohen, *International Encyclopedia of Dance* (New York: Oxford University Press, 1998); and Gerald Jones, *Dancing: The Pleasure, Power and Arts of Movement* (New York: Harry N. Abrams, 1992). On the importance of Ephraim Amu to Ghanaian culture in general and to choral music in particular, see Kofi Agawu, "The Amu Legacy," *Africa*, 66:2 (1996), 274–86.

Index

Aboakyer festival, 45, 79, 150–152; food and drink, 113

Aborigines' Rights Protection Society, 23, 74

Abruquah, Joseph, 66

Accelerated Development Plan for Education, 10

Accra, 2, 12–13, 48, 53, 71, 147, 160; architecture, 101–102; festivals, 150, 152, 165; media, 73, 76–78; music and dance, 178, 184, 186; population, 4, 8

Accra Arts Centre, 93

Accra Community Centre, 102

Accra Hearts of Oak, 157

Accra Herald, 73

Accra Orchestra, 181

Acheampong, Ignatius Kutu, 27

Achimota School, 10, 90, 93–94

Acquaye, Saka, 90, 179

Ada, 8

Adae, 153

Adaklu, 154

Adangbe, 8, 9, 168; proverbs, 60–61

Adinkra, 87–89, 114, 115, 117–118. *See also* Textiles

Adowa, 177

Afahye, 79, 113

African American Heritage Association, 90

African Brothers, 184

African Morning Post, 75

Afro-beat, 184

Afro-rock, 185

Agbada, 53

Agbekor, 172

Agriculture, 13–15, 19, 49, 134, 142, 163, 165

Ahanta, 113

Ahl ul-Sunna, 56

Ahmadiyya Muslim Mission, 4, 50–51, 53–55

Aidoo, Ama Ata, 66, 68–69

Akan: art, 61, 85–86, 91–92, 94, 100; ceremonies, 85, 127–131, 153; cuisine, 107–110; dress, 117–118, 120; festivals, 151–153; history, 6–7, 19; language, 8–9; literature, 64; music and dance, 168, 171, 173–175, 181–182; poetry, 61–62; proverbs, 60–61; religion, 35, 39–45, 100; social relations, 97, 126, 136–138, 141–142; worldview, 35–36, 43–44. *See also individual groups and art forms*

Akan Trio, 181
Akosombo Dam, 3, 24
Akpalu, Hesino, 59
Akuaba, 89–90, 94, 127
Akuapem, 7–8
Akuffo, Frederick W.K., 27
Akwamu, 7
Akyem, 7
Alliance Française, 191
Ambolley, Gyedu Blay, 186
AME Zion Church, 47
American Embassy, 191
Amoah, Kofi, 94
Ampaw, King, 161
Amsterdam, 176
Amu, Ephraim, 50, 121, 189–190
Ananse, 64–65, 70
Anatsui, El, 94
Anglican Church, 46
Anglo-Asante wars, 20–21, 73
Ankroba River, 3
Annan, Kofi, 19, 37
Ansah, Elizabeth, 94
Ansah, Kwaw, 161
Antwi, Kojo, 186
Anyanfuri, 16
Anyidoho, Kofi, 66
Apostle's Revelation Society, 48
Apostolic Church, 47, 188
Architecture, 83, 95; Islamic, 54, 100; rural, 97–101; urban, 25, 30, 101–103
Armah, Ayi Kwei, 67–68
Armed Forces Revolutionary Council, 27
Armstrong, Louis, 182
Art, 83–95, 156, 186. *See also* Traditional art
Asafo, 61, 100, 151–152, 168, 172
Asante: art, 85–88, 90–92, 94, 100; ceremonies, 127–131, 153; cuisine, 107–110; dress, 115, 117–119; festivals, 153; history, 6–7, 19–21; language, 9; literature, 64; music and dance, 168, 171–175, 177–178, 181–

182; poetry, 61–62; religion, 3, 35, 39–45, 100; social relations, 97, 102–103, 126, 136–138, 141–142; worldview, 35–36, 43–44
Asante Cultural Centre, 93, 102
Asante Empire, 6, 12, 19–21, 51, 86, 90–91, 118
Asante Kotoko, 157
Asantewaa, Yaa (Queen Mother of Ejisu), 20
Asanthene, 102, 118–119, 177
Asare, Kwame, 189
Ashanti Pioneer, 75
Ashanti Region, 3–4, 12, 157
Ashitey, Nii, 179
Assemblies of God, 47
Atanga, Rebecca, 176
Atenteben, 173
The Atlantic Monthly, 68
Atta-Mills, John E., 29
Attoh Ahuma, Rev. M., 74
Atumpan, 168, 173–174, 177
Atwia, 70
Avengers, 184
Awoonor, Kofi, 66–68
Axim Trio, 72
Azikwe, Nnamdi, 75

Bakatue, 113
Bannerman, Charles, 73
Basel Mission, 46, 73
Basketball, 157
Basketry, 92. *See also* Art
Baule, 6
Bayete, 176
Beads, 92, 119, 129. *See also* Art
The Beautyful Ones Are Not Yet Born, 67–68
Beverages, 110–112, 128, 135, 164
Bibiani, 16
Birim River, 3
Birth. *See* Rites of passage
Black Beats, 183
Black Star Square, 25, 102, 155, 184
Black Stars, 157

Blay, J. Benibengor, 69
The Blinkards, 67
Bolgatanga, 176
Bono, 6
Bonwire, 88
Boombaya, 185
The Boy Kumasenu, 161
Boxing, 157–158
Brass bands, 168
Brazil, 8
Bremen Mission, 47
Brew, James Hutton, 73
Bridewealth, 49, 117, 131–132
British, 7, 17; colonial rule, 21–24. *See also* Anglo-Asante wars; Colonialism
British Broadcasting System, 77, 79, 149
British Council, 93
Brong-Ahafo Region, 4,
Brotherhood of the Cross, 47
Bruce, King, 183
Buddhism, 34
Build Your Own Ark, 80
Buk Bak, 187
Burgher highlife, 185
Burkina Faso, 2, 5, 176
Burns Constitution, 23
Busia, Kofi A., 26

Cape Coast, 5, 6, 12–13, 67, 147, 165; architecture, 102; media, 73, 77; theater, 69–70
Cape Coast Sugar Babies, 181
Casely-Hayford, J. E., 67, 74–75
Castles: Cape Coast; 21; Castle of St. George, 21; Christiansborg Castle, 21, 23, 102
Catholicism, 47, 50–51, 133, 189
Central Region, 12, 18, 53, 157
Changes, 69
Chaplin, Charlie, 72
Charismatic church. *See* Pentecostalists
The Chatechist, 67
Checker, Chubby, 179
Chicago, 187

Chieftaincy, 18, 21–22, 43, 119; art, 84–86; festivals, 151, 153–155; music, 173; 176, 177; poetry, 61–62
Childbirth, 127–128
Children's Library, 100
China, 12, 121
Christ Apostolic Church, 47
Christian Messenger, 73
Christian Reporter, 73
Christian Scientists, 48
Christianity: demographics, 34, 46–47, 55; education, 9, 46, 49; history in Ghana, 4, 34, 45–51; holidays, 33, 55, 155–156; impact, 4, 30, 38–39, 45, 48–51, 65, 84, 100–101, 167–168; and indigenous religion, 44–45, 48–51, 56; marriage practices, 131, 133–134; missionaries, 4, 9, 30, 46–49, 121; music, 47, 50–51, 188–190; worldview, 38. *See also individual religions*
Church Missionary Society
Church of Jesus Christ of Latter-day Saints, 48
Church of Pentecost, 47
Cinema, 38, 144, 149, 160–162, 165
Cities. *See individual cities*
Climate, 3–4
Clinton, William, 117
Cloth. *See* Textiles
Clothing. *See* Dress
Clottey, Emmanuel, 158
Cocoa, 1, 3, 13, 15, 17, 22–24, 28–29, 37
Cole, Bob, 72
Colonial economy. *See* Economy
Colonial Film Unit, 160
Colonialism: culture, 29, 98, 101, 121; drama and film, 69, 160–161; history, 21–24, 30; literature, 66–68; media, 73–74, 76–77; music, 168, 189; sports, 157–158
Columbia University, 94
Commonwealth of Nations, 18
Commonwealth Writers Prize, 69

Concert party, 71–72, 79–80, 182
Congo, 184
Constitution: of 1946, 23; of 1951, 24;
    of 1954, 24, of 1969, 8; of 1992, 8,
    17–18, 28, 76
Convention People's Party (CPP), 10,
    23–26, 75, 94, 102
Converted Muslims' Christian Associa-
    tion, 55
Côte d'Ivoire, 2, 6, 14–15, 27
Coups. See Military coups
Cricket, 157
Cuisine, 105, 156, 164–165, 171; eti-
    quette, 106–107, 148; festival use,
    33, 112–113, 152–155; interna-
    tional, 105, 110; meats, 109; pat-
    terns of consumption, 106–108;
    regional differences, 107–109; sea-
    food, 109; staples, 107–109
Culture of silence, 76
Customary Marriage and Divorce Law,
    131
Customs House, 102

Dagbani, 8–9. See also Mole-Dagbani;
    Northern cultures
Dagbon, 173, 179–180
Dagomba, 6, 19, 87, 97, 128; music
    and dance, 168, 179–180. See also
    Mole-Dagbani; Northern cultures
Dagomba (music), 181
Daily Graphic, 75
Daily Mail, 75
Damba, 53, 154
dan Fodio, Uthman, 51
Dance. See Music
Dangme, 119
Danquah, J.B, 75, 90
Danquah, Mabel Dove, 75
Darko, George, 185
Daughters of Glorious Jesus, 189
Dawuni, Rocky, 186
Decca, 182
Dede, Amakye, 186

Dei-Anang, Michael, 66
Delaquis, Ato, 94
Denkyira, 7
Densu River, 3, 8
Deportation Act, 25
Development. See Economy, develop-
    ment
Diamonds, 15–16
The Dilemma of a Ghost, 68
Divination, 44, 50, 119, 127
Divine Life Power Ministries, 47
Divorce, 132–133
Doctor in the House, 79
Donno, 168, 173
Drama, 69–72. See also Concert party
Draughts, 159
Dress: ceremonial, 87, 116–118, 129,
    152; elite, 116; etiquette, 113–115,
    149; fashion, 123; and identity, 22,
    53, 120–12149; ornamentation,
    113, 118–120, 129; traditional, 50,
    87, 113–120, 149; Western influ-
    ence, 22, 94, 113, 120–123
Drinking. See Beverages
Du Bois, W.E.B., 1, 25
Dunkwa, 15
Duodu, Lee, 185

Eastern Region, 18
Economic Community of West African
    States, 19
Economic Recovery Program, 17, 28–
    29
Economy: changes, 17, 142–145, 163–
    165; colonial, 21–23; development,
    16–17, 24–25, 29, 31, 70; informal
    sector, 13–14; modern, 13–16; per-
    formance, 17, 24–29, 161; tradi-
    tional, 13–15, 163. See also Trade
Education, 9, 12, 60; and gender, 9–
    11, 140–142; Islamic, 38, 54–55;
    missionary, 9, 30, 38, 46, 48–49;
    music programs, 176, 190–191; tra-
    ditional, 9; Western-style, 8–12, 22,

24, 30, 38, 143–145, 163–164; of women, 11, 134, 139–143, 164. *See also* Universities

Education Act, 47

Effutu, 45, 152

Egypt, 7, 92

Eid-el-Adha, 33, 55, 156

Eid-el-Fitr, 33, 55, 156

Eighteenpence, 67

Elections: of 1951, 24; of 1969, 26; of 1979, 27; 1992, 1, 28–29; of 2000, 29, 55

Elites, 22–23, 49, 52, 66–67, 69, 141, 145; culture, 116–117, 121, 123, 165, 181

Elmina, 21, 46, 69, 113

Emancipation Day, 16

Emancipation Fair, 186

English, 8–9, 30; in literature, 66–69; in media, 73, 77

Environment, 3, 13–14

Ethiopia, 25

Ethiopia Unbound, 67

Ethnic groups, 4–8. *See also individual groups*

Ethnicity, 5–8

Ewe, 76, 189; art, 84, 87–88; ceremonies, 128–129; cuisine, 107–110; festivals, 154; history, 7; language, 9; literature, 65; marriage practices, 130–132; music and dance, 168, 172; poetry, 61, 63; religion, 39–45, 47; social relations, 136; worldview, 35, 43–44

Ex-Doe, 187

External Service, 77

Family, 147; benefits, 127, 144; gender, 126, 142–145; modern, 138, 141–143, 165; responsibilities, 126–127, 138–142-145, 163; status, 135, 138, 143, 148–149, 164; structure, 125–126, 135–138, 142–145, 163. *See also* Lineage

Fante, 100; history, 6–7, 19–20; language, 9; music and dance, 172, 180–181; poetry, 61; religion, 46, 100. *See also* Akan

Farming. *See* Agriculture

Farrakhan, Louis, 53

Festivals, 30–31, 41–42, 49, 191; dress, 116–119, 150–151; food and drink, 112–1113; music and dance, 150–155, 177. *See also individual festivals*

Fiawoo, Ferdinand Kwasi, 65

Field hockey, 158

Film production, 79–80

First Republic, 24–26

Fishing, 13, 152

Five Pillars of Islam, 52

Flack, Roberta, 184

Foes, Okulay, 178

Folktales, 39, 63–65, 138

Fon, 7

Fontomfrom, 168, 173

Food. *See* Cuisine

Fourth Republic, 17, 28–29

France, 7, 21, 47, 173

Frequency Registration and Control Board, 77, 79

Funerals, 43, 50, 85–86, 134–135; dress, 116–118, 134–135; music and dance, 171, 173, 176–177, 179–180

Ga, 158; ceremonies, 128–129; cuisine, 107–110, 128; festivals, 150, 152–153; history, 7–8, 20; language, 9, 187; marriage practices, 143; music and dance, 152, 168, 173, 178–180; religion, 39–45, 51; social relations, 136–137, 141; worldview, 35–36, 43–44

Ga-Adangbe: festivals, 50; history, 7–8; language, 9; poetry, 61; religion, 39–45; social relations, 136, 142. *See also* Ga

Gambaga, 6

Gender roles, 126, 138–142-145, 149,

163, 171; in marriage, 132–134, 136–138
General Post Office, 102
Genesis Gospel Singers, 188
Geography, 2–4, 18
Germany, 17, 21, 173, 185. *See also* Togo
Ghana, ancient empire, 4
Ghana Association of Writers, 70
Ghana Broadcasting Corporation. *See* Radio Ghana
Ghana Broadcasting System, 77
Ghana Builds, 79
Ghana Christian Council, 51, 55
Ghana Dance Ensemble, 190–191
Ghana Drama Studio, 70
Ghana Evening News, 75
Ghana Experimental Theatre Project, 70
Ghana Pentecostal Council, 55
Ghana Statesman, 75
Ghanaian Times, 76
Glass and Grant, 72
Glidzi, 154
Globalization, 30–31, 81, 144, 149; in music 169, 180, 187–188
Glover, Ablade, 94
Goethe Institute, 191
Gold: 37, 90–92; export and trade, 15–17, 19–22, 28–29; ornamentation, 86, 91, 119, 153; mining, 15–16,
Gold Coast Aborigines, 74
Gold Coast Leader, 74
Gold Coast Methodist Times, 74
Gold Coast Times, 73
Golden Stool, 19–20, 86
Gome, 173, 178–179
Gonja, 5–6, 19, 39–45
Gonje, 173
Government, 17–19; control of media, 73–79; support for culture, 30–31, 71, 93–94, 190–191
Grand Reggae Festival,, 186
Greater Accra Region, 3, 8, 12, 157

Greenwich Meridian, 2
Griots, 167
Guan, 5, 61, 168, 173
Guggisberg, Gordon, 9–10, 90
Guinea, 176
Gulf of Guinea, 2
Gullah, 65
Gyamfuaa-Fofie, Akosua, 69
Gyil, 174

Haiti, 65
Halo, 63
Happy Trio, 72
Harper's, 68
Hausa, 6, 54, 66, 168, 179–180
Hausa Constabulary Force, 6
Hearts of Oak, 157
Hedzolleh, 185
Highlife, 31, 72, 178–181, 185, 187–188; dance band, 182184; gospel, 188–190; guitar band, 181–182
Hinduism, 34
Hip-hop, 31, 185–186-187
Hiplife, 31, 181, 186–188
History, 1; Asante, 19–21; colonial, 20–22, 30; independence era, 23–30; precolonial, 4–8, 19–21. *See also specific topics*
Hodgson, Sir Frederick, 20
Hogbetsotso, 154
Holidays, 33, 55, 155–156
Homowo, 42, 50, 79, 150, 152–153; food and drink, 112–113, 153
The House By the Sea, 68
Housing: traditional, 95–98, 136–138; urban, 101–103, 138, 165

I Told You So, 72
Independence Day, 155
Independence movements, 23–24
India, 53
Indirect rule, 22,
Industry/manufacturing, 16, 24, 164
Inheritance, 126–127, 163

Institute of African Studies, 190
International African Choral Festival, 190
International Charismatic Church, 47
International School of Music and Dance, 190
International Trade Fair, 191
Intestate Succession Law, 126
Islam: demographics, 34, 51–53, 55; dress, 53; history, 4, 19, 29, 34, 51–56; holidays, 33, 55, 155–156; impact, 4, 19, 29, 38–39, 44–45, 52–56, 84, 90–91, 100, 118, 154, 167; literature, 65; marriage practices, 130–131, 134; worldview, 38
Islamic Reformation and Research Centre, 53

Jamaica, 65, 173, 185
James Town, 8, 13, 101
Japan, 17
Jazz Kings, 181
Jehovah's Witnesses, 48
Johnson, "Bob" Ishmael, 72
Johnson Wax Conference Center, 90
Jolson, Al, 72
Jongo, 168, 177
Judaism, 34
June 4 Movement, 28

Kanbonwaa, 168
Kasena, 174, 177. *See also* Northern cultures
Kente, 37, 61, 87–88, 94, 129; dress, 114–118, 121, 123. *See also* Textiles
Kenya, Lord, 187
Keta, 47
Kete, 177–178
Keteke, 187
King, Nana, 188
Kinship, 30, 92, 101, 125–127, *See also* Lineage
Kodzidan, 70
Kofi, Vincent, 83, 94

Koforidua, 77
Kolomashie, 179
Konadu, Asare, 67, 69
Konkomba, 98. *See also* Northern cultures
Kora, 167
Korle Bu, 90
Kotei, Amon, 94
Kowalski, Nicholas, 94
Kpanlogo, 94, 173, 178–180
Kristo Asafo Christ Reformed Mission, 48
Krobo, 8, 129
Kru, 181
Kuduo, 91–92
Kufuor, John. A., 18, 29
Kukurantumi, 161
Kumase, 3, 19–20, 48, 52, 88, 160, 165; architecture, 102–103, 147; media, 76–77; population, 4, 12–13
Kundum festival, 113
Kusum Agoromba, 70
Kuti, Fela Anikulapo, 184, 187
Kwame Nkrumah Memorial Park, 155

La, 8
Lake Bosumtwi, 3, 109
Lake Volta, 3, 5, 13, 109
Laloi lagoon, 8
Language, 5–9, 30, 54, 168, 188–189; in media, 8–9, 73, 76–77, 79–80
Larteh-Kyerepong
League of Nations, 7, 21
Leatherwork, 92. *See also* Art
Lebanon, 12, 26
Legal system, 18
Legon School of Performing Arts, 71
Leisure, 38, 72, 157–165, 169, 171
Liberia, 19, 181
Lifestyle, 163–166
Lighthouse Chapel International, 47, 80
Limann, Hilla, 27–28
Lincoln, Otoo, 178

Lineage, 125–126, 127, 144–145, 147, 164–165; duolineal descent, 126–127; matrilineal descent, 126, 132–133, 136; patrilineal descent, 126, 132–133, 136

Literature: English, 66–69; indigenous, 65–66. *See also specific writers;* Oral literature

Love Brewed in an African Pot, 161

MacCarthy, Charles, 73

Magazines. *See* Newspapers and magazines

Magic. *See* Witchcraft

Makaa, Maka!, 186

Mali, 6, 51, 167

Mamprusi, 6, 19, 39, *See also* Mole-Dagbani; Northern cultures

Mande, 6, 9, 51

Manufacturing. *See* Industry/manufacturing

Marley, Bob, 185

Marriage, 30, 116–117, 130, 136–137; customary, 130–133; monogamy, 130–133; music, 171, 177, 180; polygyny, 130, 133–134. *See also* Bridewealth; Divorce

Marriage of Mohammedans Ordinance, 130–131

Marriage Ordinance, 130–131, 133

McCann, Les, 184

Me Na Me Kae, 187

Media, 8, 38, 81, 121. *See also* Newspapers and magazines; Radio; Television

Medicine, 38, 49

Mensah, E.T., 181–183

Mensah, Joe, 187–188

Metalwork, 90–92. *See also* Art

Methodists, 9, 46, 47–48

Metro TV, 79

Midim Ne Miase Nyatepe La, 76

Migration, 38; pre-colonial, 4–8, 152, 154, 172; rural-urban, 12–13, 52, 125, 134, 142, 144–145, 161, 163–165, 176. *See also* Urbanization

Military coups, 25–28, 67

Military rule, 26–28

Mineral resources, 15–16

Mining, 15–16

Missionaries, 4, 30, 38, 46–49, 84, 180; dress, 121; literature, 65; media, 73–74. *See also* Christianity; Education

Modern art, 93–94. *See also* Art

Mohammed (Prophet), 52–53, 154–155

Mole-Dagbani, 5–6, 9, 19. *See also* Northern cultures

Morning Telegraph, 75

Mossi, 6. *See also* Mole-Dagbani; Northern cultures

Musama Disco Christo Church, 48

Music, 135 156, 164, 167–170, 191; choral, 168, 189–190; Christian, 47, 50–51, 168, 188–190; festival, 152–155, 165, 190; functions, 171–173; instruments, 167–16, 171–181; popular, 150, 176, 180–188; neo-traditional, 178–180; on television, 79–80; traditional, 39, 177–178; Western, 30–31

Muslim Representative Council of Ghana, 54

Nanumba, 6. *See also* Mole-Dagbani; Northern cultures

The Narrow Path, 67

Nation of Islam, 53

National Catholic Secretariat, 51, 55

National Commission on Culture, 191

National Congress of British West Africa, 23

National Democratic Congress (NDC), 18, 29

National Festival of Arts and Culture, 31, 191

National House of Chiefs, 18
National Liberation Council (NLC), 26
National Music and Dance Troupe, 184
National Redemption Council (NRC), 27
National Sports Festival, 158–159
National Stadium, 157, 191
National Theatre, 31, 71, 190, 191
National Times, 75
Nationalism, 23–24; and culture, 29–31, 37, 121
Navrongo, 47
Nelson, Azumah, 158
New Patriotic Party (NPP), 18, 29
Newspapers and magazines, 38, 73–76, 156
Nigeria, 6–8, 12, 26, 52, 54–56, 75; music, 168, 185
Nima, 52, 101
Nimo, Koo, 182
Nkrumah, Kwame, 1, 3, 23–26, 37, 88, 94, 102; criticism, 68, 183; dress, 121; newspapers, 75; praise poetry, 62–63
No Sweetness Here, 68
Nobel Peace Prize, 19
Northern cultures, 4, 29, 148; architecture, 54, 95, 97–100, 103; art, 88, 92; cuisine, 107–109, 111; dress, 53, 114, 118, 149; festivals, 53, 154–155; history, 19; language, 8–9; literature, 65–66; marriage practices, 131–132; music and dance, 167–168, 173–174, 176–177, 179–180; poetry, 66; religion, 4, 34, 46, 52–56; social relations, 97–100, 136. *See also specific ethnic groups*
Northern Region, 18; population of, 4; Northern Territories, protectorate of, 6, 20, 21
Novels, 66–69

Nungua, 8
Nyame, E.K., 181, 183
Nzema, 113

Obeng, R.E., 67
Obrafo, 187
Obuasi, 16
Occupations, 13–16, 49; associated with art, 93–94; modern, 22, 163–165; traditional, 9, 162–164
Odamtten, Vincent, 66
Odansam, 70
Odwira, 42, 153
Offin River, 3, 15
Oge, 178–179
Okai, Atukwei, 66
Okomfo Anokye hospital, 103
Okyeame, 67–68, 70
Olympics, 158
Opoku-Agyemang, Eugene, 66
Oral culture, 149
Oral literature, 59–65, 71, 164
Oral tradition, 5–6, 70–71, 152
Organization of African Unity (OAU), 18, 25, 102
Ornamentation. *See* Dress
Osibisa, 185
Osibisaba, 181
Osofo Dadzie, 79
Osu, 8, 90
Our Heritage, 79
Outdooring (naming), 34, 85, 116, 128, 173, 180
Oware, 159

Padmore, George, 1, 25
Painting, 94, 119. *See also* Art
Palladium Cinema, 77
PANAFEST (Pan-African Historical Theatre Festival), 16, 70–71, 156
Pan-Africanism, 24–25, 37, 70, 102, 156
Parkes, Frank Kobina, 66

Parliament Building, 102
Pastoralism, 163
Patriarchy
Peki, 154
Pele, Abedi, 158
Pentecostalists, 45, 47–48, 50–51, 188
Peoples, 4–8. *See also individual groups*
People's National Party, 27
Petals of Blood, 66
Pickett, Wilson, 184
Pidgin, 9, 80, 184, 187
Poetry, 61–63, 66, 186
Political authority, 49
Political culture, 43–44
Polygamy. *See* Polygyny
Polygyny, 49, 53, 133–134, 137–138
Pop Chain, 191
Popular culture, 164–165. *See also* Cinema; Concert party; Literature; Music; Sports
Population, 2, 4, 13
Portugal, 4, 20–21, 46
"Positive action" campaign, 24
Possession, 48
Posuban, 100
Pottery, 92. *See also* Art
Pra River, 3
Praise songs, 59, 61–63
Prampram, 8
Prempremsiwa, 174, 181
Presbyterian Teacher Training College, 189
Presbyterians, 9, 47, 121, 189
Presley, Elvis, 179
Preventive Detention Act, 25–6,
Progress Party, 26
Proverbs, 39–40, 60–61, 125, 138
Provisional National Defence Council, 28–29
Puberty rites, 85, 119, 128–130, 171

Qadariyya, 53
Quadiani, 53

Quarshie, Tetteh, 15
Quartey, Ike, 158

Radio, 8, 31, 38, 47, 76–79, 156, 164, 169, 187
Radio and Television Rehabilitation Programme, 78
Radio Eye, 78
Radio Ghana, 77–78
Radio Universe, 77
Railways, 22,
Ramadan, 54, 99, 156
Rastafarians, 185–186. *See also* Reggae
Rawlings, Jerry John, 76, 78–79, 117; and AFRC, 27–28; and NDC, 18, 28–29; and PNDC, 28
Rawlings, Nana, 121
Rediscovery and Other Poems, 66
Reggae, 181, 185–186
Religion, 33–56; art, 84; ceremonies, 48–49, 152–155; change, 44–45, 150; demographics, 34; holidays, 33, 55, 155–156; indigenous, 19, 39–45, 151; and politics, 43–44, 55; tension, 55–56, 150. *See also* Christianity; Islam
Riots, 23–24, 55, 190
Rites of passage, 34–35, 85; birth, 127–128; death, 43, 50, 85, 116, 134–135; marriage, 130–134; puberty, 85, 119, 128–130, 171. *See also* Funerals; Marriage; Outdooring (naming)
Rock 'n' roll, 178, 184–185
Rockstone, Reggie, 186–187
Roman Catholics. *See* Catholicism
Royal College of Art, 94
Royal Gold Coast Gazette and Commercial Intelligencer, 73

Saltpond, 53
Sankofa, 89, 91
Santana, 184

Saudi Arabia, 53, 56

Sawaaba Sounds, 185

Sculpture, 89–90, 93–94. *See also* Art

Second Republic, 26

Sekondi-Takoradi, 4, 12–13, 17, 77, 147, 160

Sekyi, Kobina, 67

Selormey, Francis, 67

Seprewa, 167, 174, 181

Seventh-Day Adventists, 48

Shai Hills, 8

Shari'a (Islamic law), 52–53

Shiites, 52

Sierra Leone, 19

Sika Nsona Sanegbalo, 73

Simpa, 179–180

Slave trade, 19–21, 110, 180

Soccer, 150, 157–158

Social change, 22, 29–31, 126, 150; dress, 120–123; family, 132–133, 142–145; lifestyle, 163–165; religion, 48–51, 53–56

Social organization, 95–97, 142, 151. *See also* Family

Social relations, 84, 95–98, 125–127, 131–134, 138–142; etiquette, 147–149

Solid Rock Chapel, 80

Songhai, 4, 19, 51

Soul (music), 184

Soul to Soul concert, 184

South Carolina, 65

Sports, 37, 150, 155, 157–159, 171,

Staple Singers, 184

Station ZOY. *See* Ghana Broadcasting System

Stools, 42, 84, 86, 89–90, 102, 126, 129

Sufism, 53

Sugar, Ayitey, 178

Sunday Mirror, 75

Sunna, 52

Supreme Military Council (SMC), 27

Sutherland, Efua, 70–71

Tagoe Sisters, 189

Talking Drums, 75

Tallensi, 98. *See also* Northern cultures

Tamale, 12–13, 52; architecture, 102

Tamale Cultural Centre, 94

Tano river, 3, 6

Tarkwa, 16

Taxi Driver, *80*

Television, 8, 38, 76–77, 79–81, 121, 144, 156, 161, 164

Tema, 2, 8, 12–13, 17, 90; population, 4; port, 12, 24

Tempos, 182–183. *See also* Mensah, E.T.

Teshie, 8, 152

Textiles, 37, 85, 87, 115–118; symbolism in, 61, 88–89. *See also* Art; Dress

This Earth My Brother, 67

Tic Tac, 187

Tijaniyya, 53

Timber, 14, 16, 17, 28

Togo, 2–3, 7, 15, 24, 27, 154; under German rule, 7, 21

Toko Atolia, 65

Tourism, 16

Tourist art, 94–95. *See also* Art

Track and field, 158

Trade: precolonial, 4, 15,19, 168; trans-Atlantic, 19; trans-Saharan, 4, 15, 19, 21, 51, 65, 91, 167. *See also* Slave trade

Traditional art, 83–93; artists, 93; functions, 84–87, 89–90, 92–93. *See also* Beads; Sculpture; Textiles

Transportation, 3, 17, 22, 24, 165, 169

Trokosi, 134

Turner, Ike and Tina, 184

Tutu, Osei, 19–20, 118

TV Theatre, 71

Twi, 6, 9, 181, 186–187, 189. *See also* Asante

Uhuru Band, 72
United Gold Coast Convention (UGCC), 23, 75
United Kingdom, Ghanaian music in, 185–187
United Nations, 18–19, 37, 61, 79
United States, 17, 47, 71, 117; Ghanaian art in, 87, 90; Ghanaian cuisine in, 110
Universities, 10–12, 26; Islamic, 53–55; music and drama, 70
University of Development Studies, 11, 103
University of Ghana, Legon, 11, 70, 78, 176, 190. *See also* Legon School of Performing Arts
Upper East Region, 18, 176; population, 4
Upper West Region, 18, 174; population, 4
Urbanization, 12–13, 38; impact on culture, 60, 130, 138, 142–142-145, 157
Ussher Town, 8, 101

Vaudeville, 71–72
Vegetation, 3
Video, 144, 161–162, 164–165. *See also* Cinema; Television
Villages, types of, 95, 97–101
V.I.P., 187
Voice of America, 79, 149
Voice of Ghana, 77
Volleyball, 157
Volta Aluminum Company (Valco), 17
Volta Region, 7, 18, 154
Volta River, 3, 21; settlement around, 5–8

Wala, 168
Wangara, 51

Ware, Opoku, 20, 118
Wassa, 7, 15
Wesleyan mission, 73
West African Graphic Company, 75
West African Students' Union, 23
West African Times, 75
Western Echo, 74
Western education. *See* Education
Western culture, 120–123, 144–145, 149, 156, 165; music, 169, 178, 180–184, 186–188; television and films, 80–81, 160–162. *See also* Globalization
Western Region, 12, 113
Wharton, Arthur, 158
Why Are We So Blest?, 68
Winneba, 5, 45, 113, 150, 152, 180
Witchcraft, 35–38, 43–45, 50, 127, 132
A Woman in Her Prime, 67
World Beat, 187
World Council of Churches, 51
World Cup, 37, 157
World War I, 7, 21
World War II, 77, 157, 160–161, 167, 182
Worldview: traditional, 34–37, 127–135, 176; Western influence, 37–38, 44–45. *See also* Christianity; Islam
Wulomei, 179

Yalley, Teacher, 72
Yam festival, 154
Yoruba, 7
Youth, 9, 31, 51–52, 156; dress, 115, 122, 149; music, 171, 178–180, 184–188, 191; rites and ceremonies, 30, 34, 127–130; and urbanization, 12–13, 158
Yua, 176

Zamfara, 6

About the Authors

STEVEN J. SALM is a William S. Livingston Fellow in the Department of History at the University of Texas at Austin.

TOYIN FALOLA is the Frances Higginbothom Nalle Centennial Professor in History at the University of Texas at Austin. He is the author of *The History of Nigeria* (Greenwood, 1999) and *Culture and Customs of Nigeria* (Greenwood, 2001).

THE
PHYSICS OF PULSARS

Topics in Astrophysics and Space Physics

Edited by A. G. W. Cameron, *Yeshiva University*, and
G. B. Field, *University of California at Berkeley*

A. LENCHEK   *The Physics of Pulsars*

Additional volumes in the series:

H. REEVES   *Nuclear Reactions in Stellar Surfaces and their Relations with Stellar Evolution*

3 ⌒ C. R. COWLEY   *The Theory of Stellar Spectra*

T. ARNY   *Star Formation in Interstellar Clouds*

1 ⌒ V. L. GINZBURG   *Elementary Processes for Cosmic Ray Astrophysics*

2 ⌒ V. L. GINZBURG   *The Origin of Cosmic Rays*

⌀ S. GLASSTONE   *The Book of Mars*

⌀ D. B. MELROSE   *Plasma Astrophysics*

⌀ K. APPARAO   *Composition of Cosmic Radiation*

8 ⌒ K. GREISEN   *The Physics of X-ray, Gamma-ray and Particle Sources*